THE RIGHTS OF ANIMALS.

THE

RIGHTS OF ANIMALS,

AND

MAN'S OBLIGATION TO TREAT THEM WITH HUMANITY.

Hamilton

BY WILLIAM H. DRUMMOND, D.D. M.R.I.A.

AND HONORARY MEMBER OF THE BELFAST NATURAL
HISTORY SOCIETY.

Is not the earth
With various living creatures, and the air
Replenished, and all these at thy command
To come and play before thee? Know'st thou not
Their language and their ways? They also know
And reason not contemptibly; with these
Find pastime and bear rule; thy realm is large.
Paradise Lost, viii. 369—375.

Taught by the Power that pities me,
I learn to pity them.—*Goldsmith*.

LONDON:

JOHN MARDON, 7, FARRINGDON STREET;
SMALLFIELD AND SON, AND GREEN, NEWGATE-STREET.
DUBLIN: HODGES AND SMITH.

1838.

Recently published by the Author,

THE PLEASURES OF BENEVOLENCE, a Poem, in four books, with
Notes and Illustrations.   Price Four Shillings.

Webb and Chapman, Printers, Great Brunswick-street, Dublin.

MEMBERS OF THE SOCIETY

FOR

THE PREVENTION OF CRUELTY TO ANIMALS.

MY LORDS AND GENTLEMEN,

Being in London in the year 1829,
I had the honor of being requested by you to advocate
the cause of your Society. Accordingly, on my return
to Dublin, I delivered a Discourse entitled " Humanity
to Animals the Christian's Duty," which, with numerous
notes, was published at the desire and expense of a large
and respectable congregation, by whom many copies
were gratuitously distributed. My attention having being
thus called to the subject, when you proposed a prize
for the best Essay on " Man's Obligation as respects
the Brute Creation," I was led by the advice of a friend,
after some delay and hesitation, to become a competitor.
The task was in perfect accordance with my own feelings; though I could not command success, there was
some merit in trying to deserve it; and, at all events,
no disgrace could attend a failure in so honourable a
competition. Eventually the Essay was written, and

forwarded to London; but arriving a day too late, found the door closed against its admission. It is now published, with several additions to its original form, not from a presumptuous belief that it would have been successful, had it been permitted to enter the lists, nor with any desire to challenge comparison with the fortunate Essay; but simply from a wish that my labours, such as they are, may not be entirely lost, and with a hope that they may make an impression on my own friends and countrymen. Some passages of the printed Discourse before alluded to are incorporated with this Essay, which I now beg leave to inscribe to you, with all due sentiments of respect; and with esteem for your zeal in a cause, by which not only the good of the animal creation, but the great Christian virtues of brotherly kindness and charity, are promoted. I have the honor to be, my Lords and Gentlemen,

Your friend and advocate,

THE AUTHOR.

DUBLIN, *November*, 1838.

CONTENTS.

RIGHTS OF ANIMALS,

AND

MAN'S OBLIGATIONS TO TREAT THEM WITH HUMANITY.

CHAPTER I.

INTRODUCTION.

THE existence of a Society in London for the " Prevention of Cruelty to Animals" argues well for the cause of humanity. Since its establishment in 1824 it has been zealously and successfully employed in promoting the benevolent design of its founders, by calling on the ministers of religion to advocate its cause both in Great Britain and Ireland, by enforcing legislative enactments, and restraining, by the arm of authority, the cruelty of those who would not listen to the persuasive voice of mercy. It has given a great and a good example, which, in due time, we hope to see extensively followed by the institution of similar societies. Some of the most degrading species of cruelty, as that of bull-baiting, have become nearly extinct under its exertions; and let us hope that all of them will soon cease to be known except by description. The various tracts, reports, and sermons published under its auspices have also, it may be presumed, been of no small service in drawing public attention to a subject that has long been too much neglected; which legislators have deemed too unimportant to merit their consideration, and which even some preachers of the gospel have thought beneath the dignity of the pulpit; as if

B

aught in which the interests of humanity are concerned should be deemed unworthy either of the serious attention of the legislative wisdom of the country, or of the pious labours of the ministers of that Great Being whose "tender mercies are over all his works."

There are many men of true benevolence and humanity to their fellowmen who yet seem unconscious that these virtues should be extended to the animal creation. Their compassionate feelings, which are sensibly touched by a tale of human wo, are never excited for the sufferings and labours of animals whose strength is wasted and life sacrificed in the service of man. This want of sympathy must be the result of inattention to a subject which formed no part of their early education, and which has at no time been properly brought before them as a theme for moral consideration. They have never been led to reflect that many animals are as delicately constituted and as sensible to pain as themselves—that all of them, as well as man, have their rights, which it is both unjust and cruel to violate or infringe—that man's dominion over them is a delegated trust, which he is required to use with discretion and lenity—that he is responsible to a higher than an earthly tribunal for the exercise of his power, and may not with impunity subject them to unnecessary suffering, nor wantonly revel in their destruction. Assuredly no sensible man, who will take the trouble of due reflection, can long remain under an error so egregious as to suppose it should be otherwise. He must soon learn to distinguish between being the lord and the tyrant of God's creatures, and find that in the charter of his dominion over them, there is no clause to justify or authorize any such treatment of them as can be taxed with cruelty.

There are some men again who, from an instinctive kindliness of disposition, would not give any creature a moment's pain, but yet would not put themselves to the slightest inconvenience to prevent its infliction. They think no harm in crushing a fly, or treading on a worm or snail in their path, when by the least effort they might spare the life of an unoffending creature, from whose death no possible good can result. Such carelessness has the appearance of positive cruelty, and the consequences are the same. The attention of such men requires to be particularly directed to the subject. They should be taught that humanity has not only man, but all animated being for its object—that to follow its dictates is a virtue —to violate them, a crime.

The Society for the "Prevention of Cruelty to Animals," by their meritorious exertions will dissipate such apathy, and introduce reflection to the bosom of the thoughtless. May the present Essay successfully co-operate in promoting so benevolent a design!

CHAPTER II.

THE OBLIGATION OF MAN TOWARDS THE INFERIOR AND DEPENDENT CREATURES.

"Of Law no less can be acknowledged than that her seat is the bosom of God, her voice the harmony of the world. All things in heaven and earth do her homage; the very least as feeling her care, and the greatest as not exempted from her power."—HOOKER.

"The essay required is one that shall morally illustrate and religiously enforce the obligation of man towards the inferior and dependent creatures." To comply with this requisition shall be the author's first endeavour. The other topics suggested in the printed proposal shall receive due attention in the sequel.

Man's obligation to practise humanity to "the inferior and dependent creatures" rests on the same basis as all other moral obligations—the *will of God*.* On what foundation rests the obligation to be just—to speak the

---

* In affirming that the will of God is the basis of all moral obligation, the author would by no means be understood as excluding the moral sense or 'conscientiousness,' reason, or Dr. S. Clarke's natural fitness or unfitness, which we acknowledge in certain actions. By these the Divine will is indicated—and he would say with Burlamaqui, " They have each their particular force; but in the actual state of man they are necessarily united. It is sense that gives us our first notice; our reason adds more light; and the will of God, who is rectitude itself, gives it a new degree of certainty; adding withal the weight of his authority. It is on all these foundations united, we ought to raise the edifice of natural law or the system of morality."—BURLAMAQUI's *Principles of Natural Law*, p. 172.

truth—to fulfil your promise—to pay your debts ? The same voice, speaking either by nature or revelation, which says 'do justly,' says also, 'love mercy.' Humanity being founded on the divine will, has ample provision made for its exercise, in the constitution, and in the wants and necessities of man. Whence or for what end are the benevolent affections, but that we may participate in the good or ill, the pleasures or the pains of all creatures capable of suffering or enjoyment? The instinctive feelings and sympathies of our own breasts prompt us, prior to all reasoning on the subject, to assist those who are afflicted by hunger, thirst, cold, nakedness, accident, or disease. There was no invention in that part of the poet's description of the pious pastor which says,

"His pity gave ere charity began."

Nor are these feelings limited to our own species. Man's wants necessarily bring him into contact with various other species of creatures. Sociability produces friendship, and claims and secures protection for the weaker. Were we to restrain the sweet influences of benevolence, and prevent them, if this were possible, from flowing forth and visiting other beings besides man, we should deprive ourselves of the most delightful enjoyment; and in resisting the stimulants of a benignant nature, frustrate as far as we could the designs of a kind Providence. But where the benevolent affections exist in purity and vigor they are not to be so confined. They seek objects for their gratification not only among mankind, but in the animal creation. Nature asserts her rights in the bosoms even of the selfish, and where philanthropy is wanting, perhaps you may find a passionate fondness for horses, lap-dogs, parrots, canary-birds, or other creatures in some degree capable of reciprocating the kindness of their benefactors. The being in whom there is no sweet sympathy either with man or beast can scarcely be placed within the pale of human nature.

Though it may seem supererogatory to confirm these observations by the testimony of philosophers, since they must find a response in the reader's breast, yet it may not be deemed superfluous to corroborate them by the authority of 'the greatest, wisest of mankind.' Bacon says, *(de Augmentis Scientiarum*, lib. viii. cap. 2) " There is a noble and excellent affection of mercy implanted in the mind of man by nature herself, which extends to the brute animals subjected by divine command to his dominion. This affection is analogous to the mercy of a prince to those whom he has subdued. And this is most certain, the more noble the soul the more does it compassionate. But narrow and degenerate minds think that affairs of this nature pertain not to them; but that which is the nobler portion of the universe is affected by a community of feeling. Wherefore we see that under the old law [the law of Moses] there were precepts not a few, and not merely ceremonial, but the institutes of mercy, as that forbidding to eat flesh with the blood, and the like. Also in the sects of the Essæans and Pythagoreans, they abstained altogether from eating animals; as do some subjects of the Mogul empire at this day. The Turks, too, though cruel and sanguinary by origin and discipline, raise charitable contributions for the support of brutes; and cannot endure that animals should be subject to vexation and torture."*

It would be well if some who call themselves Christians would condescend to take a lesson from the Turks, though they should learn humanity from other teachers, and particularly from the Great Teacher, who said, " Blessed are the merciful, for they shall obtain mercy."

In a country like England, where the duties of morality and religion have such a host of able and eloquent advocates, it seems strange that this duty of humanity to animals has not occupied a much larger portion of their time and advocacy. Is it only now that men are beginning to discover that they have obligations to their fellow-commoners of the earth? Benevolence, pity, mercy, compassion, are all moral virtues taught by reason, inculcated by religion; and surely no one will affirm that they should not be extended to every being susceptible of benefit from their influence. The inferior animals have passions, feelings, sensibilities, as well as the lordly

---

* BACON's WORKS, folio, London 1730, vol. i. p. 221 :—" Inditus est, ab ipsa natura, homini, misericordiæ affectus nobilis et excellens, &c."

creature man. Many of them have the conjugal, the paternal, and maternal affections strong and indomitable, even in torture and death. They are grateful to their benefactor, and some of them, as the dog, would venture life and limb in his defence. Their strength, their cunning, their fleetness, their labours, the fruits of their industry, are all for man's service—not for his food and raiment only, but for his luxury and ornament. The furs of quadrupeds, the plumage of birds, the pearly covering of the testaceous families, are the tributes which are paid him. Even the insect tribes work for his gratification—one concocts the sweetest of fluids for his beverage—another spins the most beautiful thread for his clothing.

A consideration of the physical benefits derived from animals should teach man to reciprocate them as far as may be practicable, or suited to creatures so differently constituted—to regard them not with cold selfishness as automata, constructed, like the toys of children, for his pleasure only; but with kindness, as being susceptible of feelings analogous to his own, and at the same time with pious gratitude to the Giver of all, for having ordained him to be the lord of so extensive and varied a creation. It might also be salutary to reflect, what would be the condition of man without those creatures of whose services he is too unconscious, and which he too often repays with tyranny and oppression.

That cruelty to a fellow-creature is a crime no one will dare to dispute—that cruelty to the inferior animals is also a crime is equally true, though it may not be so readily admitted, because it is allowed to pass without due cognizance, and seldom has any penalty been exacted for its atrocities. But the passion is the same whether indulged on a man or an insect; and though the life of an insect is not to be estimated as the life of a human being, the sentence of just history has consigned to merited infamy the imperial tyrant who found a pastime in killing flies, not less than Phalaris, who tortured men in his brazen bull. Animals writhing under the merciless strokes of the lash or the club, or the wounds of the goad, or the dissector's knife, have seldom an advocate to prosecute

their wrongs in a court of justice. They cannot utter
their complaints in articulate sounds—they can fee no
lawyer; and laws have been more frequently enacted for
their destruction than preservation. For as to the game
laws they were framed, not from any principle of mercy
to creatures coming under the denomination of game, but
to keep them in store for general butchery by the privileged few. We might be almost led to imagine that
some legislatures had passed a decree against many genera
and species of animals, similar to that of Rome against
Carthage, *Delenda est Carthago;* or rather like that of
Haman against the Jews, " to destroy, to kill, and to cause
them to perish.". Thus, " by an ancient statute, viz.
8 ELIZ. c. 15, entitled, *An Act for the Preservation of
Graine*, it was required that the churchwardens should
levy an assessment, and pay for the heads of every three
old crowes, choughes, or rookes, 1d.; of six young crowes,
choughes, or rookes, 1d. ; and for every sixe egges of any
of them, 1d.; for every twelve stares heads, 1d.......for
the heade of every woodwall, pye, jay, raven, kyte, or
king's-fisher, 1d.; bulfynce or other bird that devoureth
the blowth of fruit, 1d." Similar rewards are offered for
the heads of a variety of birds and beasts of prey. The
head of the " hedgehogge" was valued at 2d. and that of
the " moldwarpe" at one fourth of that sum. " By another ancient statute, 24 HEN. VIII. c. 10, every township
was required to keep a crow-net, to destroy rooks, crows,
and choughs."* Why an " Act for the Preservation of
Graine" should spread its meshes for the beautiful king-
fisher, it is not easy to discover; and as for the poor bullfinch and its confreres, they might have been spared for
their song, though at the expense of a little "blowth of
fruit." The ignorance and barbarity evinced by such
enactments are equally conspicuous. The crow, the rook,
and the chough are warred against for destroying grain,
whereas it is notorious that they live on insects, carrion,
and worms; beetles are the favourite food of the hedgehog; the mole feeds on worms, and the bullfinch renders
great service to the garden and orchard by destroying

* See Burn's Justice of the Peace, Lond. 1776, vol. 11, p. 283.

insects in the young buds. But game-law legislators are seldom to be ranked with such "senators" as are taught "wisdom from above." It would have been well if they had learned grammar, and penned their enactments in a style that could be understood. Blackstone says of these that they are "not a little obscure and intricate; it being remarked that in one statute only, 5 ANN. c. 14, there is false grammar in no fewer than six places, besides other mistakes : the occasion of which, or what denomination of persons were probably the penners of the statutes" he prudently forbears to inquire.* Legislators of the present day have evinced more wisdom and a better spirit. Let us hope that they will use the power with which they are invested, to prevent cruelty—to promote the interests of humanity in every department where its influence is wanted or can be felt—that they will advocate the cause of the oppressed, and spread the ægis of their protection over the defenceless. It is cheering to reflect that many members of the British legislature are zealous in making such a laudable use of their power—who, knowing what they owe to their country as true patriots, would put an end to the cruel practises by which her moral character is degraded—who, knowing what they owe to their God as dependents on his bounty, would extend that mercy in which he delighteth to every order of being. May all who are in authority remember that "he who allows oppression shares the crime," and that governments are responsible for all such sins of the people as they are fully competent to abolish.

---

* *Blackstone's Commentaries*, book iv. c. 13, § 9: "As the law stands at present, (1810) no man is punishable for an act of the most extreme cruelty to a brute animal, but upon the principle of an injury done to the property of another : of course the owner of a beast has the tacit allowance of the law to inflict upon it, if he shall so please, the most horrid barbarities."

"In the trial of William Parker (July sessions, 1794) for tearing out the tongue of a mare, Mr. Justice Heath said, "In order to convict a man for barbarous treatment of a beast, it was necessary it should appear that he had malice towards the prosecutor." Thus we see, had the mare been the property of this fiend, he had escaped punishment. In November, 1793, two Manchester butchers were convicted in the penalty of twenty shillings each, for cutting off the feet of living sheep, and driving them through the streets. Had the sheep been their own property, they might with impunity either have dissected them alive, or burned them alive, particularly if in imitation of certain examples, they could have made any allegation of profit."—LAWRENCE'S *Treatise on the Horse*, vol. 1, p. 132, 133.

Many acts of cruelty, however, are perpetrated, which no act of Government can reach. Humanity must appeal to a higher tribunal for redress : she must invoke Religion to raise her solemn voice—to speak to the conscience—to show how the Almighty has " fixed his canon" not only against " self slaughter," but against the commission of every deed which can be justly considered as cruel.

That the Sacred Scriptures inculcate the duty of humanity to animals a single text might suffice to demonstrate: "a righteous man is merciful to his beast." Mercy to an animal is here made a striking characteristic of righteousness—righteousness is every where enjoined in Scripture—mercy is one of its principal attributes, and where this is wanting it is vain to lay claim to the title of righteous. This might suffice as to Scriptural authority, but it may be useful to pursue the subject farther, and show that the same doctrine is enforced directly and virtually in various other passages of Holy Writ.

It has been questioned whether the divine permission was granted to man in his primitive state, to eat the flesh of animals. Yet we read that Abel brought as an offering to the Lord " of the firstlings of his flock and the fat thereof;" and as in most sacrifices part of the flesh was eaten, we may reasonably conclude that it was permitted from the first. But whether this be so or not, we can scarcely doubt that the ' giants' and men of violence and blood who subsequently peopled the earth, were eaters of flesh ; and after the flood, it was probably to prevent a revival of the cruel practise of devouring animals before life was quite extinguished, that it was said to Noah, " The flesh with the life thereof, which is the blood thereof, shall ye not eat." This prohibition may have been levelled not only against the excision and eating of the flesh of animals while they were yet alive—a practise, as we learn from Bruce's Travels, still extant in some parts of Africa—but, according to Selden, against all cruelty.*

---

* See SELDEN *De Jure Naturæ et Gentium*. "Sic enim Deus homines sine immanitate brutis utendum docuit; nam cum effundi eorum sanguis nequit, sine celeri morte, per exquisita veluti supplicia non esse occidenda ostendit; ne homines primum brutis vescentes, permissione a Deo accepta crudeliter forte abuterentur, et sævitiæ assuescerent."—J. CLERICI, *Comm. in Gen.* ix. 4.

It was afterwards repeated in a more amplified form in the Levitical Law. "Whatsoever man there be of the children of Israel, or of the strangers that sojourn among you, which hunteth and catcheth any beast or fowl that may be eaten; he shall even pour out the blood thereof, and cover it with dust, for it is the life of all flesh." Lev. xvii. 13. Now though it be admitted that the primary object of such injunctions was to guard the Israelites against certain superstitious and idolatrous rites of the heathen, they involved the virtue of humanity; for many of those rites were attended with circumstances of shocking barbarity. Thus the sorceresses Canidia and Sagana are described by Horace, in the performance of their necromantic ceremonies, as tearing a black lamb to pieces with their teeth, and pouring the blood into a trench, as an offering to the Manes evoked to give a reponse to their enquiries.

Scalpere terram
Unguibus, et pullam divellere mordicus agnam
Cœperunt; cruor in fossam confusus, ut inde
Manes elicerent, animas responsa daturas.

"Soon with their nails they scrap'd the ground,
And filled a magic trench profound
With a black lamb's thick streaming gore,
Whose members with their teeth they tore,
That they may charm the sprights to tell
Some curious anecdotes from hell."—FRANCIS.

The pouring out of the blood of a beast, at once, and while it was yet warm from the chace, would speedily terminate its sufferings. For similar reasons, it was forbidden to "seethe a kid in its mother's milk." The goat was sacrificed to Bacchus for being injurious to the vine. To render him propitious, the milk of a she goat, in which her own kid had been boiled, was poured round the root of his favourite tree. Or according to a Karraite manuscript on the Pentateuch, quoted by Cudworth, "It was a practise of the ancient heathens, when they had gathered in all their fruits, to take a kid, and boil it in the dam's milk; and then, in a magical way, to go about and besprinkle with it their trees, fields, gardens, and orchards; thinking that by this means they would fructify, and bring forth fruit the more abundantly the following year." " Maimonides, Thomas Aquinas, and Nicholas de Lyra, as they are quoted by Tostatus, make this to be a sacrifice to the rural gods."* It was therefore justly forbidden as idolatrous; and—if the kid was subjected to any torture in the process, if dissevered like Canidia's lamb, or immersed alive in the fluid and boiled to death—as most revolting to humanity. Moreover, every mind possessed of the least sensibility must feel it to be an aggravated cruelty to make the very provision designed by an all-wise and beneficent Creator for the sustenance of a young interesting creature, the means of destroying it by a painful, lingering death.

By the law of Moses it was forbidden to increase the distress of a bird robbed of her nest, by making her a captive. " If a bird's nest chance to be before thee in the way, in any tree or on the ground, whether they be young ones or eggs, and the dam sitting upon the young or upon the eggs, thou shalt not take the dam with the young: but thou shalt in any wise let the dam go, and take the young to thee." Deut. xxii. 6, 7. This injunction is enforced by the same consideration as the fifth commandment, " that it may be well with thee, and that thou mayest prolong thy days." Were the ministers of religion sometimes to expatiate on this text, and endeavour to put a stop, in their rural districts, to the barbarous amusement of " Birdnesting," by which some species of our singing birds are in danger of becoming extinct, no good or sensible man would blame them for going beyond their province, nor affirm that they did more than their duty.

Mercy being thus required to be shown to wild animals, we might justly expect that the claims of those in the immediate service of man should not be forgotten. One reason for the institution of the Jewish sabbath is expressly stated to be for the benefit of the labouring classes of domesticated brutes: " that thy ox and thy ass may rest as well as thou." It was forbidden to " muzzle the ox when he treadeth out the corn"—a noble dictate of justice and tenderness; for " the labourer is worthy of his hire," and it would be cruel to tantalize the patient steer

---

* YOUNG's *Dissertations on Idolatrous Corruptions in Religion*, vol. 1. p. 273. London, 1734.

with the sight of a favourite food, which he was hindered
by an unnatural species of prevention from tasting, in the
very midst of the plenty which he was preparing for the
use of his master. Such was the mercy of the Jewish
law, that it extended its protection to the ox and the ass
even of an enemy: " If thou meet thine enemy's ox or
his ass going astray, thou shalt surely bring it back to
him again. If thou see the ass of him that hateth thee
lying under his burden, and wouldest forbear to help him,
thou shalt surely help with him." Ex. xxiii. 4, 5.

Here again is a subject on which it would well become
Christian divines sometimes to expatiate. Such a passage
as this might afford a fit occasion to enlarge on the sin-
fulness of indulging a resentful spirit; and on the enormous atrocity of wreaking revenge on an enemy by
houghing his kine, maiming his horse, or slaughtering
his sheep—crimes as dastardly as they are cruel, originating in the direst passion of the soul, and stamping an
indelible stigma on every country where they are perpetrated. Such crimes, though committed in midnight
darkness and escaping the vigilance of human law, are
not unseen by that Omniscient Being, who, as we are
taught by the highest authority to believe, " careth for
oxen," and suffereth not a hoof to be injuriously treated
without his cognizance. Among the reasons assigned in
Holy Writ, by the Eternal himself, for sparing Nineveh,
contrary to the wishes of an angry and disappointed
prophet, was its " much cattle"—and shall we suppose
that such atrocities as those to which we have alluded,
shall escape righteous retribution ? A dumb animal was
once endued with " miraculous organ" of speech to reprove her master for given her three unmerited strokes—
and does not the same power, who gave the mouth of an
ass to utter articulate sounds, still exist to note and
avenge the wrongs of his creatures ? " Behold, the Lord's
hand is not shortened that it cannot save ; neither is his
ear heavy that it cannot hear."

Holding, as I do, this subject to be of great importance,
and not wishing to skim over it superficially, I must beg
permission, even at the hazard of being prolix, to notice
some other instances, recorded in scripture, of God's care

of oxen. " For whatsoever things were written afore time, were written for our instruction," and were they adverted to and commented on more frequently, the sin of cruelty to animals would be less prevalent.

As it appears to some preachers* that humanity to animals is a subject beneath their dignity, so may it appear to some readers beneath the dignity of Sacred Scripture, to notice the mode in which certain agricultural operations should be performed—and so it might, provided these operations were altogether unassociated with moral or religious principle. In this respect it can be of no consequence in what mode seed is scattered in the ground, or trees planted in an orchard. But if in conducting such operations, any cruel or superstitious practices be introduced, it then becomes the moralist and divine to interfere, and if possible, prevent them. And should a law be enacted for the prevention of any one cruelty in connexion with some of the common occupations of life, it might suffice for a whole class of similar cruelties, judging, as we ought, of the intentions of the lawgiver in framing the law, more by its spirit than the letter. If one law written in blood betrays the soul of a Draco, one written in the milk of human kindness manifests the disposition and the wishes of mercy. A single precept in behalf of humanity to the brute creation shows the humane nature of the preceptor. When the Jewish law forbids to " plough with an ox and an ass together," for the obvious reason that they are discordant yoke-fellows—the one being much stronger and larger than the other, the weaker, of consequence, must be oppressed by a task disproportioned to his powers, though in other respects they might chance to be suitable associates—we conclude that the law is not limited to that single act, but that it extends to all such cruel and unnatural coalitions. The law then is designed for the abolition or prevention of all oppressive treatment of animals, and particularly of those employed in our service. No doubt it admits of a symbolical interpretation, and the Apostle Paul is supposed to allude to it in this way in the second Epistle to the Corinthians, vi. 14,

---

* For instance, foxhunting parsons.

C

when he admonishes—" be ye not unequally yoked together with unbelievers ;" but it needs scarcely be questioned
that the symbolical or figurative was not its primitive
meaning. This may serve as an answer to those who
affirm that humanity to animals is not enjoined in Scripture ; and parsons may learn from it that the Jewish law
and the Levitical priesthood did not think it ' beneath
their dignity' to enjoin that the brute creation should be
treated with clemency. Nay more, in the twenty-fifth
chapter of Leviticus, where Jehovah himself is introduced
speaking to Moses on Mount Sinai, and commanding
him what he should say to the children of Israel respect-
ing the year of jubilee, the quadrupeds are particularly mentioned, and classed with the different orders of
the people ordained to enjoy the rest and participate
the blessings of that institution :—" And the Sabbath of
the land shall be meat for you; for thee and for thy
servant, and for thy maid, and for thy hired servant, and
for thy stranger that sojourneth with thee; and for thy
cattle, and for the beasts that are in thy land, shall all
the increase thereof be meat."*

---

* The distinction of animals into clean and unclean among the Jews,
was for one special reason to "teach them *morality* even in their food ; for
the birds and beasts allowed were of the tame and gentler kinds, and not
of fierce and voracious natures, to teach them the great truths of justice,
moderation, and kindness."—ARISTÆUS in EUSEB. *Præp. Evang.* lib. viii.
c. 9. quoted in DR. HARRIS's *Nat. Hist. of the Bible.* p. 29.
    Lowman, after stating that the food allowed to the chosen nation was "of
the milder sort of the most common and domestic animals," asks, " was not
this far better than to license and encourage the promiscuous hunting of
wild beasts and birds of prey, less fit for food, more difficult to be procured,
and hardly consistent with a domestic, agricultural, and pastoral life ?
Did not the restrictions in question tend to promote that health and ease,
that useful cultivation of the soil, that mildness, diligence, and simplicity,
that consequent happiness and prosperity, which were among the chief
blessings of the promised land ?"—*Id.* p. 31.

CHAPTER III.

HERE is a question which could be proposed by no one who was not either an enemy to Christianity, or altogether ignorant of its principles; for no one, though but superficially acquainted with that divine religion, can for a moment question that humanity to animals is a duty accordant with its whole spirit; and that every act of cruelty, though to a reptile or a fly, is in direct hostility to its nature. Christianity is throughout a religion of mercy—of mercy not limited to any tribe or nation, nor to the sphere of rationality itself, but extending to the extreme limit of life and sense. If humanity was taught by the Jewish law, much more is it included in the dictates of him who came not to destroy but to fulfil—not to abolish the moral law but to confirm it, by lending it additional sanctions, and arming it with new authority from heaven. He who said, " Blessed are the merciful, for they shall obtain mercy," and " Be ye therefore merciful, as your Father in heaven is merciful," could never have meant that the animal creation should be excluded from the sweet influences of that virtue. We can conceive nothing more abhorrent from his nature, or that would have called forth his more indignant reprehension than cruelty to animals. Why then, it may be asked, do we not find some of that indignant reprehension in his numerous discourses ? Why ? Wherefore reprehend what did not exist ? The Jews, though chargeable with many offences and trangressions of the divine law, remembered the declaration of their wise king, that " a righteous man is merciful to his beast." They might be justly reprehended, many of them at least, with avarice, selfishness, bigotry, and hypocrisy; and these vices the

Great Teacher did not spare; but they could not be taxed with cruelty to the animal tribes. They had no gladiatorial sports, nor *Ludi Circenses,* and were altogether ignorant of those refined amusements which are fostered by some of the enlightened and christianized nations of Europe, at such an expense of life and suffering. They kept cattle for such uses as Providence designed, and let the working classes of them rest on the seventh day, according to the commandment. They did not tax the horses beyond their strength and fleetness by running them against time. They had no bull-baiting, nor cockfighting, nor bear-garden, nor worrying of dogs and cats, nor any of those spectacles which afford so much delight to our sons of the "Fancy." Neither had they schools for vivisection; nor were they skilled in those culinary arts which are taught by gluttony and cruelty to gratify the taste of the gourmand and epicure. Had such practises been tolerated by the Jewish law or followed by the people, we may be well assured they would not have escaped the special condemnation of the great benevolent Reformer, as the whole spirit of his religion condemns them now. Not only were the Jewish customs, but the criminal code of the Jewish legislature, humane and merciful compared with those of modern times, boastful as we are of our superior refinement, our philosophy, and our science. The Jewish law demanded restitution only, where our laws are not satisfied with less than the offender's perpetual exile or death. Compare the "forty stripes save one" with the lacerating flagellations of the English cat-o'-nine-tails, or the horrible Russian *knout,* and say in which is the spirit of mercy most apparent. But did not the Jews slaughter numerous animals for the altar? Unquestionably. Their religion demanded the sacrifice of both birds and beasts. But even in these as much lenity was manifested as is compatible with the act of depriving animals of life. They did not fatten their birds by arts which nature detests, nor bleed their calves to whiten their flesh, in the modes practised by our accomplished butchers, nor madden their beeves by baiting them with bull-dogs. By such acts they would have thought, and justly thought, their offerings profaned, desecrated, and turned to an abomination in the eyes of the God of mercy. They brought their victims in prime condition from the stall, or the fold, or the dove-cote, and by a single stroke or section (*una sectione*, BUXT.) disse-vered the cords of life without subjecting them to any previous injury. They had officers properly trained up to the performance of this necessary duty, who, with in-struments keenly edged and properly adjusted as to form and size, executed their task speedily and effectually. This we learn from Buxtorf, Maimonides, and other writers on Jewish antiquities.*

All Christians admit that they are bound to follow the example of Christ, according to the express injunctions both of himself and his apostles. Now if it can be shewn that he was eminently distinguished for his humanity and compassion, these are virtues which we are under an obli-gation to practise. In some respects, indeed, the Saviour was of too exalted a nature to be imitated by imperfect mortals, but in others he is the great model to which they should assiduously labour to conform. They cannot work miracles as he did, but they may cherish a spirit of bene-volence similar to that which prompted him to work them. They cannot satisfy the hunger of thousands with a few loaves and fishes, but they can show compassion to the poor, and contribute of their abundance to relieve the wants of the distressed.

Our Lord's compassion was no doubt chiefly exercised on the human race; but it is no more than just to con-clude that it flowed thence to the animal creation; for had it not, that virtue would in him have been incomplete. In the inspired annunciations of his character which we read in the Prophets, he is described as pacific, merciful, and just. " He shall not cry, nor lift up, nor cause his voice to be heard in the street. A bruised reed shall he not break,

---

* " Qui artem hanc discit, per aliquot annos perito lanio mactanti adesse debet."—*Buxtorf. Synag. Jud.* c. xxxvi. p. 612.

" Peculiaribus ad mactationem utuntur cultris, magnis ad animalia magna, parvis ad parva. Magni quidem mucrone carent, sed exactissimæ sunt aciei, alioqui illis uti non liceret." " Guttur una resecant plaga."

" Since it is necessary," says Maimonides in his *More Nevochim*, " that animals should be killed for the sake of good food and nourishment, the law enjoined that kind of death that was easiest, and forbade them to be tortured by a cruel and lingering mode of slaughtering."

and the smoking flax shall he not quench." Is. xlii. 2, 3.
In the description of his peaceable kingdom it is written,
" The wolf also shall dwell with the lamb, and the leopard shall lie down with the kid; and the calf and the
young lion and the fatling together; and a little child shall
lead them. And the cow and the bear shall feed; their
young ones shall lie down together: and the lion shall
eat straw like the ox. And the sucking child shall play
on the hole of the asp, and the weaned child shall put his
hand on the cockatrice's den. They shall not hurt nor
destroy in all my holy mountain; for the earth shall be
full of the knowledge of the Lord, as the waters cover the
sea." Is. xi. 6—9. This passage is highly figurative,
and descriptive of men who, in the violence of their propensities, should resemble the fierce creatures mentioned,
but under the benign influences of Christianity should
assume a new character, and become fit associates of the
gentle and the meek. It shows us that all the milder
virtues should predominate, and consequently that cruelty
and its kindred vices should be unknown in the kingdom
of the Messiah. Accordingly, when Christ appeared he
fully realised the prophetic description of his character,
not more by the incomparable wisdom of his discourses,
than by the mildness, the meekness, and captivating
sweetness of his manners. Of him it might be truly said
that he did not " hurt nor destroy," in the whole range
of existence. The foxes could repose in their dens, and the
birds in their nests, unmolested by the Son of Man when
he had not where to lay his head. He shot no arrow—
he handled no spear—he laid no snare to capture the
creatures that God made free. The very idea is revolting
to all the ideas we have been taught to entertain of the
Saviour's virtues. By his example, and all moralists
assure us that example is far more efficacious than words,
he taught the great lesson of humanity, and so strikingly
too, that it is really marvellous how any one pretending
to be a follower of Christ does not see and feel its importance. When the Great Teacher in his own faultless
conduct exemplified the beauty and obligation of mercy,
and showed how carefully all cruelty should be avoided,
was it necessary that he should give a formal disquisition

on the subject, and paint to the imagination of the villagers of Galilee, or the citizens of Jerusalem, such scenes of violence and outrage against the animal creation as are disgraceful not only to the name of Christian, but to the name of man? There are some crimes of so detestable a nature that we are admonished by an apostle not to let them be " once named among us"—crimes too on which no Christian preacher would venture to expatiate in his pulpit, lest his congregation should think he meant to insult them. When the prophet went forth and stood upon the mount before Jehovah, behold Jehovah passed by! but he was not in the tempest that rent the mountains and brake in pieces the rocks, nor in the earthquake, nor in the fire—but in " a still small voice." The very silence of the Saviour on the subject of cruelty to animals, is more impressive than the most eloquent declamation; and it comes home to the heart of the reflecting with an effect similar to that of the "still small voice" on the mind of the prophet. In the early times of the Roman history, it is said there was no law against parricide: a crime of so black a dye could not be anticipated, and therefore it was left unnoticed. So among men professing Christianity, cruelty in every shape and disguise is so repugnant to the spirit of their religion, that its Author might have deemed it superfluous to proscribe it by any special law. No man stained with its guilt has any right or claim to rank himself as a follower of Him whose glory it was not to destroy but to save.

This argument might be deemed sufficient; but that no species of refuge or excuse may be left for the sin against which we protest, let us examine whether any farther reasons may be found in the words or actions of Christ, for the practice of humanity to brutes, from which it must necessarily follow that inhumanity is forbidden.

It is worthy of observation, then, that our Lord approved of the customary attention being paid to domesticated animals even on the sabbath day. For when reproving the over-righteousness or hypocrisy of the ruler of the synagogue, who had expressed ' indignation' because Jesus had performed a miraculous cure on that day, "the Lord answered him and said, thou hypocrite, doth not each one of you on the sabbath loose his ox or his ass from the stall, and lead him away to watering ?" (Luke xiii. 15.) Here he not only does not reprove them for performing those offices on the sabbath, but deduces from it a justification of his own conduct, and proves, by their own example, that not only does an office of humanity to a fellow-creature, but to a beast, supersede the observance of an instituted duty. Again did he exemplify the same truth when he healed the withered hand, and was asked if it was "lawful to heal on the sabbath day ; and he said unto them, what man shall there be among you that shall have one sheep, and if it fall into a pit on the sabbath day, will he not lay hold on it and lift it out ? How much then is a man better than a sheep ? Wherefore it is lawful to do well on the sabbath days." Matt. xii. 11, 12. It is commendable to be kind to a brute ; *a fortiori*, to a man. "The sabbath," said our Lord, "was made for man, and not man for the sabbath;" and by a warrantable extension of the idea we may affirm that beasts were created not for the sanctification of the seventh day, but the seventh day was sanctified for the rest and refreshment of the labouring classes of beasts : and so we find it in the commandment. If the owner of one of these useful creatures had neglected to supply its provender, to lead it to watering, or to relieve it from the effects of any accident, under the mistaken idea that such offices would violate the sanctity of the sabbath, we may suppose that instead of being commended, he would have been reproved by the Saviour for not understanding better the object of the divine institutions : and admonished to " go and learn what this meaneth—I will have mercy, and not sacrifice."

Many of our Saviour's discourses are illustrated with incomparable beauty, by allusions to external nature, and images taken from the vegetable and animal kingdoms, from which we are persuaded of his love to both. When he teaches us to confide in the constant superintending providence of God, and not to be too anxiously engrossed by the cares of life, perplexing our thoughts about food and raiment, he desires us to consider the lilies of the field which neither toil nor spin, and yet Solomon in all his glory was not arrayed like one of these. " Behold the fowls of the air," said he, " for they sow not, neither do they reap, nor gather into barns ; yet your heavenly Father feedeth them." Matt. vi. 26. The very idea that God has such a love for them as to feed them induces the belief that he requires all under whose dominion they may be subjugated, to show them equal kindness, and that he will not suffer them to be injuriously treated without rebuke or castigation. To FEED is to do an act of beneficence, and implies a regard for the comfort and well-being of the creatures that are fed. A man who has a number of animals under his protection, for the mere pleasure of observing their instincts and habits, would not willingly see any of them in the ruffian hands of a spoiler, nor subjected to any species of abuse. He considers an injury to his hound, his hawk, or his singing-bird as done to himself, and demands such apology or compensation as the case may require. Much more then may we suppose that it must be highly offensive to the all-bounteous Creator, who formed them and gave them peculiar faculties, to see them wantonly molested and injured. We think it therefore incontrovertible that the Saviour, by this single expression, " GOD FEEDETH THEM," teaches a lesson of humanity to every reflecting mind, not less strongly than if he had inculcated it by the most positive precepts, and armed it by sanctions the most awful. God feedeth them ! This single consideration is pregnant with instruction. They are God's pensioners—he fills their hearts, as the hearts of the children of men, with food and gladness ; provides for them their mossy couch, gives them a shelter in the umbrageous foliage, or allots them their habitation in the cliffs or depths of the ocean ; and furnishes them with abundance of nutriment in the rich produce of the fields, in the insect-loaded gale, or the waters of the fishy sea : and though he gives man the privilege to use them as his wants and necessities require, he gives no authority to abuse the privilege, and convert liberty into lawless licentiousness. What ! shall the Blessed Author of All have thus declared they are his, and under his protection—shall he have displayed his power, his wisdom, his munificence in creating, clothing,

and feeding them, only to lure the sportsman to go forth
girt with the instruments of death to ravage and destroy;
and where God gave the music of birds, with the animat-
ing sounds of life, and all the cheerfulness of love and
joy, to spread the stillness of desolation, and turn the
fair aspect of nature into a scene of carnage and slaughter? Let us not suppose it. Neither let it be imagined
that any animal is so insignificant as not to form an important link in the chain of being. There may be some
men who, if they think at all, may persuade themselves
to believe that animals are of too little value to be objects
of divine cognizance or regard; and who, when admonished or rebuked for their destructive cruelties, are ready
to assert with some atheistical sinners of old, "The Lord
shall not see; neither shall the God of Jacob regard it;"
and we would repeat the same luminous argument that
was addressed to them in refutation of their ignorance
and folly: "Understand, ye brutish among the people,
and ye fools, when will ye be wise? He that planted
the ear, shall he not hear? he that formed the eye,
shall he not see? he that chastiseth the heathen, shall not
he correct? he that teacheth man knowledge, shall not
he know?" Ps. xciv. 7, 10. In their blindness and
their hardness of heart they impeach the wisdom and
brave the justice, not less than they deny the knowledge
of the Omniscient God. But to leave them without excuse or subterfuge, has not he who can best instruct us
as to the nature, office, and extent of the divine attributes,
declared that God not only "feedeth the fowls," but that
"not a sparrow falleth to the ground without his knowledge?" No; not a drop from their veins, nor a feather
from their wings can escape the glance of his all-seeing
eye. Since his liberal hand provides for the sustenance
and enjoyment of all his creatures—all! from the zoophyte
at the bottom of the ocean to the dolphin and the whale
that sport on its surface; from the small winged insect
that battens on a flower, to the swift-footed ostrich that
finds her provender in a wilderness of sands—it is virtual
atheism to affirm that he cares not how wantonly and
cruelly they are destroyed.

The benevolent mind of the Saviour had not failed to

witness the tender solicitude with which a hen protects her brood, and he dignifies the act by comparing to it his own compassion for the people of Jerusalem when he anticipated the approaching calamities of the devoted city: "O Jerusalem, Jerusalem, thou that killest the prophets, and stonest them which are sent unto thee, how often would I have gathered thy children together, even as a hen gathereth her chickens under her wings, and ye would not!" Matt. xxiii. 37.

Our Lord again shows the benevolence of his nature, when he compares the joy that shall be in heaven over a repentant sinner, to that of a shepherd who goes to the mountains in quest of a lost sheep; and when he finds it, instead of treating it with harshness, and belabouring it with his staff for having wandered from the fold, to spare it the fatigue of farther travel he lays it on his shoulders, carries it home rejoicing, and invites his friends to come and participate his joy. Will any one betray such a total destitution of taste, as not to admit that this beautiful pastoral illustration of a most important doctrine, manifests such a spirit of tenderness and compassion as would have felt warmly indignant at an act of cruelty? Has it not the force of an injunction to be lenient and merciful? Sure we are that many a stronger conclusion is drawn from more feeble premises. Our Lord admonished the disciples to be "wise as serpents and harmless as doves;" and none of his admonitions, the latter part especially, has been less heeded, nor violated more grossly. The serpent is described in sacred writ as the subtlest or wisest beast of the field; and wisdom is a virtue which we should by all lawful means endeavour to acquire. The dove is the emblem of innocence and peace, the bearer of the olive branch; the form in which the Holy Spirit was manifested at the waters of Jordan, when it descended on the Saviour's head. To be harmless as doves implies that we should be as free from all violent and sanguinary deeds. What figure could the most tasteful ingenuity supply that would more strongly or beautifully inculcate the duty of humanity? But the conduct of too many evinces that they have never thought of the precept at all, or if they did, they would seem to have understood it as if it enjoined them to be rapacious as—I was going to say vultures,—but vultures are contented with prey which has been killed for them; and therefore the butcher-bird or hawk will suggest a more appropriate comparison.

The Saviour himself is compared in Scripture to one of the most gentle and innocent of creatures. He is denominated the "Lamb of God;" and "he was led like a lamb to the slaughter." If to be a Christian be to resemble Christ, here is another powerful argument for humanity. How shall any one be said to resemble the Lamb of God, whose dispositions and conduct bear a much more close similitude to the savage instincts of a wolf or the ferocity of a tiger?

Again, our Lord inculcates the duty of humanity to animals, when he directs our attention to the omniscient providence of God, as extended to the lives of creatures held the most cheap of any amongst the Jews: "Are not two sparrows sold for a farthing, and one of them shall not fall on the ground without your Father." Mat. x. 29. Or, as Luke has it, (xii. 6) "Are not five sparrows sold for two farthings, and not one of them is forgotten before God." All sound philosophy and all natural theology must concur with revelation in asserting the truth of this beautiful declaration. The inference from it is irresistible. If God regards the life of a sparrow, is it wise, is it becoming, is it not impious, in man to disregard it? Or is he privileged to take that life merely for his sport, and in contempt of that mercy which is God's darling attribute? But they are a numerous race, it may be said, and a few of them taken in a trap, or singled out as marks for the incipient efforts of young sportsmen, will not be heeded. Thus "fools make a mock at sin," and say, "Jehovah shall not see, neither shall the God of Jacob regard it?" But what says the voice of inspiration? "NOT ONE of them is forgotten before God." Insignificant as they seem to proud man, drest in his 'little brief authority,' they hold their proper station in the scale of existence, and are no more hidden from the all-seeing eye of the Omniscient, than the purple tyrant or the sceptered potentate. The gunner may make his wretched boast of the number he can bring down at a shot; but let him remember that though they were numerous as the ocean-sands, "not one of them falleth to the ground" without the knowledge of their Maker; and unless he can plead necessity or use, there is a tribunal to take cognizance of his offence.

It may be scarcely necessary to observe that our Lord's declaration extends to all animated beings, and that the sparrow* is selected only for example, because it was among the cheapest of the feathered tribes, and universally known. Besides, the species to which the allusion is made obtains the specific name of house-sparrow, from its being so familiar with man, and seeking the protection of his roof. On this ground it has a special claim to humane consideration; and as it would be inhospitable to deny it a lodging in the eaves, so would it be a pitiful parsimony to refuse it, in conjunction with the red-breast, a share of the crumbs which fall even from the poor man's table. Therefore, it is not without feelings of horror, that the author has read in a public paper the following account of a barbarous association, designated by the name of the " SPARROW CLUB," having for its object the wholesale slaughter of these cheerful interesting birds :—

" April 19, 1832.—At the parish of Hursterpoint a Sparrow-club was formed in September last, to continue until the following April, each member, during the continuance of that period, to produce, under a forfeiture, if deficient, two dozen sparrows' heads per month. Three prizes to be awarded to the members who should produce the greatest number. A few days since the members and their friends dined together, at the inn at Hursterpoint, when the *twelve* members present produced the heads of 3,978 sparrows which had been slaughtered in the interim" ! ! !—*London Morning Post.*

The existence of such a horrible fraternity is a disgrace to the nation. *Twelve* Apostles of the Demon of Cruelty would be enough to pollute the land, and fix an indelible stigma on its character—were there not some society, like that for "the Prevention of Cruelty," to

---

* "TSIPPOR. The Hebrew word is used not only for a sparrow, but for all sorts of clean birds, or such whose use was not forbidden." HARRIS's *Nat. Hist. of the Bible.*

D

counteract their mischief, and show that humanity is no stranger to the bosoms of Englishmen. May all such diabolical combinations as the Sparrow Club sink under the people's unmitigated abhorrence and execration ! Cruelty is the ally of every vice and every crime; and the sparrow-butcher and the assassin are the progeny of the same parent.

From the frequent introduction of various animals into holy writ to illustrate the divine attributes, to teach man his moral and religious duties, and above all to exemplify the paternal care and providence of the Father of All, we might reasonably conclude, independently of any positive precept, that none of them is a proper object of contempt, much less of inhumanity. As Peter, when in a vision, he beheld a sheet of vast dimensions let down from heaven, " wherein were all manner of four-footed beasts of the earth, and wild beasts, and creeping things, and fowls of the air," was commanded not to call " what God cleansed, common or unclean ;" so may we suppose ourselves commanded by a voice from universal nature, not to vilify or contemn, much less abuse or torture aught which owes its formation to infinite wisdom and Almighty power. But when we find the Son of God himself breathing mercy and compassion, and illustrating his heavenly doctrine by images and examples taken from the animal kingdom, can we for a moment doubt whether humanity to animals be an evangelical virtue; or whether he who delights in perpetrating acts of cruelty does not forfeit all just pretensions to the name and character of disciple to the meek and benevolent Jesus ? Notwithstanding, how many who are proud of their Christianity never consider the kind treatment of animals as in any manner connected with Christian duty ? How many start, and wonder, and exclaim, when it is recommended to them under the sanction of religion ?

CHAPTER IV.

MAN'S RIGHT TO THE FLESH OF ANIMALS.

" Every moving thing that liveth shall be meat for you."—Gen. ix. 3.

The question of man's right to the use of animal food has given rise to much discussion. Those who acknowledge the right contend for it on various principles, but chiefly on the Creator's power to transfer any share he pleases of his absolute dominion over the creatures of his hands, to other beings in subordination to himself. Of this dominion he has given to man a portion on certain conditions; and according to Puffendorf, not on the grounds of mutual friendship between God and man, as alleged by Diogenes the Cynic, who syllogised thus :—" All things belong to God; wise men are the friends of God; all things are common amongst friends; therefore all things belong to wise men." But in this case what becomes of the fool? Does his folly exclude him from a participation of the entrusted right? Aristotle held an opinion which egregious pride and arrogance may still defend—that as nature has made nothing imperfectly or in vain, she must of necessity have made all things for man—a conclusion which the premises by no means warrant; as if man were the sole object of creation, and that the thousand and ten thousand species of creatures could not exist happily, many of them might say much more happily, without him. Seneca thought more wisely, *Nimis nos suscipimus, si digni nobis videmur propter quos tanta moveantur.* (See Puff. p. 284.) We should indeed hold an overweening idea of our own importance, were we to imagine that the magnificent frame of nature was formed solely on our account, and not for myriads of other animated beings.

Since God has given life to man, it follows that he has given all things necessary, not only for the support but the enjoyment of that life; and therefore we conclude that man derives a right from the divine permission clearly indicated by the fact of his creation; and this conclusion is

ratified by the authority of Scripture. The prohibition
of the Jews to feed on some animals does not impair but
rather establish his right, the exception being proof of the
general rule; and besides there were special reasons for
the prohibition. Whether Adam was forbidden to eat
flesh, as some rabbins have affirmed, is of no importance,
since permission was specially granted to Noah. Gen. ix. 3.

Some of the ancient philosophers, like the modern
Brahmins, were strongly opposed to the eating of flesh,
on principles of humanity. Pythagoras in particular forbade it, contending that animals have the same common
right as ourselves to the enjoyment of life κοινον δικαιον
ημιν εχοντων ψυχης. This, says Diogenes Laertius, was
the ostensible reason; but the true one was that men might
live entirely on vegetable food, of which he supposed there
was always abundance, and that they would in consequence
be more independent of the culinary art, and also enjoy
more health of body and greater activity of mind. The
doctrine of the transmigration of souls also furnished a
strong argument against the use of animals for food.*
Porphyry participated in the sentiments of Pythagoras,
and founded his objection principally on the idea that
animals are partakers of reason, and consequently of the
same nature as man. To this it has been objected that
there is no mutual right or obligation between men and
brutes; but rather antipathy and discord. Hence results
a state of mutual warfare, and they may do each other all
the harm in their power, or whatever may best suit their
respective comfort and convenience. The argument, however, is valid only as it respects the more untameable and
ferocious creatures.

Poets and others, who form their ideas of the primitive
state of nature from imagination, are adverse to the opinion that animals were originally intended for mutual
support and destruction. On the contrary, as they inform
us, all at first was peace and harmony :—

> " Then birds in airy space might safely move,
> And timorous hares on heaths securely rove ;
> Nor needed fish the guileful hooks to fear,
> For all was peaceful and that peace sincere."

---

* See Stanley with his authorities in the " *Lives of the Philosophers,*" p. 553."

This state, however, did not long endure. Animals began to indulge their carnivorous appetites, and man to delight in feasts of blood. He was justifiable however in killing beasts of prey; but to murder innocent animals to glut his appetite was an inexcusable enormity.

> " Had he the sharpened steel alone employed
> On beasts of prey that other beasts destroyed,
> Or man invaded with their fangs and paws,
> This had been justified by nature's laws,
> And self-defence : but who did feasts begin
> Of flesh, he stretched necessaity to sin."
> To kill man-killers man has lawful power,
> But not th' extended licence to devour."

Pythagoras, who had travelled in the east, and probably studied under the Indian Brahmins, is introduced by Ovid teaching these lessons to the people of Crotona; and however unfounded we must deem them in reason and in fact, they are worthy of commendation for their merciful spirit. It is gratifying to find such humane sentiments advocated by a Grecian philosopher, and celebrated by a Roman poet. But we are admonished by our subject to turn from the fascinations of poetry to the stern realities of truth.

Paley, in the eleventh chapter of his Moral and Political Philosophy, affirms that man has " a right to the flesh of animals," and that " some excuse seems necessary for the pain and loss which we occasion to brutes, by restraining them of their liberty, mutilating their bodies, and, at last, putting an end to their lives (which we suppose to be the whole of their existence) for our pleasure or conveniency."

" The reasons alleged in vindication of this practice are the following : that the several species of brutes being created to prey upon one another, affords a kind of analogy to prove that the human species were intended to feed upon them; that, if let alone, they would overrun the earth, and exclude mankind from the occupation of it; that they are requited for what they suffer at our hands, by our care and protection."

Upon these reasons he alleges, " that the analogy contended for is extremely lame ; since brutes have no power to support life by any other means, and since we have ; for the whole human species might subsist entirely on fruit, pulse, herbs, and roots, as many tribes of Hindoos actually do." He then proceeds to state that "it would be difficult to defend this right by any arguments which the light and order of nature afford ; and that we are beholden for it to the permission recorded in Scripture." Gen. ix. 1—3.

Is there not a law, and consequently a permission, antecedent to this, founded in the constitution and absolute necessities of man ? Dr. James Johnson very justly observes, that "the first law of Nature is ' Eat or be eaten.' Life can only subsist by death. Every organized being, and particularly man, slays thousands of other organized beings, either in the vegetable or animal kingdom, to build up or maintain his own corporeal fabric."*

However lame the "analogy" may appear to Paley and his admirers, the destruction of one creature by another must always have afforded an argument in justification of man's use of animal food. If trouts kill flies, why should not man kill trouts ? If a hawk feed upon partridge, or if the nord-caper, *balæna glacialis*, may swallow three hundred cod-fish or a ton of herrings at a meal,† why should man be refused the use of similar viands ? Dr. Franklin, when a young man, "had read a treatise on the Pythagorean regimen, and fully convinced by its reasoning, abstained from the use of meat for a long time, until a cod-fish caught in the open sea, having its stomach full of little fishes, overturned his whole system. He concluded that since fishes eat each other, man might very well feed upon other animals."‡

Paley's declaration, that "the whole human species might subsist entirely on fruit, pulse, herbs, and roots, as many tribes of Hindoos actually do," requires to be greatly qualified ; nay, it may, without hazard of confutation, be absolutely contradicted. Though it be admitted that human life may be well sustained in tropical regions abounding in esculent roots and vegetables, how

---

* See *The Influence of Civic Life, Sedentary Habits, and Intellectual Refinement on Human Health and Human Happiness, &c.* by JAMES JOHNSON, M.D. London, 1820, p. 8.
† See *Shaw's Lectures on Zoology,* vol. 1, p. 145, note.
‡ *Warville's Travels in America,* p. 218.

will the argument apply to regions of perpetual sterility ?
In most countries within the temperate zones, animal
food from the earliest ages has been found indispensably
necessary; and in savage or semi-barbarous states of society, in a soil where agriculture is unknown and vegetation feeble, how could life be supported without it ? The
Greenlanders and Esquimaux derive almost their whole
subsistence from fish, seals, and whale blubber; aliments
suited by a kind Providence to the dreary regions of
cold in which they dwell. They could not, like the Hindoos, subsist on rice, though it were furnished to them in
abundance. They are impelled by strong and invincible
necessity to employ the arts in which they are dexterous,
for the capture of animals, the flesh and fluids of which
they have proved by experiment to be peculiarly adapted
to their climate and constitution. In one of Parry's expeditions in search of a north-west passage, " the seamen
sought to treat their visitors (the Esquimaux) to such de-
licacies as their ship afforded, but were for some time at
a loss to discover how their palate might be gratified.
Grog, the seamen's choicest luxury, only one old woman
could be induced to taste. Sugar, sweetmeats, ginger-
bread, were accepted only out of complaisance, and eaten
with manifest disgust; but train oil, entrails of animals,
and any thing consisting of pure fat or grease, were swallowed in immense quantities, and with symptoms of exquisite delight."* " The Greenlander," says Marchand,
in his Voyage, vol. 1, page 340, " swallows a glass of
train oil as the European would swallow a glass of TOKAY.
Fish oil, in general, is a liquor of which the inhabitants
of frozen climates, settled on the borders of the sea, and

---

* *Narrative of Discovery and Adventure in the Polar Seas and Regions,*
p. 284.
  Captain Ross, in his Second Voyage to the Arctic Regions, says, " It
would be very desirable, if in a polar region the men could acquire the
Greenland food; since all experience has shown that the large use of oil
and fat meats is the true secret of life in those frozen countries; and that
the natives cannot subsist without it, becoming diseased and dying under
a more meagre diet." Were sailors made sensible of its advantages, they
might easily be brought to the use of train oil, which independently of its
nutritive quality, is of such a stimulating nature as to support the system
against the debilitating effects of cold. I have somewhere read that this
oil has been long used in the Manchester Infirmary as an internal remedy
for rheumatism, and though much disliked by the patients at first, they
soon get so fond of it, that they beg for more than the physician thinks
necessary to prescribe.

living on its productions, make a habitual and necessary use ; it developes the heat concentrated in the stomach, and by driving it towards the circumference, by carrying it to the extremities, it maintains throughout the whole habit of the body the circulation of the fluids, it protects the members from a numbness which would end by causing their action to cease, and occasion their loss."

Some of our intrepid navigators have proved by their own experience, that draughts of animal oil enabled them much better to endure the intense cold of those " thrilling regions of the thick-ribbed ice." We conclude then, that it is the law of their nature that the inhabitants of those shores should subsist on animal food, and therefore they have an indisputable claim to its use. It is the *will of God*, manifested by proofs not to be mistaken. Their right is based upon this, the most stable of all foundations.

The stern law of necessity has impelled men in want of subsistance to devour human flesh. If that necessity has been pleaded in justification of the deed, much more may a similar necessity justify the taking of animal life.

Farther, among the proofs that it is the will of God that " every moving thing that liveth shall be meat for man," is the structure of his corporeal frame. Anatomists demonstrate this by a consideration of his organization— his teeth, his intestines, constructed for the mastication and digestion of animal as well as vegetable aliment. Add to this the pleasure of having a nutriment so congenial to the taste and appetite. Would this pleasure have been given, had it been in the plan of Providence that it should never be gratified ? Of all men, Paley would be the last to answer in the affirmative.

Plutarch, in his treatise, περι σαρκοφαγιας, *on eating flesh*, combats our opinion, because man is deficient in those powers of rending and digesting which are possessed by the carnivorous animals. " But if you contend," says he, " that you have an inborn inclination for animal food, kill what you want for yourself, without the help of a chopping knife, mallet, or axe, as wolves, bears, and lions do, who kill and eat at once. Rend an ox with thy teeth, worry a hog with thy mouth, tear a lamb or a hare in pieces, and fall on it and eat it alive as they do." We reply, no. For though we desire animal food, we must have it in a manner to suit our taste; bears and lions prefer it raw; we choose to have it boiled or roasted. When we wish to have an animal for our table, as we have neither the teeth of bears not the paws of lions, we must use the arms which nature gives, with such auxiliary instruments of art as can supply the defect with most ease to ourselves, and at least expense of pain to the creature.

The argument founded on the want of vegetable or farinaceous food, in countries which for nine months in the year are covered with ice and snow, is irresistible. But even in more favoured countries, the fruits of the ground cannot be so multiplied as to be adequate to the wants of a numerous population. Even Egypt had seven years of unproductive harvests; and we read in the history of Ireland, that in seasons of dearth the inhabitants of that fertile island have been obliged to take blood from their cattle to save them from famishing. How often have the people of many a district been preserved from a similar fate by the seasonable supply of animal food, brought to them, I might almost say miraculously, as the quails to the Israelites in the wilderness; for certain, providentially, in flights of birds, irruptions of quadrupeds, or shoals of fishes cast upon their shores ? It is a part of the wise economy of nature to supply the deficiency of one kind of her productions by the redundance of another. She seems to act on the principle recommended by the Saviour to the disciples, when they had been fed by a miraculous multiplication of the loaves and fishes, to " Gather up the fragments, that nothing might be lost." When a bird, a beast, or an insect dies, she suffers it not to be lost; for immediately it becomes the prey of other creatures, which find in it a delicious repast. Thus the atmosphere is preserved from contamination, and the hungry are fed.

The absolute prohibition of animal food would be of little service to the animal creation. Such a prohibition would involve the necessity of cultivating every spot of ground for the production of vegetable nutriment. The flocks and herds must consequently be deprived of their pasture, and should we not kill or cause them to perish, we must ourselves become the victims of hunger and want. But by no art, in our present state, can we possibly avoid depriving some creatures of life. The Brahmin who supposed that he had lived all his days on rice and vegetables only, was convinced of the contrary when he saw a new world of life rendered visible to him by the microscope. We swallow down thousands of animalcules in our " dinner of herbs," in our common beverage, and in the atmosphere we breathe. The life so destroyed is, perhaps, attended with little or no pain ; and as it is unavoidable and irremediable, not being an object of sense, it does not become an object of moral consideration. There is no cruelty, nor even a consciousness of the act in which we are engaged. But we must employ stratagem and violence to gain a superiority over the larger and more ferocious creatures. These, when we master them, we should treat with lenity, and when we find it necessary to put them to death, it should be done with the infliction of no pain which can possibly be avoided. A ball or a dagger sent at once to the seat of life is a merciful dispensation.

It may seem, perhaps, beside the object of this essay, to contend for the use of animal food ; but it may not be useless to show, that the author who undertakes to advocate the cause of humanity, is not actuated by any such morbid sensibility or false refinement as would lead him to argue against the lawfulness of taking a creature's life under any circumstances. Conscious that prejudices may be excited, and a good cause injured by carrying it to an extreme, he would discuss the subject on principles sanctioned by Scripture and reason ; and while he defends the rights of the inferior animals, would allow to man for his comfortable subsistence, and for the purposes of science, all the latitude of dominion over them which he can justly claim.

CHAPTER V.

MAN'S RIGHT TO HUNTING AND FISHING.

" Take, I pray thee, thy weapons, thy quiver and thy bow, and go out
to the field, and take me some venison."—GEN. xxvii. 3.

If it has been proved, as we think it has, that God has
given to man a right to the use of animal food, it follows
that all animals being originally in a wild state, they must
be taken by such means as man can most successfully
employ, by force or stratagem, by the inventions of art,
or by such auxiliaries as nature herself suggests and
provides. Many species, when taken, can be so tamed
and domesticated, as to render the arts by which they
were captured, so far at least as they are concerned, no
longer necessary; but others are of so wild and ferocious
a nature, that their capture cannot be easily effected, nor
the captor's safety secured, except by their death. Thus
we arrive, by a short argument, at a justification of the
practices of hunting and fishing, to which shooting may
be added.

These practices, however, are reckoned by many friends
of humanity as altogether inconsistent with the character
of Christian benevolence. They regard such sports as
exceedingly cruel, and think them indefensible by any
sound principle of religion or philosophy. Our sentimental
poets, particularly, speak of the chase with unqualified
abhorrence. Thus Thomson, in such exaggerated terms
as poetry may justify and admire, reprobates

" the steady tyrant, man,
Who, with the thoughtless insolence of power,
Inflamed beyond the most infuriate wrath
Of the worst monster that e'er roamed the waste,
For sport alone pursues the cruel chase."

He says,

" Poor is the triumph o'er the timid hare !"

and sympathizes deeply in her perplexities when she is pursued by the hounds. He is also distressed for the hunted stag, when

> "he stands at bay,
> And puts his last weak refuge in despair.
> The big round tears run down his dappled face;
> He groans in anguish, while the prowling pack
> Blood-happy, hang at his fair jutting chest,
> And mark his beauteous chequered sides with gore.

He justifies, however, the chase of the "roused-up lion," with the grim wolf, and says, when

> "The brindled boar
> Grins fell destruction, to the monster's heart
> Let the dart lighten from the nervous arm."

But as there are no lions, wolves, nor wild boars in Great Britain, he admonishes the British youth to indulge their cynegetic propensities in the fox-chase, which he describes *con amore.*

> "Give, ye Britons, then
> Your sportive fury pitiless to pour
> Loose on the nightly robber of the fold.
> * * * * *
> * * * * *
> Pour all your speed into the rapid game;
> For happy he who tops the wheeling chase;
> Has every maze evolved and every guile
> Disclosed; who knows the merits of the pack;
> Who saw the villain seized, and dying hard,
> Without complaint, though by an hundred mouths
> Relentless torn."

Now there seems no good reason why a poet should be lacrymose for the death of a hare, and triumphant with joy at the laniation of a fox. The one is as much an object of compassion as the other, and has as many virtues to give him a claim to respect. The fox is one of the most beautifully formed quadrupeds, and he is distinguished above all animals for his ingenuity, and the number and variety of his resources; and when he is pursued by the hounds, and his fate becomes inevitable, he "dies hard," that is, with a fortitude which entitles him to the commendation of the brave. But in his tastes he is too *recherché;* like many of the unfeathered biped race, he is a gourmand, and delights, when rabbits are scarce, to dine and sup on poultry; and because he follows

the instinct of his nature, in taking a chicken or gosling
for his repast, he is stigmatized as a " robber," and a
" villain," and it is deemed a subject of exultation to see
him " by a hundred mouths relentless torn !"

Hare-hunting is reprobated by Cowper as a

> " detested sport,
> That owes its pleasure to another's pain,
> That feeds upon the sobs and dying shrieks
> Of harmless nature."

It would be an easy matter thus to become sentimental
with the gentle and amiable poet. But we are discussing
an important subject, not in the spirit of poetry but of
philosophy—as a friend also to humanity,. and though
having no partiality or fondness for the chace in any form,
yet constrained to believe that there is such a provision
made for it by an all-wise Providence in the constitution
of man, the instinct of hounds, and even in the stratagems and fleetness of the hare herself, who may often
have a gratification in eluding or out-stripping her pur-
suers, as to afford some justification of the practice.* It
has been strongly argued that the great propensity to
field sports, which operates on many like an uncontrollable
instinct, is a sure indication of the intention of the Deity
not only to permit, but to stimulate to those pursuits.
And here, as in all things else, we may discern wisdom
and goodness. Such pleasure is annexed to the quest of
game, as enables the sportsman to endure hunger and
fatigue—the winter's storms and the summer's heats ; to
explore the passes of Alpine glaciers, and scale the regions
of eternal snow; to mount to the long hidden source of
rivers ; to penetrate deep forests, and make discoveries in
regions hitherto unknown, *studio fallente laborem.*

To man in a savage or semi-barbarous state the capture

* " The hare," says Beckford, p. 138, " is a little timorous animal, and
we cannot help feeling some compassion at the very time we are pursuing
her to destruction: we should give scope to all her little tricks, and not
kill her forcibly and over-matched. Instinct instructs her to make a good
defence when not unfairly treated, and I will venture to say, that as far
as her own safety is concerned, she has more cunning than the fox, and
makes many shifts to save her life far beyond all his artifice. Without doubt
you have often heard of some, who from the miraculous escapes they have
made have been thought *witches;* but I believe you have never heard of a
fox that had cunning enough to be thought a wizard."

E

of animals is necessary to his subsistence, and often would
he find his labours intolerable, were it not for the pleasure
combined with them, independently of the provision
which success affords. To lessen the pain which he might
feel in taking the life of an animal, God has given him,
as a phrenologist would say, the organs of combativeness and destructiveness, and allows them, for wise purposes in the economy of his Providence, to be gratified.
And since the lives of animals, in all stages of society,
must be taken for human support, it was benevolent in the
Creator to make necessity a pleasure; for were it otherwise, the hunter and his family might often be in a state
of starvation. Those who participate in the sports of the
field will tell us that there is mingled with them such a
spirit of enterprise, such a stimulating joyous excitement,
as renders them incomparably superior to all other recreations. Health, with air and exercise, is found in
search of amusement. The meal purchased by fatigue
has a delicious relish; sound and refreshing is the sleep
of the sportsman. "See," says Hume, in the essay entitled The Stoic, "See the hardy hunters rise from their
downy couches, shake off the slumbers which still weigh
down their heavy eye-lids, and ere Aurora has yet covered
the heavens with her flaming mantle, hasten to the forest.
They leave behind in their own houses, and in the neighbouring plains, animals of every kind, whose flesh furnishes the most delicious fare, and which offer themselves
to the fatal stroke. Laborious man disdains so easy a
purchase. He seeks for a prey which hides itself from
his search, or flees from his pursuit, or defends itself from
his violence. Having exerted in the chace every passion
of the mind, and every member of the body, he then
finds the charms of repose, and with joy compares its
pleasures to those of his engaging labours."
    In some regions of the world man must wage perpetual
war against the ferocious animals by which his own safety
is endangered. He must either slay or be slain. If he
has herds or flocks, they demand his protection, and it is
equally his duty and interest to guard them from the
beast of prey by the most efficient means in his power.
Proud is the triumph of the courageous hunter, who, like

the stripling shepherd David, has slain a lion or a bear in defence of his fold. Virgil happily illustrates the observation of Hume in a passage just quoted, that "Laborious man disdains an easy purchase," when he tells us that Ascanius in his hunting excursion, wishes that a boar or a tawney lion would descend from the mountain, and yield him a nobler triumph than the death of a flying deer :—

Spumantemque dari pecora inter inertia votis
Optat aprum, aut fulvum descendere monte leonem.—Æn. iv. 158.

Impatiently he views the feeble pray,
Wishing some nobler beast to cross his way;
And rather would the tusky boar attend,
Or see the tawney lion downward bend.—DRYDEN.

Hunting, though the proper and necessary employment of savage life, is also the precursor of a better state of society, as has been remarkably exemplified in the wilds of North America. Tucker, in his Life of Jefferson, informs us that "the brunt of the border conflicts (with the Indians) was borne by a small number of adventurers on the frontiers, who have been properly called the *pioneers of civilisation,* and who thus voluntarily made themselves the advanced guard of the colonists, from their *passion for hunting,* together with their spirit of adventure, which preferred the exciting hazards of even Indian hostility to the tame and quiet occupations of civilized life."

Hunting has ever been considered as a sport worthy of royalty, at least since the days of Nimrod, that "mighty hunter before the Lord." As it presents an image of war, it is thought a befitting exercise for potentates and kings, and a suitable preparative for military expeditions. Well indeed might a warlike spirit be excited and fostered by such hunting enterprises as we read of, in the histories not only of ancient but of more recent times, especially those which are sometimes achieved in the dominions of Asiatic sovereigns, and which appear more like affairs of great national importance than of amusement or recreation. In these the wild beasts of an extensive territory are driven together into one confined circle ; and all the princes and nobles of the land, with horse and hound, and spear and javelin, and all the apparatus of the chace, come forth invited to participate in the glory and the danger of the sport. In our boyish days we have read with deep interest the pursuit of Actæon in Ovid, and the hunting excursion of Dido and her gallant train in the fourth book of the Æneid. But no one equals Somerville's admirable description of the oriental style of hunting in the second book of the Chace; which though in poetry, and powerfully descriptive, is not invention. He compares such enterprises with the royal game of war, and praises them for the benefit they confer on mankind, by the destruction of so many noxious creatures as perish in the onslaught.

> " A nobler cause
> Calls Aurengzebe to arms. No cities sack'd,
> No mother's tears, no helpless orphan's cries,
> No violated leagues, with sharp remorse
> Shall sting the conscious victor; but mankind
> Shall hail him good and just: for 'tis on beasts
> He draws his vengeful sword ; on beasts of prey,
> Full-fed with human gore.

They who are fond of the chace in our own country speak of it in terms of rapture. They become eloquent and even poetical as they speak of the sunny landscape, the balmy breath of morn, the sound of the horn re-echoing among the mountains, the baying of the hounds, the starting and curvetting of the steeds, impatient to ' swallow up the ground," the shouts of the hunters, the gallant feats of horsemanship, and all the speed and thunder of the chace. In scenes so exhilarating and of such stimulating energy, the moralist may justly fear that the voice of pity would be vainly raised to its loftiest pitch ; or poured in its most pathetic accents in behalf of the timid fear-struck animal, for whose pursuit so much preparation has been made and so much excitement produced. The huntsman would only reply in the words of the song, " This day a stag must die," and hasten on to the fulfilment of his prediction.

That such pursuits are not prohibited by the laws of nature, or the will of God, seems to be clearly indicated by the instincts of animals themselves, whether they pursue or are pursued. A horse trembles with instinctive dread at the roar of a lion; and the hen at the appearance of a *hawk* instantly calls her brood under the wing, and assumes a posture of defence. The scent of the *pointer* is evidently given to enable him to discover the game, and the fleetness of the grey-hound that he may overtake it. These are man's auxiliaries in his shooting and hunting excursions, and so obviously intended for their specific purpose, that no one can reasonably start a question on the subject. Then as to the animals pursued, they generally lose their lives without much pain. The death of a hare or a rabbit in the chase, is nothing compared to its suffering by some other processes which there will be occasion to mention. A true sportsman has no pleasure in the protracted suffering of the bird he has wounded, or the beast he has ensnared.

Farther, must it not be admitted that such sports are designed by the wise Creator, to operate as a check to the excessive multiplication of various tribes of creatures? Throughout the whole of the animal kingdom various causes are in operation to prevent the unlimited increase of any one species; and the most constant and effectual of these is their destruction by each other. Beasts of prey are less prolific than the graminivorous and the ruminating tribes, for the obvious reason that they are less easily subjugated or destroyed; and by preying on the weaker animals, they prevent them from becoming the sole occupants of the soil. Lions and tigers in their turn become the prey of a superior foe. They are taken in the hunter's trap, or fall by his missile fires; man, the great destroyer, is sometimes himself the victim of brutal rage; he is gored by a bull, or struck down by a lion—and thus is the balance of life in the animal tribes adjusted.

The fecundity of some species of animals is of all the phenomena of Natural History the one most calculated to fill the mind with astonishment; while it demonstrates as clearly as that grass grows for the support of cattle, that they are designed for the nutriment of each other. Were they not destroyed thus, or by some other adequate means, the world could not contain them. A single herring, or cod-fish, would in an incredibly short space of time fill the whole capacity of the ocean with its progeny; and the rabbit and the rat would cover the entire surface of the terrestrial globe. Leuwenhoeck computed that there are no less than 9,344,000 eggs in a single cod,* and Pennant has calculated that a single pair of rabbits in the lapse of four years would have an offspring of one million, seventy-four thousand, eight hundred and forty.

Almost all the islands of the Archipelago are, at particular seasons, covered with quails. "On the coast of Naples, within a space of four or five miles, have been taken no less than 800,000 in a day."† Great crowds of these birds, according to Buffon, are occasionally seen to alight on the French coasts; and hence it may be almost literally said, in the language of Scripture, to "rain food from heaven." But these, multitudinous as they are, fall short of the numbers of the migratory pigeons of the American woods. These birds are seen like clouds of great depth, stratum upon stratum, and extending as far as the eye can reach, millions behind pressing upon millions before, for several successive hours, as they pass in rapid flight to their roosting or feeding localities. Wilson made a rough calculation of one of these clouds; and supposing it to be a mile in breadth, though in reality much more, and in length 240 miles, and three pigeons in each square yard, it contained 2,230,272,000 pigeons. "An almost inconceivable multitude, and yet probably far below the actual amount!" "Heaven has wisely and graciously given to these birds rapidity of flight, and a disposition to range over vast uncultivated tracts of the earth, otherwise they must have perished in the districts where they resided, or devoured up the whole productions of agriculture, as well as those of the forests." Add to this, that being palatable and nutritious food, their increase is abridged not only by hawks, buzzards, and eagles, but by the destructive arts employed to take them for the sustenance of man.

---

* Schonfeld observes, that the Icthyophagi of those barren regions of the North that are unfit for the production of grain, "not only furnish themselves with a substitute for bread by drying this fish, but send a vast quantity of their surplus stores to add to the supply of other nations." The cattle in some of those regions are fed in winter on dried pounded fish.
† *Shaw's Lectures on Zoology,* vol. i. page 212.

The grey or Norwegian rat *(Mus decumanus,* Linn.) exemplifies well the necessity of a constant check to its increase; and it so happens that, having no friend, but numerous enemies, even in its own species, its numbers are thinned and kept within due bounds. Fothergill, in his excellent Essay on the Philosophy, Study, and Use of Natural History, reckons that "a number not far short of *three millions* might be produced from a single pair in the course of four years. Now," he continues, "the consequence of such an active and productive principle of increase, if suffered continually to operate without check, would soon be fatally obvious. We have heard of fertile plains being devastated, and large towns undermined in Spain by *rabbits;* and even that a military force from Rome was once requested of the great Augustus to suppress the astonishing numbers of the same animals which overran the islands of Majorca and Minorca: but if *rats* were suffered to multiply without the restraint of the most powerful and positive natural checks, not only would fertile plains and rich cities be undermined and destroyed, but the whole surface of the earth in a very few years would be rendered a barren and an hideous waste, covered with myriads of famished *grey rats,* against which man himself would contend in vain." pp. 138, 139.

That it is among the ordinances of Providence, that one tribe of animals should prey upon another, to keep the number of each in proper bounds, is what no observer of nature will dispute. In the *Amœnitates Academicæ* it is observed, that "if the species destined to prey upon any particular animal were to perish, the greatest calamities might result from it. Nature has appointed the *Quiscula* to watch over the *Dermestes pisorum;* these being extirpated in North America by shooting, the peas have been totally ruined. If all the sparrows were to be destroyed here, our plantations would be ruined by the Grylli; America, deprived of swine, would be infested with serpents to an intolerable degree; and we must believe the same with respect to the other servants of the great family of nature, since its Author has permitted nothing to be without sufficient reason." When any genus or species ceases to be reduced to the proper standard by one engine of destruction, another is employed. A murrain among beasts may effect what the jaws of the tiger and lion have failed to accomplish. "Seals have in some seasons been observed floating in incredible numbers; and their dead bodies were so thickly strewed on some parts of the North coast of Scotland and the Northern islands, that they tainted the air."—MUDIE's *Guide to the Observation of Nature.* "Many analogous instances of mortality in particular tribes, for which no cause could be, or at least has been assigned, are recorded; and because nothing is known of the means by which they are produced, these mortalities are, in the case of animals, called 'Epizooty,' that is, 'On the Life,' because they as it were fall on the life itself, without any apparent derangement of the organization, or other disease of which the symptoms can be observed."*

Man may be considered as one of the principal instruments designed by Providence to check the redundance of other creatures. His physical wants stimulate to the invention and the employment of those arts by which this object is effected. Some animals he must sacrifice for food—others for safety and for health. Cleanliness and comfort demand the extermination of vermin, when they come to infest us; and we must consider it not as a virtue but an act of blind and excessive superstition to found such hospitals as that of Surat, mentioned in Forbes's Oriental Memoirs, for the support not only of birds and quadrupeds, but "vermin of the most loathsome description." It was the spirit of a false philosophy that led the Emperor Julian "to celebrate his shaggy and *populous* beard, which he fondly cherished after the example of the philosophers of Greece." Gibbon justly observes, that " had Julian consulted the simple dictates of reason, the first magistrate of the Romans would have scorned the affectation of Diogenes, as well as that of Darius."—*Decline and Fall*, vol. IV. page 45.

Enough has now been said to prove that man is obliged by necessity to take the lives of animals. They are part of the provision on which he subsists, and which God

---

* Lord's *Popular Physiology.*

created for his use, and he must take them by such arts as he finds most available; whether by the dog, the net, or the gun.

"The Canonists allow fishing with rods to be a proper recreation for clergymen, but prohibit them the diversion of hunting. Yet there are doctors of great authority, on the contrary, who allow them that liberty for health, and not merely for pleasure."* But this is a distinction that is seldom if ever regarded. Few would think of either hunting or fishing for mere health, though this may be the pretext, when pleasure is the real object. It is well observed in the thirty-seventh number of the Adventurer, that " there is great difference between killing for food and for sport. To take pleasure in that by which pain is inflicted, if it is not vicious is dangerous ; and every practice which, if not criminal in itself, yet wears out the sympathizing sensibilities of a tender mind, must render human nature proportionably less fit for society." It is not, however, of the legitimate acts of hunting, fishing, and shooting, as necessary to the sustenance and well-being of man, that the friends of humanity complain, but of a wasteful and useless expenditure of life, the destruction of animals for mere amusement, and the putting of them to death with circumstances of cruelty, whether it be to gratify an epicurean taste, or a too audacious curiosity, designated as a love of science. Against all such acts they must record their solemn protest, and against the sacrifice of any life, though it be that of a worm or a fly, if it cannot be justified by strong claims of use or necessity. There are some who go still farther, and proscribe hunting and fishing; and certainly, where they are pursued by gentlemen for mere amusement, they shall have no praise of mine. But as occupations, the latter particularly, they are necessary and therefore allowable. The Saviour did not condemn fishing as an employment. His disciples were fishermen, and he was sometimes present with them in their piscatory labours. On one occasion he said to Peter, "Go thou to the sea, and cast an hook, and take up the fish that first cometh up," (Matt.

---

* Wood's *New Institute of the Imperial and Civil Law*, page 103.

xvii. 27,) and on another directed them where to cast the net for a miraculous draught of fishes. The gentle and more prolific animals are required for man's support; the more ferocious must be destroyed, that the weaker may not perish under their fangs. If we would preserve the fold, the wolf must be slain; if we would save the poultry, we must kill the fox. But still animals have their rights as well as men; rights that are not to be infringed or trampled down with guiltlessness or impunity.

CHAPTER VI.

MAN'S RIGHT TO THE USE OF ANIMALS LIMITED.

" He causeth the grass to grow for the cattle."—Ps. civ. 14.

All charters and privileges have their limits. Though it be admitted that man has a right to the use and services of animals, he is not permitted by any just law, human or divine, to inflict upon them any pain which can be avoided, or to carry destruction among them without some imperative necessity. The same beneficent being who formed man, and gave him this beautiful world for his residence, also formed them, and allotted to them their respective habitations in the waters, the earth, and the air; some in depths where man has never penetrated, and others in elevations where he has never soared; where he can neither strike them with his trident nor reach them with his arrows; but where they live free and independent of him as he of them. He who said to our first parents, " Have dominion over the fish of the sea, and over the fowl of the air, and over every living thing that moveth on the earth"—said also, " To every beast of the earth, to every fowl of the air, and to every thing that creepeth on the earth wherein there is life, I have given every green herb for meat." (Gen. i. 28, 30.) Thus we find that the wants of the animal tribes were, by the bounty of God, provided for at their creation ; and in other passages, par-

ticularly in the 104th Psalm, we read of their distribution
into various localities adapted to their nature. Hence
the inference is unquestionable, that they are not to be
maltreated by man, nor deprived of that which a kind
Providence designed for their use. An apocryphal writer
says, " God ordained man through his wisdom, that he
should have dominion over the creatures which he hath
made, and order the world according to equity and righteousness, and execute judgment with an upright heart."
Wisdom, ix. 2, 3.   And once more, " Thou lovest all
things that are, and abhorrest nothing which thou hast
made ; for never wouldest thou have made any thing if
thou hadst hated it ; and how could any thing have endured, if it had not been thy will ? or been preserved, if
not called by thee ? But thou sparest all ; for they are
thine, O Lord, thou lover of souls." xi. 24. 26.

The charter given to man invests him with the privilege to *reign*, not with authority to *tyrannise;* such a
charter as a wise and powerful monarch would give to his
vicegerent, to govern with righteousness and mercy.
What can be more abhorrent from all just notions of the
beneficent Parent of all, than to imagine it could be for
any but a merciful end, that he constituted man the lord
of the lower creation ? The very superiority of man's
powers is a reason for discretion and lenity in their use ;
for they are seldom withstood, or exasperated by opposition. He triumphs in his undisputed dominion over
the animal tribes, and boasts that though he be surpassed
by one or another in fleetness, or muscular strength, in
hearing, or in sight, he surpasses them all in the combi-
nation of his faculties under the guidance of reason ; the
strongest cannot cope with his potent enginery, nor the
fleetest escape his arrows and his balls. But though
amply empowered to conquer, to subdue, and to tame,
he has no privilege from heaven to go forth, like a demon
of destruction, wantonly and unsparingly to slaughter and
destroy. The indulgence to use is not to be misinter-
preted into a liberty to abuse the gifts of Providence.
We may pluck the fruit, but not hew down the tree. We
may urge the nerves and sinews of the courser, but we

may not strain them till they snap asunder. Man's powers have their limits, and animals have their rights.

The creative energy of the Deity was originally employed, and still continues to be employed in providing for the sustenance of animals. The grass of the field was formed for their special use, and it is only by their instrumentality that it is converted into nutriment for human beings. Man cannot live on grass. It must be eaten and elaborated into flesh, not only by such mechanical and chemical processes as no mortal art has ever been able to effect; but by the still more necessary and mysterious agency of those vital energies which the living God alone can bestow and preserve.

Let any man of sense, after reading the 104th Psalm, that beautiful and sublime descant on the creation, ask of his own understanding, on what principle can it be believed that the allwise Creator formed such an infinite variety of creatures, only to furnish subjects to gratify the cruel and destructive propensities of man? Is there no distinction to be made betwixt a privilege and an absolute independent right? Beasts, birds, fishes, insects, as well as men, were formed to taste the pleasures of existence; and they, as well as men, are furnished with innumerable sources of enjoyment, passions, appetites, affections, feelings, solitary or social, conjugal, parental, and to a certain extent intellectual and moral, all of which have their proper objects of gratification. If man, urged by no necessity, but for his sport or gust, cruelly destroys that happiness of which they are living in the enjoyment, does he not endeavour to frustrate the will, and counteract the benevolent designs of the Deity?

As the Supreme Being is possessed in himself of infinite blessedness, he created the world and its tenants not to enhance his bliss, but to diffuse happiness among creatures capable of enjoying it. We see benevolent design in every region, and in all the grand phenomena of nature. The sun was formed to give light, to warm, to vivify; not to scorch, consume, and destroy; to show the brilliancy of the peacock's plumage, and the diamonds on the beetle's shard, not less than to illumine the habitation and exhilarate the heart of man. The ocean has poured forth its multitudinous waters to be the abode of innumerable myriads of creatures, from the tiny *beroe*, almost invisible in its translucency, up to the leviathan " that plays therein," not less than to be an inexhaustible source of exhalations to bedew and fructify the earth, and to form a connecting link between the most distant regions of the world. So with all the other parts of the universe above, around, beneath: and as Paley, when speaking of the human frame, observes that there is a marked design in every part for some beneficent end, we may extend his observation to the universe; and see all things cooperating by their various laws and influences, for the preservation of harmony and order, not only in the world of unorganised matter, but for the general welfare and happiness of all animated beings. This we see demonstrated by the bounteous provision made for their wants, for their pleasures, their dwelling, their clothing, their armour, and weapons of offence. And hence we conclude, that God clearly intending the good of his creatures, for man by any means to prevent that good, to injure, to abuse, to maim, torture, or inflict upon them any pain which can be avoided, is to act in opposition to the will of Heaven, and rise in rebellion against his Maker.

It seems to be a favourite opinion with many, that because they have the power, they have also the right to treat animals in whatever way their whim or caprice may dictate, without any regard to the claims of humanity. Might, with them, constitutes right. But how many actions have we the power to perform, which it would be criminal even to think of attempting ? For, as a heathen poet, speaking in the very spirit of Christianity, (see Mat. v. 28,) informs us,

" ——— Scelus intra se tacitum qui cogitat ullum Facti crimen habet."—JUV. *Sat.* xiii. 209.

" For, in the eye of Heaven, a wicked deed Devised, is done."—GIFFORD.

A strong man can tyrannise over a weak one; he may embitter his life by vexatious tasks, by stripes, and by blows; and because he calls him his own, his slave perhaps, and is responsible to no earthly tribunal for his oppressive deeds, dares to think that his right to perpetrate

F

them should not be questioned. But what is he in the
" eye of Heaven ?" What, in the estimation of all good
men ? Pharaoh thought he had a right, because he had
an armed chivalry for enforcing his commands, to make
" the children of Israel to serve with rigour," and to make
" their lives bitter with hard bondage, in mortar and in
brick, and in all manner of service in the field." (EXOD.
i. 13, 14.) Thus do some treat their brute dependents,
giving convincing proof that they want only an opportunity to rival the Egyptian oppressor, and show that the
rationality of their subjects should be no obstacle to the
malice of the despot.

> " Oh ! 'tis excellent
> To have a giant's strength ; but it is tyrannous
> To use it like a giant."

No idea can be more erroneous than this, that all animals were created for the sole purpose of being subservient
to the uses of man ; and in nothing are his arrogance and
self-conceit so obnoxious as in upholding such a belief,
though maintained by philosophers, and sanctioned by
divines. They were formed for their own enjoyment of
life, and from a principle of benevolence in the Deity,
which delights in being diffused, and whose very existence,
it might almost be said, depends on its diffusion. Some
creatures, indeed, as the horse and the dog, are admirably
adapted to be the friends and companions of man ; and
others, as the sheep and the cow, to afford him sustenance ;
and it may be admitted, that these, with the rein-deer of
Lapland and the camel of Arabia, were created with a
special regard to the comforts of the inhabitants of their
respective climates ; a consideration which should always
secure to them protection and kindness. But how many
myriads of creatures exist, that are not, and do not appear
to have ever been intended to be subservient to man's
use, except as constituting a part of the universal plan of
which man himself is a part ? Though he is said to be
omnivorous, and insatiable in his eating propensities, there
are many creatures which, happily for them, he cannot
use as food, or render palatable by all the condiments and
appliances of luxury. Some are protected from his voracious jaws by their loathsome smell ; some by a tough-

ness that will yield to no mastication; and others by
their poisonous qualities. The medusæ are too liquid,
and the star-fish (*asteriæ*) too earthy to provoke his
appetite. He does not feast on the toad, nor prepare
ragouts of the slow-worm, nor luxuriously gorge on a
fricasee of scorpions; nor, unless in cases of extreme necessity, such as occurred to Vathek, does he venture to prey
on the wolf and the vulture. What generations of the insect, the molluscous and crustaceous tribes, and of higher
orders of animals too, of birds, beasts, fishes, live and propagate their kinds, and die to give place to new generations, age after age, uninjured and unknown by man;
some in the profound depths of the sea, which plummet
never fathomed; some on rocks and islands of the ocean,
where sail was never spread; some in the lonely savannah
or howling wilderness of sand, where the foot of traveller
never trod? The lion and the tiger have sometimes as
good reason to say that man was made for them, as they
for him; and the raven and the vulture, hovering over a
field of battle, have still more reason for making a similar
affirmation. The locusts lead forth their armies to desolate the earth, and devour the fruits of man's industry, as
if he had toiled only to glut their rapacity; and having
before them a land blooming like "the garden of God,"
leave it behind them turned to a desert exhaling stench and
rottenness. The polypi construct their coral bowers in
the recesses of the deep, without asking permission of the
biped who plumes himself as Lord of the creation; and
when the war-ship is shivered to atoms on their rocky
citadel, they may boast how low they can level the pride
of those who came forth in the pride of their strength,
chanting, "Britannia rules the waves."

By what limits, it may be asked, is man's right to the
use of animals bounded? In moral questions we cannot
adjust boundaries as in geometrical measurements. We
must be guided here by reason, by conscience, and a
sense of duty to God, and the limits will be extended or
contracted according as each of these principles acts with
strength or weakness. We should use such liberty here,
as in other cases, according to an apostolic admonition,

not " for an occasion to the flesh," not for the gratification
of any cruel or luxurious propensity, but for what our
real uses and necessities require. We should never kill
for the mere sake of killing, nor for sport, nor pastime,
nor for gluttonous appetite, nor epicurean taste, nor from
antipathy, nor idle curiosity to see what nature has concealed. Neither should we cause any pain that can possibly be avoided, nor tax the working animals beyond
their strength, nor bring into contact those that are naturally hostile to each other. We should attend to the
precept of Horace in its moral and physical sense, as well
as in its poetical application, and not couple serpents with
birds, and lambs with tigers,

> " Ut placidis coeant immitia,
> Serpentes avibus geminentur, tigribus agni."
> HOR. *De Arte Poetica*, 12, 13.

unless it may be for the not illaudable purpose of shewing how kind treatment can reconcile formidable enemies,
and overcome the most ferocious instincts. Cats have
been taught to frolic with birds and mice, and hounds
with hares. So may, and so ought the influence of moral
and religious principles acting on the minds of men, lead
them to subdue their destructive propensities, and become
gentle and humane.

Cowper has well expressed, in a few lines, the extent
of man's privilege to take the lives of animals :

> " If man's convenience, health,
> Or safety interfere, his rights and claims
> Are paramount, and must extinguish theirs.
> Else they are all, the meanest things that are,
> As free to live, and to enjoy that life,
> As God was free to form them at the first,
> Who in his sovereign wisdom made them all."

Now it would be well if every man, before he ventures
on taking away that which no mortal ingenuity can restore—life, the precious gift of God to his creature—were
seriously to consider, and ask his own heart, does my
convenience necessarily demand the death of this animal,
or shall I be greatly incommoded if it be suffered to live ?
Shall I suffer so much in my person or property, that it
becomes an object of importance to have it exterminated ?
Is it required for my health ?   Has my physician recom-

mended it as a restorative, or a remedy for my growing
infirmities ? Will it act on my mind as the hellebore of
the ancients, and save me the expense of a voyage to Anticyra ? Is its existence incompatible with my own
safety ? Shall I incur from it any danger of a lacerating
bite, or an envenomed sting ? Then I am permitted to
consult my own profit by its loss. But if none of the
mischiefs or benefits contemplated would result from its
death, wherefore should it be destroyed ? Let it live,
and unmolested enjoy the life that God has bestowed :
and let me not bear the reproach of having extinguished
a single spark of vitality.

Were men to pause and ask themselves such questions
as these, there would be less useless waste of animal life,
and fewer acts of cruelty. But how often is there occasion to lament that they place no value on that life at all,
and are never for a moment impeded in their efforts to
destroy it, by the reflection that of all phenomena life is
the most interesting and the most wonderful, exclusively
the work of God, an emanation from his spirit, which
God alone can bestow, and which when once dislodged
from its corporeal tenement, can by no art or persuasion
be induced to return ? Every spark of life, though in
the feeblest insect, attests the power, the wisdom, and
consummate contrivance of the Deity, not less than the
stars that glitter in the firmament, or the sun which enlightens the system. In the external form even of a
worm or a fly, how much do we see to excite profound
admiration ! What a display of minute and elegant
workmanship, which no human ingenuity can rival or imitate ! Or, admitting that human art might imitate, and
of the materials that nature affords (for, as to absolute
creation, *that* the Almighty alone can effect) man might
form the similitude of a bird, a beast, or an insect, still it
would be only a similitude, a fine specimen of machinery,
perhaps, as compared with the common productions of
mechanism, but no more to be compared to a real living
creature, than deformity to beauty, or darkness to light.
Though, on superficial observation, it might be mistaken
for what it represents, how infinitely short must it fall of
the matchless beauty and perfection of the reality ? Con-

sider the true animal, the adaptation of its structure to its mode of life, its food, its habitation, its arts to capture its prey or elude its enemy. What a knowledge of anatomy, of mechanics, acoustics, optics, was requisite for its formation; to mould the ear with its winding auditory grottoes, and the eye with its crystalline lens and its " chamber of imagery ;" and to bind all the parts together with such incomparable symmetry, by membranes, muscles, and sinews. Then contemplate its power of voluntary motion, its sensations, instincts, appetites, all so admirably adjusted to its situation, climate, office, and rank in the scale of creation. Man might try to organize matter till the day of doom, if permitted, but still the work of his hands would be inert. He could never construct an eye to see, nor an ear to hear. God alone can impart life, that principle which is superadded to organization to form animated beings, or which rather is the organizing principle itself; a principle emanating from God : and accordingly it is written, " He sendeth forth his spirit, and they are created." Ps. civ. The emission of the quickening influence precedes the formation of the creatures ; and when it is recalled or taken back to its parent source, the forms which it organized, in which it was lodged, and which it preserved from dissolution, fall to pieces. " Thou takest away their breath (spirit), they die and return to the dust."

We are told of an atheistical physician, who in dissecting a human body, saw such irresistible evidences of design, that he was constrained to acknowledge the existence of a God all-powerful and all-wise. King David, on the contemplation of his own frame, was moved by such pious emotions of admiration and awe, that he exclaimed he was " fearfully and wonderfully made." The same may be predicated of all animal beings ; they are all fearfully and wonderfully made, insomuch that it might seem marvellous how any one can seriously contemplate them, without experiencing similar emotions, mingled with some pious dread lest he should not sufficiently honour the Deity, by not duly appreciating the superlative excellence of his works.* Justly might we

* See DERHAM's *Physico-Theology*, Book xi. Sec. 24.

suppose, had we not sad experience of the contrary, that the striking beauty of their forms, and the inimitable perfection of their organization, would prevent men from ruthlessly destroying them, as if they were created for no end but destruction. Most men in the civilized world could not see without pity, or some attempt to prevent the catastrophe, any curious piece of mechanism, an orrery, a chronometer, the model of a steam-engine, or war-ship, smashed to atoms by the hands of a barbarian ; and yet what are works like these in beauty, execution, or design, compared to the structure of a bee or a butterfly, to say nothing of the higher orders of animals ? And yet, beautiful as they are, adorned with Heaven's precious workmanship, God permits us to take and to use them, when our " convenience, health, or safety" requires. And is not this enough, but we must act the part of barbarians, rashly abuse a privilege that should be used with the greatest discretion, and prodigally destroy life, when neither convenience, health, nor safety can advance a single plea in our justification ? Can such monstrous ingratitude escape the condemnation of Heaven ? Is not such cruelty to God's creatures a sin against God himself ?

It is lamentable to see how unconscious men are of what they owe to the Creator, and how they let that very profusion of his bounty which should draw from them many a pious sentiment, and many a grateful thanksgiving, only tempt them to riotous extravagance, and the indulgence of passions which his law condemns. What folly, what sin, to make the exuberance of blessings, and the kindness of their donor, an argument for their perversion and abuse ! Is the munificence with which the table is furnished, any excuse for the gluttony and ebriety of the guests invited to the entertainment ? In the midst of plenty, produced by miracle, Christ admonished the disciples to gather up the fragments, that nothing might be lost.

We should highly extol the generosity of a rich and powerful nobleman, who, having spent large sums in ornamenting his demesne, and stocking it with various kinds of exotics and of rare game, should give free admission to all to enter its precincts, to enjoy its beauties, and, under certain restrictions, to take of his pheasants, his hares, and his deer. But what should we think of those who, turning their license to licentiousness, should find pleasure in doing all the mischief in their power—in trampling down the precious shrubs, placing bird-lime twigs in the aviaries, poisoning the fish-ponds, and laying snares and traps in every winding of the parks ? Justly might we denounce such destroyers as vile ingrates, who had forfeited a privilege of which, by abusing it, they proved themselves to be unworthy. Now what is this fair earth which we inhabit but the demesne of the Creator, in which he gives us permission to expatiate freely, and to enjoy, as discretion dictates, all the blessings with which it is so richly stored, but surely not to waste and ravage, and spread desolation and solitude where he had given fertility and animation ?

Waterton, in his amusing and instructive " Wanderings in South America,"* speaking of the wilds of Demerara, says, in accordance with these observations, " The genius which presides over these wilds will kindly allow thee to slay the fawn, and to cut down the mountain cabbage for thy support, and to select from every part of her demesne whatever may be necessary for the work thou art about; but having killed a pair of doves in order to enable thee to give mankind a true and proper description of them, thou must not destroy a third through wantonness, or to show what a good marksman thou art; that would only blot the picture thou art finishing, not colour it."

Suppose a race of beings as much superior to us as we to the irrational creatures, can we imagine any thing more shocking or horrible than that they should exercise their superiority for our destruction ? Should they come with hostile arms to seize our property, to dislodge us from our habitations, put us to the torture, and in the hope of discovering some secret of nature, dissect us alive ; or if, on some high festival, a jubilee, or coronation, when all the princes and nobles of the land were congregated, they should discharge among them repeated vollies of chained thunderbolts and fire, as Milton's satanic crew on the ce-

---

* London, 1825, 4to. pp. 15, 16.

lestial host, in what terms sufficiently strong could we reprobate their cruelty? and if, instead of pleading necessity
or use for their conduct, they should add insult to injury,
and say that it was for their sport, and that they delighted
as men do when they assail creatures which have no power
either to resist or escape, to see the ground strewed with
our mangled carcases, our limbs palpitating in blood, and
expiring in excruciating tortures; well might we believe
that the fiends had broken loose from the infernal regions,
to vent their malice and cruelty on the works of God.
As such might the weak and unresisting tribes of animals
regard man, when he comes with his devilish enginery and
murderous shot, to mow them down for his sport.

A humane man feels no small reluctance to take the life
even of such animals as injure his property. Melmoth,
after stating that the snails had more than their share of
his peaches and nectarines, says, " I deem it a sort of
cruelty to suffer them to be destroyed. ... ... To confess
the truth, I have some scruples with respect to the liberty
we assume in the *unlimited* destruction of these lower
orders of existence. I know not upon what principle of
reason and justice it is, that mankind have founded the
right over the lives of every creature that is placed in a
subordinate rank of being to themselves. Whatever claim
they may have in right of food and self-defence, did they
extend their privilege no farther than these articles would
reasonably carry them, numberless beings might enjoy
their lives in peace, who are now hurried out of them by
the most wanton and unnecessary cruelties. I cannot,
indeed, discover why it should be thought less inhuman
to crush to death a harmless insect, whose single offence
is that he eat that food which nature has prepared for its
(his) sustenance, than it would be were I to kill any more
bulky creature for the same reason. There are few tem-
pers so hardened to the impressions of humanity, as not
to shudder at the thought of the latter, and yet the former
is practised without the least check of compassion."

Dr. Edward Stillingfleet, observes that " Man regulates his actions towards his *fellow men* by *laws* and
customs. But certainly there are laws also to be observed

them should not be questioned. But what is he in the "eye of Heaven ?" What, in the estimation of all good men ? Pharaoh thought he had a right, because he had an armed chivalry for enforcing his commands, to make "the children of Israel to serve with rigour," and to make "their lives bitter with hard bondage, in mortar and in brick, and in all manner of service in the field." (Exod. i. 13, 14.) Thus do some treat their brute dependents, giving convincing proof that they want only an opportunity to rival the Egyptian oppressor, and show that the rationality of their subjects should be no obstacle to the malice of the despot.

> " Oh ! 'tis excellent
> To have a giant's strength ; but it is tyrannous
> To use it like a giant."

No idea can be more erroneous than this, that all animals were created for the sole purpose of being subservient to the uses of man ; and in nothing are his arrogance and self-conceit so obnoxious as in upholding such a belief, though maintained by philosophers, and sanctioned by divines. They were formed for their own enjoyment of life, and from a principle of benevolence in the Deity, which delights in being diffused, and whose very existence, it might almost be said, depends on its diffusion. Some creatures, indeed, as the horse and the dog, are admirably adapted to be the friends and companions of man ; and others, as the sheep and the cow, to afford him sustenance ; and it may be admitted, that these, with the rein-deer of Lapland and the camel of Arabia, were created with a special regard to the comforts of the inhabitants of their respective climates ; a consideration which should always secure to them protection and kindness. But how many myriads of creatures exist, that are not, and do not appear to have ever been intended to be subservient to man's use, except as constituting a part of the universal plan of which man himself is a part ? Though he is said to be omnivorous, and insatiable in his eating propensities, there are many creatures which, happily for them, he cannot use as food, or render palatable by all the condiments and appliances of luxury. Some are protected from his voracious jaws by their loathsome smell ; some by a toughness that will yield to no mastication; and others by their poisonous qualities. The medusæ are too liquid, and the star-fish (*asteriæ*) too earthy to provoke his appetite. He does not feast on the toad, nor prepare ragouts of the slow-worm, nor luxuriously gorge on a fricasee of scorpions; nor, unless in cases of extreme necessity, such as occurred to Vathek, does he venture to prey on the wolf and the vulture. What generations of the insect, the molluscous and crustaceous tribes, and of higher orders of animals too, of birds, beasts, fishes, live and propagate their kinds, and die to give place to new generations, age after age, uninjured and unknown by man; some in the profound depths of the sea, which plummet never fathomed; some on rocks and islands of the ocean, where sail was never spread; some in the lonely savannah or howling wilderness of sand, where the foot of traveller never trod? The lion and the tiger have sometimes as good reason to say that man was made for them, as they for him; and the raven and the vulture, hovering over a field of battle, have still more reason for making a similar affirmation. The locusts lead forth their armies to desolate the earth, and devour the fruits of man's industry, as if he had toiled only to glut their rapacity; and having before them a land blooming like " the garden of God," leave it behind them turned to a desert exhaling stench and rottenness. The polypi construct their coral bowers in the recesses of the deep, without asking permission of the biped who plumes himself as Lord of the creation; and when the war-ship is shivered to atoms on their rocky citadel, they may boast how low they can level the pride of those who came forth in the pride of their strength, chanting, " Britannia rules the waves."

By what limits, it may be asked, is man's right to the use of animals bounded? In moral questions we cannot adjust boundaries as in geometrical measurements. We must be guided here by reason, by conscience, and a sense of duty to God, and the limits will be extended or contracted according as each of these principles acts with strength or weakness. We should use such liberty here, as in other cases, according to an apostolic admonition, thousand "procreant cradles" rocked by the wind in the branches, may be offered up a sacrifice equal to a hecatomb, to the demon of cruelty. Unawed by the rooks lamenting for themselves and their young in such tones as nature gives them to utter, deprecating the gunner's wrath, and imploring to be spared, he plies his sulphurous fires, till the soil around is darkened by the carnage, or till wearied by the *sport* he desists, and goes elsewhere in quest of nobler game. Anon—behold him at the base or on the brow of some steep promontory, or in a skiff by the shores of a cliff-girt island, frequented by thousands of birds that adorn the scene by their airy flight, and swell the concert of nature by their hoarse music. Though these birds, as has been already observed, are useless when dead, neither their flesh nor their feathers being objects of domestic economy, they are highly useful while living, cheering to the seaman as he bounds over the billows, heralds of success to the industrious fisherman, ornamental to the sombre iron cliffs of the ocean, and giving a vivacity to the scene which every painter endeavours to imitate in his picture, and every poet in his song. But our sportsman careth for none of these things. His pleasure is to prove and afterwards to boast that he is "*a good shot,*" and with this view he kills as fast as he can prime and load, if not from night till morn, "from morn till dewy eve," till his ammunition or strength be exhausted; or the setting sun or falling tide warns him to be gone. The Genius of the rocks might enquire wherefore he dared to intrude, as a fiend, with his fatal artillery, into a province which God allotted to the birds of ocean as their dwelling-place: by what injury to his person or property, his health or his pleasure, had they provoked his wrath? What benefit did he expect from staining the rocks with their blood; from leaving an unfledged progeny to perish by hunger amidst the remains of their slaughtered dams; and from shrouding in misery and death a scene which till he came was all animation and joy? But the Genius would address him in these, or in more forcible terms, in vain. He would not listen to "the charmer though charming ever so wisely." The proprietor of the soil might accost him in a language that he would better understand.

There cannot be a more beautiful spectacle than a sea-bird floating on the bosom of the air, with smoothly-balanced wing, in the very luxury of motion; nor to a mind susceptible of pleasure from the contemplation of beauty, or of sympathy in the happiness of God's creatures, can there be an object that he beholds with more delight; nor aught, on the other hand, with more pain, than that same bird struck on the wing by a merciless shot, brought down in a moment from its towering elevation, and for ever deprived of its wonted enjoyment. Happier its fate to be struck dead at once, than taken captive, maimed and disfigured, to spend the residue of its brief existence in scenes altogether foreign to its habits. Even the bird of prey with which we may have less sympathy, the hawk or the eagle, chained in captivity amid the fetid relics of herons, or other birds which have been given it to devour—the fire of its eye extinguished, its plumage ruffled and sordid; its whole aspect sullen, hopeless, and sad—is a melancholy sight which few sensitive minds behold without pity; especially when they contrast its present state of captivity with its former freedom, when pursuing the game on the mountain heath, having the vast amplitude of heaven for its range, and

> Sailing with supreme dominion
> Thro' the azure depths of air.—GRAY.

Pope describes a shot pheasant with his usual descriptive powers, but he exhausts his pity in a single interjection :—

> " See from the brake the whirring pheasant springs,
> And mounts exulting on triumphant wings :
> Short is his joy ; he feels the fiery wound,
> Flutters in blood, and panting beats the ground.
> Ah! what avail his glossy, varying dyes,
> His purple crest, and scarlet circled eyes,
> The vivid green his shining plumes unfold,
> His painted wings, and breast that flames with gold ?"

The poet proceeds to describe what he calls the "pleasing toils" of the woods and fields; and how the fowler roves with "slaughtering guns," "where doves in flocks the leafless tree o'ershade;" but he expresses no disap-

not " for an occasion to the flesh," not for the gratification
of any cruel or luxurious propensity, but for what our
real uses and necessities require. We should never kill
for the mere sake of killing, nor for sport, nor pastime,
nor for gluttonous appetite, nor epicurean taste, nor from
antipathy, nor idle curiosity to see what nature has concealed. Neither should we cause any pain that can possibly be avoided, nor tax the working animals beyond
their strength, nor bring into contact those that are naturally hostile to each other. We should attend to the
precept of Horace in its moral and physical sense, as well
as in its poetical application, and not couple serpents with
birds, and lambs with tigers,

> " Ut placidis coeant immitia,
> Serpentes avibus geminentur, tigribus agni."
> Hor. *De Arte Poetica*, 12, 13.

unless it may be for the not illaudable purpose of shewing how kind treatment can reconcile formidable enemies,
and overcome the most ferocious instincts. Cats have
been taught to frolic with birds and mice, and hounds
with hares. So may, and so ought the influence of moral
and religious principles acting on the minds of men, lead
them to subdue their destructive propensities, and become
gentle and humane.

Cowper has well expressed, in a few lines, the extent
of man's privilege to take the lives of animals :

> " If man's convenience, health,
> Or safety interfere, his rights and claims
> Are paramount, and must extinguish theirs.
> Else they are all, the meanest things that are,
> As free to live, and to enjoy that life,
> As God was free to form them at the first,
> Who in his sovereign wisdom made them all."

Now it would be well if every man, before he ventures
on taking away that which no mortal ingenuity can restore—life, the precious gift of God to his creature—were
seriously to consider, and ask his own heart, does my
convenience necessarily demand the death of this animal,
or shall I be greatly incommoded if it be suffered to live ?
Shall I suffer so much in my person or property, that it
becomes an object of importance to have it exterminated ?
Is it required for my health ? Has my physician recom-

mended it as a restorative, or a remedy for my growing infirmities ? Will it act on my mind as the hellebore of the ancients, and save me the expense of a voyage to Anticyra ? Is its existence incompatible with my own safety ? Shall I incur from it any danger of a lacerating bite, or an envenomed sting ? Then I am permitted to consult my own profit by its loss. But if none of the mischiefs or benefits contemplated would result from its death, wherefore should it be destroyed ? Let 'it live, and unmolested enjoy the life that God has bestowed : and let me not bear the reproach of having extinguished a single spark of vitality.

Were men to pause and ask themselves such questions as these, there would be less useless waste of animal life, and fewer acts of cruelty. But how often is there occasion to lament that they place no value on that life at all, and are never for a moment impeded in their efforts to destroy it, by the reflection that of all phenomena life is the most interesting and the most wonderful, exclusively the work of God, an emanation from his spirit, which God alone can bestow, and which when once dislodged from its corporeal tenement, can by no art or persuasion be induced to return ? Every spark of life, though in the feeblest insect, attests the power, the wisdom, and consummate contrivance of the Deity, not less than the stars that glitter in the firmament, or the sun which enlightens the system. In the external form even of a worm or a fly, how much do we see to excite profound admiration ! What a display of minute and elegant workmanship, which no human ingenuity can rival or imitate ! Or, admitting that human art might imitate, and of the materials that nature affords (for, as to absolute creation, *that* the Almighty alone can effect) man might form the similitude of a bird, a beast, or an insect, still it would be only a similitude, a fine specimen of machinery, perhaps, as compared with the common productions of mechanism, but no more to be compared to a real living creature, than deformity to beauty, or darkness to light. Though, on superficial observation, it might be mistaken for what it represents, how infinitely short must it fall of the matchless beauty and perfection of the reality ? Consider the true animal, the adaptation of its structure to its mode of life, its food, its habitation, its arts to capture its prey or elude its enemy. What a knowledge of anatomy, of mechanics, acoustics, optics, was requisite for its formation; to mould the ear with its winding auditory grottoes, and the eye with its crystalline lens and its "chamber of imagery;" and to bind all the parts together with such incomparable symmetry, by membranes, muscles, and sinews. Then contemplate its power of voluntary motion, its sensations, instincts, appetites, all so admirably adjusted to its situation, climate, office, and rank in the scale of creation. Man might try to organize matter till the day of doom, if permitted, but still the work of his hands would be inert. He could never construct an eye to see, nor an ear to hear. God alone can impart life, that principle which is superadded to organization to form animated beings, or which rather is the organizing principle itself; a principle emanating from God: and accordingly it is written, "He sendeth forth his spirit, and they are created." Ps. civ. The emission of the quickening influence precedes the formation of the creatures; and when it is recalled or taken back to its parent source, the forms which it organized, in which it was lodged, and which it preserved from dissolution, fall to pieces. "Thou takest away their breath (spirit), they die and return to the dust."

We are told of an atheistical physician, who in dissecting a human body, saw such irresistible evidences of design, that he was constrained to acknowledge the existence of a God all-powerful and all-wise. King David, on the contemplation of his own frame, was moved by such pious emotions of admiration and awe, that he exclaimed he was "fearfully and wonderfully made." The same may be predicated of all animal beings; they are all fearfully and wonderfully made, insomuch that it might seem marvellous how any one can seriously contemplate them, without experiencing similar emotions, mingled with some pious dread lest he should not sufficiently honour the Deity, by not duly appreciating the superlative excellence of his works.* Justly might we

* See DERHAM's *Physico-Theology*, Book xi. Sec. 24.

suppose, had we not sad experience of the contrary, that the striking beauty of their forms, and the inimitable perfection of their organization, would prevent men from ruthlessly destroying them, as if they were created for no end but destruction. Most men in the civilized world could not see without pity, or some attempt to prevent the catastrophe, any curious piece of mechanism, an orrery, a chronometer, the model of a steam-engine, or war-ship, smashed to atoms by the hands of a barbarian; and yet what are works like these in beauty, execution, or design, compared to the structure of a bee or a butterfly, to say nothing of the higher orders of animals? And yet, beautiful as they are, adorned with Heaven's precious workmanship, God permits us to take and to use them, when our "convenience, health, or safety" requires. And is not this enough, but we must act the part of barbarians, rashly abuse a privilege that should be used with the greatest discretion, and prodigally destroy life, when neither convenience, health, nor safety can advance a single plea in our justification? Can such monstrous ingratitude escape the condemnation of Heaven? Is not such cruelty to God's creatures a sin against God himself?

It is lamentable to see how unconscious men are of what they owe to the Creator, and how they let that very profusion of his bounty which should draw from them many a pious sentiment, and many a grateful thanksgiving, only tempt them to riotous extravagance, and the indulgence of passions which his law condemns. What folly, what sin, to make the exuberance of blessings, and the kindness of their donor, an argument for their perversion and abuse! Is the munificence with which the table is furnished, any excuse for the gluttony and ebriety of the guests invited to the entertainment? In the midst of plenty, produced by miracle, Christ admonished the disciples to gather up the fragments, that nothing might be lost.

We should highly extol the generosity of a rich and powerful nobleman, who, having spent large sums in ornamenting his demesne, and stocking it with various kinds of exotics and of rare game, should give free admission to a minister of his justice, and is associated with the eagle in punishing filial disobedience and ingratitude.—*Prov.* xxx. 17. Again we find it in the company of the cormorant and bittern, croaking the dirge of Nineveh's departed glory, or choosing her residence with the pelican and the porcupine in the ruins of Edom, and thereby declaring its utter desolation.—LOWTH's *Isaiah* xxxiv. 11.

In enumerating the blessings of disobedience, Moses says to the children of Israel, " Blessed shalt thou be in the fruit of thy cattle, the increase of thy kine, and the flock of thy sheep." In the curses of disobedience, all this was reversed; and it is added, " Thou shalt be meat unto all the fowls of the air, and unto the beasts of the earth, and no man shall fray them away." Moreover, "All thy trees and the fruit of thy land shall the locust consume."—*Deut.* xxviii. The Israelites had good reason to know what a formidable enemy they might find in the locust, though only an insect that might be crushed in hundreds beneath the foot. They had seen the desolation it caused in the land of Egypt, when it came in myriads, as the angel of wrath, and consumed every herb and green leaf. They had also witnessed in the plagues of the flies and the frogs, how the feeblest and most despicable of creatures, in the hand of the Almighty, can be made a scourge terrible as the blasting thunder and the devastating hail, that "smote both man and beast, and every herb, and brake every tree of the field."

With the plague of locusts may be conjoined " the teeth of beasts, and the poison of serpents," commissioned to execute the sentence of Jehovah in destroying their cattle, robbing them of their children, and thinning their population.—*Numb.* xxi. 6. *Lev.* xxvi. 22.

While a disobedient prophet was journeying on his way, a lion met and slew him, impelled, it would seem, by a divine impulse, and not by hunger, for neither was the carcase devoured nor the ass torn. But a whole den of lions, under the sovereign controul of Omnipotence, lose their fury, and refuse to obey the mandate of a tyrant to devour the true prophet of God.—*Dan.* vi. 22.

As a scriptural exemplification of the mode in which the Deity makes animals subservient to his gracious purposes of benevolence towards man, as well as for his chastisements, it may be mentioned that when the Israelites murmured for lack of bread, God sent them quails in such numbers that they filled the camp, or, as it is poetically expressed in the 78th Psalm, " He rained flesh upon them as dust, and feathered fowls like as the sand of the sea." The increase of their kine being among the promised blessings, David, praying for the prosperity of his country, says, "That our sheep may bring forth thousands and ten thousands in our streets, and that our oxen may be strong to labour." He would justly consider the granting of this petition as a signal instance of divine favour.

Several of the tribes of Israel seem to have manifested their estimation of animals by having one or another figured on their standards or armorial bearings, as emblematic of their respective characters, history, or occupation, and to these the patriarch Jacob is supposed particularly to allude, when he addressed his children for the last time in the language of prophecy. He says of Judah that he is a lion's whelp. Issachar he designates a strong ass couching down between two burdens; Dan, an adder in the path; Naphtali, a hind let loose; " Benjamin shall raven as a wolf, in the morning he shall devour the prey, and at night he shall divide the spoil."—*Gen.* xlix. 27.

Again we find the whole animal kingdom invoked by David to join in celebrating the praises of Jehovah, and associated with " kings, princes, and judges of the earth." *Psalm* cxlviii. 10, 13. Jehovah himself is introduced by the prophet Isaiah, xliii. 20, saying, " The beasts of the field shall honour me, the dragons and the owls;" or, as the passsage is rendered by Bishop Lowth,

" The wild beast of the field shall glorify me,
The dragons, and the daughters of the ostrich,
Because I have given waters in the wilderness,
And flowing streams in the desert,
To give drink to my people, my chosen."

The Deity himself is compared in the Scriptures to some animals: and here it may be said, that to compare that infinite and eternal Being, who is beyond all comparison great and wise and good, to any of his own creatures, is a lessening of his majesty; and, philosophically speaking, this is unquestionably true; and hence it is written, " To whom then will ye liken God ? or what likeness will ye compare unto him ?"—*Isaiah*, xl. 18. This may still be asked in confutation of image worshippers; and we may say, in the language of the heathen poet,

"Nil majus generatur ipso ;
Nec viget quicquam simile, aut secundum."

But the dealings of God towards man must be described in such language as will make a suitable impression, and by such sensible and lively images as will convey the idea meant to be expressed, more forcibly than could be done by the language of metaphysics. In treating of a subject so exalted as the attributes of the Deity, and the exercise of his providence, metaphor and comparison must be employed, in accommodation to human understanding and comprehension. Hence Jehovah is represented by the prophet Hosea, expressing the severity of his judgments, by saying, " I will be unto Ephraim as a lion, and as a young lion to the house of Judah." *Hosea* , v. 14 ; and xiii. 7, 8.

As the lion is the noblest among quadrupeds, so is the eagle the noblest among birds. The female, like that of most birds, is supposed to have a peculiarly tender care of her young ; and therefore Moses, to show the loving kindness of the Deity to the children of Israel, says, " as an eagle with affection watcheth over her young, and cherisheth and spreadeth her wings over them, so he (Jehovah) took him, (Israel) and bore him on his wings." *Deut.* xxx. 11 ; *Exod.* xix. 4.

The safety and triumph of the righteous in the most formidable perils are illustrated by animals : " Thou shalt tread upon the lion and adder ; the young lion and the dragon shalt thou trample under feet." *Ps.* xci. 13.

Numerous are the lessons both of moral and religious wisdom taught and enforced in the Scriptures, by examples taken from the animal creation. The effects of evil habits, and the difficulty of relinquishing them, are shown by asking, " Can the Ethiopian change his skin, or the leopard his spots ? then may ye do good that are accustomed to do evil."—*Jer.* xiii. 23. Apathy, indifference, and ignorance of the divine judgments are reproved by saying, "The ox knoweth his owner, and the ass his master's crib; but Israel doth not know, my people doth not consider."—*Is.* i. 3. "Yea," says Jeremiah, (vii. 7.) "the stork in the heavens knoweth her appointed times, and the turtle and the crane and the swallow observe the time of their coming; but my people know not the judgment of the Lord."

The wise king Solomon was a great and successful student of natural history; "and spake of trees, from the cedar tree that is in Lebanon, even unto the hyssop that springeth out of the wall; he spake also of beasts, and of fowl, and of creeping things, and of fishes."—1 *Kings,* iv. 33. He turned his knowledge of these subjects to the best use, and deduced from it maxims of practical wisdom. He illustrates the fugacity of riches by the flight of an eagle towards heaven; he sends the sluggard to the ant for a lesson of provident industry; and he warns the drunkard of his fate, by telling him that wine, "at the last, biteth like a serpent, and stingeth like an adder." While he admired the graceful movements of the lion and the greyhound, he led us to consider and imitate the exceeding wisdom of other animals, their intelligent foresight, their means of securing themselves from danger, their love of order equalling that of a marshalled host, and their judicious use of the means which God has given them, in finding and securing for themselves a proper residence, though it be in the palaces of kings. "There be four things which are little upon the earth, but they are exceeding wise: the ants are a people not strong, yet they prepare their meat in the summer; the conies are but a feeble folk, yet they make their houses in the rocks; the locusts have no king, yet they go forth all of them by bands; the spider taketh hold with her hands, and is in kings' palaces."—*Prov.* xxx. 24—28.

To Job we are indebted for some of the most splendid descriptions in natural history. By these he illustrates the power and wisdom of the Deity with matchless beauty. No writer of natural theology is so eloquent as Job, or makes so felicitous a use of his knowledge of the

animal creation to prove' and adorn his reasonings on
the divine attributes. Succeeding writers, as Derham and
Paley, may have considered more profoundly the anatomical structure, with the various uses of the parts of animals, and by the aid of the microscope, contemplated
numerous marks of contrivance which escape the scrutiny
of unassisted vision; but none has been more judicious
in the selection of examples, nor seized more happily on
the grand characteristics of what he describes. As in his
notices of the celestial and atmospherical, and let me add,
geological phenomena, he is always sublime; so, in his
description of animals, he is discriminating and powerful.
He places the object before us in all the vivid colouring
which language can bestow. Who has not felt transported
with admiration, as he contemplated his magnificent picture of the war-horse pawing in the valley and rejoicing
in his strength; of the eagle mounting to her eyrie in the
rocks; of the behemoth, whose bones are as strong pieces
of brass or bars of iron; and of the leviathan, whose eyes
are as the eye-lids of the morning, who counteth darts as
stubble, and whose rapid motion through the deep is
marked by a wake sparkling and ebullient with the ocean
foam?

Enough has been said on this topic; the reader, perhaps, may think too much. But the author is of opinion,
that a forcible argument for humanity to animals may
be founded on the single circumstance, that they occupy
so much of the attention of the sacred writers, and are so
often spoken of in immediate connexion with the divine
attributes. Job exalts them into the office of teachers,
and admonishes us to attend to their instruction. "Ask
now the beasts, and they shall teach thee; and the fowls
of the air, and they shall tell thee; or the reptiles of the
earth, and they will inform thee; who among all these
knoweth not that Jehovah made them; in whose hand is
the breath of every living thing?" (xii. 7, 10.)

It may confirm the argument to observe that animals
now, as of old, continue to be employed by the Deity in
the conduct of his providence, as blessings or curses, to
promote or to frustrate the designs of man, to render too
daring a project abortive, to humble the pride of the am-

bitious, and weaken the strength of the mighty. In nothing, indeed, are the power and wisdom of God more remarkable than in the silent mysterious modes by which he accomplishes his purposes, by means the most unsuspected, and apparently the most inefficient. Without giving way to any fanciful or superstitious notion, we may readily believe that by the feeblest instrument he can effect the most stupendous revolutions in the history both of nations and individuals. Men, in the management of their affairs, commonly select such causes as seem most adequate to the intended effect; they prepare mighty fleets and armies to humble the pride of their enemy, and come with well-imitated thunder and lightning, to subvert his citadels and towers. But in the hands of God a worm or a fly is armed with the might of omnipotence, and the most astonishing effects result from causes apparently the most contemptible. For, as in the propagation of the gospel, so in his moral and physical administration, " God hath chosen the weak things of the world to confound the things which are mighty ; and base things of the world, and things which are despised hath God chosen, yea, and things which are not, to bring to nought things that are ; that no flesh should glory in his presence." 1 *Cor.* i. 27, 29. We have seen how, under the Jewish dispensation, the locust and the caterpillar were commissioned to destroy ; and when God intended to desolate Judah, he declared by the prophet, that he would " hiss" for the Egyptian fly and the Assyrian bee to execute his purpose.—*Isaiah,* vii. 18. Shall we affirm, that these and similar agencies have ceased ? We dare not. The greatest events in the history of man are still accomplished by means seemingly the most trivial, really the most efficacious. The sting of an insect, the bite of a reptile, the fang of a beast of prey, may be coupled with the rise and fall of empires. " An adder in the path biteth the horse's heels, so that his rider shall fall backward," and end a dynasty of kings. We have read of a royal usurper, whose death was caused by the titillation of a fly in his nostrils ;* and the most loathsome of ver-

* See MILMAN's *History of the Jews,* vol. iii. p. 237.

min became to the vain-glorious Herod terrible as the smiting brand of the angel of the Lord.

Many instances, if necessary, might be adduced to show the instrumentality of animals in leading to important results, not only when acting under man's immediate guidance, as in the case of the Persian monarch who owed his crown to the opportune neighing of his horse; but in cases where their presence might be almost attributed to their own voluntary determination, or even to a divine commission. A belief in omens is now wisely discarded as superstitious, and birds may be seen in the heavens, either to the right or the left, without deciding the issue of a battle. But the Roman warrior, who was indebted to the assistance of a raven for his defeat of a gigantic Gaul, and an honourable title commemorative of the fact, that descended to his posterity, might well suppose so singular an incident a special mark of favour from the Gods; and well might the geese, that by their cackling saved the Capitol, be esteemed sacred. One of the most formidable wars in which Rome had ever been engaged, was brought to a fortunate conclusion by the lowliest of reptiles. Some snails, as Sallust informs us, discovered to a Roman soldier the path by which a rocky citadel, till then deemed impregnable, was scaled; the garrison was in consequence surprised, the fortress taken, and the last hope of Jugurtha extinguished. The most splendid events in the history of Scotland, the discomfiture of Edward's gallant host, and the establishment of Bruce on the throne, might be literally said to have been decided by the perseverance of a spider.—See Sir WALTER SCOTT's " Tales of a Grandfather," Vol. 1. Nay, in our own times a British man-of-war, as has been well authenticated, was indebted for a victory to the crowing of a cock.* "At this moment (when she was on the point of striking her colours) a cock having, by the wreck, been liberated from

---

* *Life of Richard Earl Howe, K.G.* &c. by Sir JOHN BARROW. " On the arrival of the ship (the Marlborough) at Plymouth, the cock was given to Lord Geo. Lennox, the governor, by desire of Captain Berkeley. Lady Hardy has been good enough to ascertain from her aunt, Lady Mary Lennox, that the story is perfectly true, that the cock lived to a good old age, and that while the Marlborough remained at Plymouth, it was daily visited by parties of her crew."—LIT. GAZ, Dec. 30, 1837.

the broken coop, suddenly perched himself on the stump of the main-mast, clapped his wings and crowed aloud. In an instant three hearty cheers rang throughout the ship's company, and no more talk of surrender."

"Such great events from trivial causes spring!"

And not only from causes deemed trivial, but most remote both as to time and place. A little spark may kindle a devouring conflagration; and the touching of some invisible spring put into motion a whole train of complicated machinery. Condorcet remarks that "the appearances we observe in a nation in any particular age have frequently their cause in a revolution happening ten ages before it, and at a distance of a thousand leagues; and the night of time conceals a great portion of those events, the influence of which we see operating upon the men who have preceded us, and sometimes extending to ourselves." We know not by what imperceptible mysterious ties the human mind is influenced; but we cannot deny that its weightiest determinations are often prompted and fixed by circumstances insignificant as the movements of a spider, or the crowing of a cock.

That God could so multiply and arm the meanest of reptiles, or microscopic animalcula, as to become a destructive annoyance, none but a fool or an Atheist will dispute. Linnæus, with the prophet Joel, speaks of insects as the armies of the Most High. "If he decrees to chastise mankind, a single species of these animals is multiplied as the sands of the sea, and perform their divine commission." We learn from the traveller Bruce what consternation the *zimb* spreads among the Abyssinian shepherds and their flocks; and to the rein-deer of Lapland the gad-fly is not less formidable. How terrible would be a legion of these "winged assassins!" The hornet, the wasp, and exasperated bee are enemies not to be despised in our own country. How often, both at home and abroad, are various species of worms and flies found to act as the scourge of God, in frustrating the labours of the husbandman! In one season "the *formica saccharivora* appeared in such myriads in the island of Granada, as to put a stop to the cultivation of the sugar-cane, and a reward of

H

£20,000 was offered for the most effectual mode of destroying them." But that power alone who sent was found efficient to remove them; and they were at last destroyed by torrents of rain accompanied by a dreadful hurricane.*—(KIRBY and SPENCE's *Entomology,* vol. i. page 184.

Such events, however, happen when they may, are seldom considered in connexion with religion. They are regarded as merely fortuitous; just as are the phenomena of wind and rain, and heat and cold, by the majority of mankind, without any reference to the Great Being who gave to nature her laws, and regulates her movements. They forget that God is in the zephyr as well as in the whirlwind; and that the moth can accomplish his purpose not less effectually than the thunderbolt.

In the apocryphal book of " The Wisdom of Solomon," we are told of certain idolaters who worshipped images in the form of beasts; "Therefore by the like were they punished worthily, and by the multitude of beasts tormented." " That they might know that wherewithal a man sinneth by the same also shall he be punished." It would not indeed, by any means be surprising if those who are merciless to animals should suffer by them in their person or property; and find by experience that the *lex talionis* is not yet altogether abrogated. " The wicked," says Solomon, " shall fall by his own wickedness; and transgressors shall be taken in their own naughtiness." The deceiver is often meshed in the net which he spread for his neighbour. The poisoner by mistake drinks the bowl which he drugged for his friend. The assassin is mistaken in the dark by his accomplice, and falls by a dagger or a ball, instead of the intended victim. In the glutton and drunkard is fulfilled the imprecation of David. " Let their table become a snare before them, and that which should have been for their welfare, let it become a trap." The exhilarating beverage is converted by excess into a deleterious poison; and the surfeit is followed by apoplexy and death. Often does it

---

* PLINY in his *Nat. Hist.* lib. 8, c. 29, to which the curious reader is referred, gives us several striking examples of the mischief caused by creatures which we deem contemptible. "Nec minus clara exitii documenta sunt etiam ex contemnendis animalibus," &c.

happen that the persecutor of animals becomes the victim of his own cruelty. There is a point, or maximum, of sufferance beyond which they cannot be pushed with safety. Oppression which drives even wise men mad, may goad the most passive creatures to resistance and revenge.

> " The poor wren
> The most dimunitive of birds, will fight,
> The young ones in her nest, against the owl."

We should not wonder to hear of a man trodden down and gored to death by the bull he has baited; nor of a dog turning on his unmerciful master, and by a lacerating bite avenging the blows and kicks he has received. The author has heard of two distressing cases of hydrophobia caused, one by the bite of a dog, the other by that of a cat; the former driven mad in a cruel experiment; the other by being hunted for sport, in a confined situation. The story of Misagathus in " Cowper's Task," is probably no fiction. This "man monster" had urged his horse " with sounding whip and rowels died in blood," to the brink of a precipice intent on self destruction. But, the wiser beast resisting all attempts to take the fatal leap, the rider at last relinquished his evil purpose, and withdrew, elated by the impious thought that as by his attempt he had bravely defied, so had he also as bravely triumphed over divine Providence. But—

> " A storm was near,
> An unsuspected storm. His hour was come.
> The impious challenger of power divine
> Was now to learn, that Heaven, tho' slow to wrath,
> Is never with impunity defied.
> His horse as he had caught his master's mood,
> Snorting, and starting into sudden rage,
> Unbidden and not now to be controll'd,
> Rush'd to the cliff, and, having reach'd it, stood.
> At once the shock unseated him : he flew
> Sheer o'er the craggy barrier ; and immers'd
> Deep in the flood, found, when he sought it not,
> The death he had deserv'd, and died alone.
> So God wrought double justice ; made the fool
> The victim of his own tremendous choice,
> And taught a brute the way to safe revenge."

Such facts as these may appear purely accidental. But in truth nothing is really so, and when we say that aught has happened by chance we only say in other words, that

we are ignorant of the means by which it was effected.
The axiom of Lucretius, *Ex nihilo nihil fit*, is as true in
morals as in physics. Events deemed altogether fortuitous
are really as much the result of certain causes, as those
of which we are ourselves the agents. " The ways of
heaven are dark and intricate;" but only to human observation. They are " a mighty maze; but not without
a plan." The springs and wheels of the great machine
of nature may be imperceptible, but the motion is seen,
and known to be uniform and constant. In the moral
world, secrets which were thought to be wrapt up in the
darkest concealment, become known and rush into public
circulation we cannot tell how; but surely from some efficient agency. " A bird of the air shall carry the voice,
and that which hath wings shall tell the matter." Birds
and beasts, as well as the cherubim and seraphim who
are represented as surrounding the throne of God, ready
to go forth and execute his high behest, are his agents to
accomplish his designs in this lower world; and, according to its present constitution, are as indispensible to the
whole of its economy as the elements of light and heat.
The worm that God prepared smote Jonah's " gourd
that it withered," and served the will of the Almighty not
less surely than if it had been the two-edged sword in
the hand of the cherub that guarded Eden. We have
read of strange discoveries, and signal acts of justice and
mercy effected by animals. A dog has detected and
brought murderers to conviction. A ship has been saved
from sinking, by a fish wedging itself in the leaky orifice.
Shall we say that such events are mere accidents ? Whatever a cold hearted sceptic may think, no person on board
the vessel thus marvellously preserved, would fail to re-
cognize the finger of God in the mode of his deliverance.
The sight of a little flower in the wilds of Africa, by suggesting or reviving a trust in him who clothes the lilies
of the field, so recruited the fainting strength of the traveller Park, that he was enabled to make a new exertion
which led him to safety. On another occasion when he
lay down sick, exhausted and almost perishing of thirst,
the croaking of frogs at some distance came as sweet
music to his ear, for it told him that water was nigh to

renovate his spirit and recruit his weary frame. The frog ever after should have been, perhaps was, as much an object of friendly regard to Park, as was the spider to king Robert Bruce. To him it was as the angel of Jehovah to Hagar in the wilderness, when the water in her bottle was spent. Vaillant, in a similar situation in Caffraria, was led by his ape and his dogs to the discovery of " a beautiful spring." More than once says he, " I received signal services from the animals I had along with me, and on this occasion they freed me from a dreadful affliction, under which I must have sunk without their assistance."*

But not to dwell on particular instances such as these, which are innumerable, let us for a moment consider how Providence, by means of animals, conducts the most important affairs in the history of our species. They form a great link in the chain of causes and effects, and by them is plenty or want created, and consequently health or disease, peace or discord, the stability or subversion of thrones. Who can tell what mighty events are produced by animalcula floating in the atmosphere, rising in miasmata, choaking the gates of life in higher orders of animals, and producing cholera, pestilence, and death? Earthworms are, of all creatures, perhaps, the most despised; and yet if lost, as White of Selborne attests, they would make " a lamentable chasm. For to say nothing of half the birds, and some quadrupeds, which are almost entirely supported by them, worms seem to be the great promoters of vegetation." Insects, of all the forms in which life is exhibited the most various and numerous, are employed in many operations conducive to the support and well-being of the general system, and especially in contributing to man's food, raiment, and health. Some of them are highly useful, as the fig-tree will testify, in puncturing and maturing the fruit, or in transporting the pollen of blossoms and flowers, by which trees are fructified. By the migratory instincts of birds and fishes, provision is made for an annual plenteous

---

* Strange that Vaillant should say "Botany neither speaks to the heart nor conveys any sentiment to the mind." Park felt differently.

variety of nutriment. Were a single species annihilated; the herring for instance, how lamentable would be the result to the poor of the country, and consequently to the rich, and the whole mass of Irish and Scotch population ? Both birds and beasts are made the unconscious agents of much good in the vegetable world, by conveying from one region to another various seeds which pass through them undigested, or which cling to their hairy coats as they are browsing in the copses. The squirrel performs the office of a good planter by depositing in the ground for future use some of the nuts on which he feeds, which being forgotten or unfound, have leave to vegetate and become a forest. The Dutch colonists of the spice islands in the East, in order to shut out all competition, and secure to themselves the whole of the nutmeg trade, seemed as if they would battle with heaven, like the giants of old, and proclaimed war against nature by endeavouring to extirpate all the nutmeg trees that grew in regions not immediately in their possession. But the winged messengers of the Most High frustrated the impious attempt, by sowing the seeds which they swallowed in districts beyond the Dutchmen's reach and jurisdiction ; thus affording another striking example of the pride, the wickedness, and the impotency of man in essaying to frustrate the designs of a gracious Providence; and at the same time demonstrating how the feeblest agents, if commissioned by the Almighty, can turn the wisest of his projects to folly, and wither up and annihilate the most gigantic efforts of human strength.

A few of the instances which have been noticed of the instrumentality of animals in producing important results, may tend, perhaps, to confirm some men's belief of a particular Providence. Many, on the other hand, may regard them as events with which Providence had no concern, and maintain that God rules the world by certain laws, of which the action is never interrupted. The law of gravitation, for instance, acts universally, and is never for a moment suspended. Fire will burn, water drown, and arsenic poison the good as well as the bad. If a virtuous man and a tyrant fall down a precipice both are dashed to pieces; or if shipwrecked both perish: nay, it may happen that the former alone shall perish, and the tyrant escape, owing to greater strength of body, to skill in swimming, or to an act of violence in seizing the plank of his companion. Thus he may preserve his life by a crime. Where, it is asked, is there a Providence here? Wherefore is the good man drowned while the criminal reaches the shore in safety? The answer has been anticipated. The latter escapes by the proper use of his limbs, and by availing himself of that law of nature by which fluids support bodies of less specific gravity than themselves. The moral character can make no change on a physical ordinance. The immutability and consistency of nature's laws are the ground of our confidence in the expected result. The bad man's faith in the buoy-ancy of the waters will support him as surely as the good man's. It is not contended that nature will suspend her laws in behalf of any one however wise and virtuous. None is more convinced of this than the wise and virtuous themselves, and therefore they are cautious how they transgress those laws, and by such transgression ' tempt God.' They do not expect that an angel will be sent to guard them from dashing their foot against a stone, should they wilfully persist in strolling among rocks and preci-pices. The Providence of the Deity is manifested in that very uniformity and consistency which are adduced as a proof of its non-existence. His laws are never found deceptive or capricious to disappoint or frustrate those who act with a firm belief in their immutability. The "law of the Lord is perfect" so as never to require change, reform, or abrogation. Sir John Herschell observes truly that " the divine Author of the universe cannot be sup-posed to have laid down particular laws, enumerating all individual contingencies which his materials have under-stood and obey: this would be to attribute to him the imperfections of human legislation ; but rather by creating them endowed with certain fixed qualities and powers, he has impressed them in their origin with the *spirit*, not the letter of the law, and made all their subsequent com-binations and relations inevitable consequences of this first impression.—*Study of Nat. Phil.* Art. 27.

We are under no necessity to allege that Bruce's spider was specially commissioned; or that Park's frogs croaked by inspiration. We need not maintain as a heathen poet might, that Mars or Neptune, or some other tutelary god of the fleet assumed the form of the martial bird to excite the flagging spirit of a war-ship's crew—*"Martemque accendere cantu."* But we must admire the wonderful adaptation of the instincts and habits of animals to answer peculiar ends in connexion with the welfare and safety of man. In the cases specified the results were not less apparent nor less extraordinary than if the animals had been created for the particular occasion. Surely the adjustment of a general law to meet a singular exigency, argues not less wisdom, less foresight, in a word, providential care, than if an angel were deputed for the specific purpose. As to the catastrophe of Misagathus, it could not have befallen a humane man; for, in the first instance, no humane man would have acted as he did. But we shall be told that the whole happened in perfect accordance with the laws of motion and animal instinct. Very true; and here is the marvel. The natural universal laws operated with such a precise and certain result in bringing the transgressor to a merited end, as if an agent from heaven had come with authority and power to tilt him over the precipice.

There are enthusiasts and fanatics, who seem to think that Providence has nothing to do but to attend to their movements, to influence their minds by secret suggestions, and for their pleasure or convenience to controul not only the operations of animal instinct, but the direction of the winds and tides, and to "annihilate both space and time," not to make "two lovers happy"—this would be something —but to gratify their silly and preposterous self-conceit. Such notions require no refutation. The Diety will not listen to human dictation; nor suffer the audacious importunities of ignorance and folly to influence his determinations. The laws which he has established will perform their office regularly and impartially, without respect of persons. The sunshine and the shower are shared by the evil as well as the good. The lightning strikes and consumes the temples of religion, when it respects and passes harmless down the thunder-rods of the tents of sin, in obedience to the laws of electricity. The sea-bird, stationed as a watchful sentinel on a rock amidst the breakers, fulfils the designs of a kind Providence in warning the mariner by its cry, of approaching danger, without enquiring whether he is white or black—a disciple of John Wesley or of Thomas Paine.

As to the multiplication of animals, that depends on the laws of their particular economy; and according as they are useful or noxious, they may prove a blessing or a curse. If in consequence of the extinction of rooks, swallows, and other insectivorous birds, grubs, flies and beetles should become so numerous as to destroy the hope of the farmer, they may well be considered as a scourge from God to chastise man for his folly in removing the checks to their increase. The Supreme Lawgiver, from the infinite perfection of his nature, must always act with unvarying rectitude and truth; and though he is not subject to his own physical ordinances, nor bound by the inflexible chains of necessity or fate, his providence is manifested, not by special interpositions, but by the constant, regular, uninterrupted action of his laws. They who best understand, and most conscientiously conform to those laws, act most agreeably to their Maker's will, and provide most securely for their own comfort and happiness. Were men more observant of the established order of things—of the laws of nature and of their own constitution, they would have less reason to think special interferences necessary. At the same time, it would be presumptuous—an assumption of knowledge beyond what it is possible to prove—to affirm, that the hand of the Deity is never stretched forth to rescue his creatures from any physical evil—to shut the mouths of lions—to still the raging of the sea—to avert the lightning and the hurricane, or arrest the progress of the "pestilence that walketh in darkness." But of this we may rest assured that as cheerful obedience to his righteous will is our highest wisdom; so is it our best protection on earth against the worst calamities that human nature deplores, and the surest foundation of our trust in the world to come.

CHAPTER VIII.

THE BENEFITS DERIVED FROM ANIMALS, THEIR DOCI-
LITY, OBEDIENCE, AND AFFECTION FOR MAN, AN AR-
GUMENT FOR TREATING THEM WITH HUMANITY.

"Belluæ, a barbaris, propter beneficium, consecratæ.—Cic.

"———— Every object in creation
Can furnish hints for contemplation;
And from the most minute and mean,
A virtuous mind can morals glean."—GAY.

For how many benefits are we indebted to the animal
creation? To enumerate them would be impossible.
They give us almost the whole of what is comprised in
the comprehensive terms of food and raiment, and contribute in a thousand and ten thousand ways to our
necessities, our comforts, our luxuries. They facilitate
our labours in the city and the field; bear our burdens;
transport us from place to place, and, with the pleasure of
locomotion, enable us to visit distant regions which, without their aid, could never be explored. The elephant
lends us his gigantic strength; the horse his speed; the
ass his patience; the camel his almost invincible endur-
ance of thirst and labour, in regions where no water
refreshes the ground. The sheep bestows her woolly
mantle; the cow supplies abundance of delicious nutriment, while the dog performs the duty of a vigilant sentinel, in guarding our dwellings. Among reptiles, what a
useful phlebotomist is the leech? Of insects, the cantha-
rides are indispensible in the medical profession, and the
coccus yields a purple that in brilliancy exceeds the
famous Melibœan dye. Of the fishy, the testaceous, and
crustaceous tribes it would be superfluous to speak, since
a moment's consideration will show how greatly man is
their debtor.

All animals, particularly those whose services are most
required, as if conscious that they were ordained to be
subject to man's dominion yield to it without reluctance,

asking in return only to be treated with humanity. The Apostle James says truly, (iii. 7.) " Every kind of beasts, and of birds, and of serpents, and of things in the sea, is tamed, and hath been tamed of mankind!" Hanno the Carthagenian is said to be the first who tamed a lion* and " led him in a slippe like a dog ;" and Mark Antony had lions yoked to his car. The well known story of Androcles and the lion would show that gratitude is no stranger to the breast of that noble animal, though there were not many other proofs of it more recent. How serpents were charmed of old, and how they may still be charmed in some countries of the East, is sufficiently notorious. The most noxious and formidable animals are seldom the first aggressors on man ; but if attacked or molested they will of course resist and use the arms which God has given them for their defence. Lucian speaks of serpents so tame that they would suck women and play with children without doing them any hurt ; and we learn from Waterton that the most poisonous snakes, even the Labarri, may be touched without fear, if approached with caution.—*Wanderings,* pp. 184, 185.

Many animals seem to forego their natural instincts or to employ them only for the service and profit of their benefactors. Certain birds in China, follow the occupation of fishing for their owners. The *parra chavaria* of South America, guards the poultry of its master, as the dog guards the shepherd's flock. The hawk returns to her lure and perches on the falconer's fist after having struck down the game for his food and recreation. Pliny tells us of a young lady of Sestos who had a favourite eagle which she had reared from the nest, which accompanied her in the sports of the field, and supplied her table with venison.—(Book x. c. 5.) The *cuculus indicator,* as Vaillant informs us, is honoured as a deity in Southern Africa ; and the Hindus hold the bird *garuda,* a destroyer of snakes, in equal veneration. The Norwegians think it impious to destroy the black-throated

* For this act of ingenuity Hanno was banished from the city, a lion-tamer, being thought dangerous to the liberty of the state. Mark Antony's feat was " a shrewd and unhappy presage of the subjection of men of an high spirit and brave mind."—PLINY, lib. 8, c. 16.

diver, *colymbus arcticus*, because it indicates approaching storms, by its restlessness and clamour. The Persians delight in singing birds: they almost idolize the *bulbul*, and would deem it ungrateful to repay them for their song by confining them in cages. What shall we say of the services of our own noble but much abused bird, the cock, with his " shrill clarion?" What of the carrier pigeon, with its

> " Wreathen or conquest, or its vows of love?
> Say, thro' the azure what compass points her flight?
> Monarchs once guard, and nations bless the sight.
> We roam on rocks, our woods and mountains rise,
> Salute her native scenes, her native skies;
> 'Tis vain, thro' ether's pathless wilds she goes,
> And lights at last where end her cares, repose."—Beaume.

After hearing of lions being yoked to the car, we need not wonder at bear cubs being accustomed to the harness, or serpents taught to hunt like dogs with their masters, or bears taught to dance, though dancing seems one of the more intricate movements; and to them we unconsciously must admit that they are indebted for whatever skill they possess in that elegant accomplishment. We are told of elephants that could not only dance, but also to instruments of music. Pliny relates some curious acts of these " half reasoning" creatures. Great ingenuity, it seems shown in the ... twelve, six male and six female elephants robed in flowered dresses, the players, and they performed ... with measured applause; reclined, and ... on couches covered with purple, and ...

The curious and affecting warmth of the name of ... between a man and his horse, his ass, and ... as sometimes with animals of a far more ... character than these, as in the case of Bisset ... Sterne's history of the poor man ... is universally known. The horse recognises ... master or groom by sounds and attitudes expressive ... Many instances are on record of the ... warm mutual attachment of the Arab and his steed. Buffon ... alleges that " there is no creature so gentle as a Turkish horse, nor more respectful to his master or the groom that dresses him. The reason is *because they treat their horses with great lenity."* That animals so capable of domestication as swine, sheep, goats, and horses, should reciprocate the gentleness of their owners is not extraordinary, but even those deemed the most untameable have been rendered so gentle by kindness, as to show the mildness and fawning affection of a spaniel. The last mentioned author informs us that one of his servants had a lynx of Assyria, that was wont to caress him with all the blandishments of love; that pined in his absence, and rejoiced at his return; and at last was so grieved by the loss of his master, that he refused food, and languished till he died. He also tells us of a Spaniard, who had a Balearic crane that attended him in his walks, knocked at his door, and was wont to greet him by "clapping her wings with such an antick posture of her body as dancers in a jig use to do; or as if she had been to prepare herself for combat with a pigmy."

" The pious Hindu has a sort of filial attachment to the creature that affords him his daily food." Something similar is told of the Irishman's love of the pig that is destined to *pay the rent* of his wretched cabin; and it is not without a praiseworthy reluctance that he is at last obliged to consign to its fate the creature that has long been the object of his care and the inmate of his dwelling. Not only are birds and beasts, but even fishes, susceptible of gratitude. The story of the boy and the dolphin has been recorded by Pliny, and celebrated in the Halieutics of Oppian. Wild beasts have been known to protect, and even to suckle children. The story of the exposure and preservation of Cyrus, and of Romulus and Remus, is not necessarily a fable. We read of young rats having been suckled by a cat, the most deadly enemy of their race. That some animals should supply the place of a human nurse, is not surprising. Bebe, the extraordinary dwarf, whose real name was Nicholas Ferry, had so small a mouth that he could never suck his mother's breast. A she-goat supplied her place, and entertained for him the affection of a parent.

" The dog," says Cuvier, " is the most complete, the most remarkable, and the most useful conquest ever made

I

diver, *colymbus arcticus,* because it indicates approaching storms, by its restlessness and clamour. The Persians delight in singing birds: they almost idolize the *bulbul,* and would deem it ungrateful to repay them for their song by confining them in cages. What shall we say of the services of our own noble but much abused bird, the cock, with his "shrill clarion?" What of the carrier pigeon, with its

> "Wreathes of conquest, or its vows of love?
> Say, thro' the clouds what compass points her flight?
> Monarchs have gaz'd, and nations blest the sight.
> Pile rocks on rocks, bid woods and mountains rise,
> Eclipse her native shades, her native skies;
> 'Tis vain! thro' ether's pathless wilds she goes,
> And lights at last where all her cares repose."—ROGERS.

After hearing of lions being yoked to the car, we need not wonder to hear of stags being accustomed to the harness; or leopards taught to hunt like dogs with their masters; of bears taught to dance, though dancing seems to be one of their instinctive movements; and to them the Kamtschadales gratefully admit that they are indebted for whatever skill they possess in that elegant accomplishment. We have heard of elephants that could not only dance, but play on instruments of music. Pliny mentions some curious facts of those "half reasoning" creatures. Cæsar Germanicus, at games shown in the reign of Tiberius, had six male and six female elephants clothed in histrionic dresses, like players, and they performed their parts with unbounded applause; reclined, after the Roman fashion, on couches covered with purple, and drank out of goblets of gold.

How often does an affection worthy of the name of friendship subsist between a man and his horse, his ass, or his dog; and sometimes with animals of a far more untractable character than these, as in the case of Bisset and his learned pig? Sterne's history of the poor man and his ass is universally known. The horse recognises his kind master or groom by sounds and attitudes expressive of delight. Many instances are on record of the fond and mutual attachment of the Arab and his steed. Busbequius alleges that "there is no creature so gentle as a Turkish horse, nor more respectful to his master or

the groom that dresses him. The reason is *because they
treat their horses with great lenity."* That animals so
capable of domestication as swine, sheep, goats, and
horses, should reciprocate the gentleness of their owners
is not extraordinary, but even those deemed the most untameable have been rendered so gentle by kindness, as to
show the mildness and fawning affection of a spaniel.
The last mentioned author informs us that one of his
servants had a lynx of Assyria, that was wont to caress
him with all the blandishments of love ; that pined in his
absence, and rejoiced at his return ; and at last was so
grieved by the loss of his master, that he refused food,
and languished till he died.   He also tells us of a
Spaniard, who had a Balearic crane that attended him in
his walks, knocked at his door, and was wont to greet him
by "clapping her wings with such an antick posture of
her body as dancers in a jig use to do ; or as if she had
been to prepare herself for combat with a pigmy."

" The pious Hindu has a sort of filial attachment to
the creature that affords him his daily food."   Something
similar is told of the Irishman's love of the pig that is
destined to *pay the rent* of his wretched cabin ; and it is
not without a praiseworthy reluctance that he is at last
obliged to consign to its fate the creature that has long
been the object of his care and the inmate of his dwelling.
Not only are birds and beasts, but even fishes, susceptible
of gratitude.   The story of the boy and the dolphin has
been recorded by Pliny, and celebrated in the Halieutics
of Oppian.   Wild beasts have been known to protect, and
even to suckle children.   The story of the exposure and
preservation of Cyrus, and of Romulus and Remus, is
not necessarily a fable.   We read of young rats having
been suckled by a cat, the most deadly enemy of their
race.   That some animals should supply the place of
a human nurse, is not surprising.   Bebe, the extraordinary dwarf, whose real name was Nicholas Ferry, had so
small a mouth that he could never suck his mother's
breast.   A she-goat supplied her place, and entertained
for him the affection of a parent.

" The dog," says Cuvier, " is the most complete, the
most remarkable, and the most useful conquest ever made

I

by man." But what can be said of this inestimable creature that has not been said already? The language of panegyric would be exhausted before his excellent virtues could be described as they merit. His fidelity, his courage, his vigilance, his gratitude, his generosity, each the theme of merited praise, win our love and respect. The favourite of children, the chosen companion of women, the watch and the guardian of our homes, the guide of the blind, the participator of man's excursions by land and sea, the defender of the shepherd's fold, the detector of the thief and robber, the fleet courser that transports the Esquimaux, in his sledge, over the arctic waste of snow. If such a benefactor to man has not a special claim to his protection and kindness, nay, to affectionate regard, what has? He ventures life and limb in our service; he explores the mountain waste, and faces the wintry tempest, in search of the traveller that has been overwhelmed by the snow-drift;* he springs into the foamy torrent to rescue its threatened victim from destruction; he breasts the boisterous surges of the ocean, to convey a rope to the shipwrecked mariners, by which he achieves their deliverance; he recognizes his beloved master after twenty years' absence, and expires at his feet in a paroxysm of joy at his return. He seems, too, to participate in the nature of man, in having his resentments. He knows his enemy, and when provoked by wrongs, becomes a formidable antagonist. Bacon says that "dogs know the dog-killer, though they never saw him before."—(vol. iii. p. 205.) And in some eastern countries where dogs are eaten, they know their butchers, and whenever one of them appears, pursue him in full cry. Vivisectors of dogs would do well to attend to this, and be on their guard. Should they scent a Magendie, they might be stimulated to try their skill in vivisection, and to practise his favorite art on himself. Their experiment would be less elegantly conducted, but more summarily, with a most certain result, and with infinitely less pain than if they followed the mode practised in his own theatre of slaughter.

---

* The dogs of St. Bernard.

> " Videre canes, primusque Melampus,
> Ichnobatesque sagax latratu signa dedere.
> Quosque referre mora est—resonat latratibus æther.
> Prima Melanchætes in tergo vulnera fecit;
> Cætera turba coit, confertque in corpore dentes.
> Jam loca vulneribus desunt. Gemit ille, sonumque
> Etsi non *hominis*, quem vel tamen edere possit
> Crudelis VIVISECTOR."

Such, however, we trust, may never be the fate even of a Magendie, though having done more to deserve it than the unfortunate Actæon. But we hope and pray that the canine race may no longer be sacrificed to the demon of cruelty, under the specious pretext of advancing science. More of this anon.

In connexion with the more important services rendered to mankind by animals, may be mentioned the beauty and cheerfulness which they impart to the aspect of nature. How cold and dead would the landscape appear, if destitute of living creatures ; did no herds or flocks browse on the lawn, nor goats hang over the precipice, to supply the painter and the poet with picturesque images ; nor birds carol in the grove, nor fishes dimple the pool, nor insects unfurl their iridescent wings in the sun, and send forth a hum redolent of life and joy ? Animals are often a happy substitute for the companionship of beings like ourselves ; often have they cheered the loneliness of solitude, dissipated the gloom of confinement, and rendered less tedious the lingering hours of exile, or of absence from beloved friends. Busbequius, whom we must be permitted to quote once more, says, " I kept a great many sorts of birds, as eagles, jackdaws, Muscovy ducks, Balearic cranes, and partridges, yea, my house is so full of them, that if a painter were to draw it, he may take from thence a copy of Noah's ark. Besides the delight that I and my family take in these creatures to counterpoise our long absence from our own country, I got this advantage by them, that now I know, by experience, what I could hardly have believed when I read it in books." (p. 120.) Alexander Selkirk found a relief to his solitude, in taming goats and teaching them to dance. Baron Frederick Trenck, during his long rigid confinement in the fortress of Magdeburg, found a companion in a mouse, which he had rendered so familiar, that it would play round him and eat from his mouth. "In this small animal," says he, " I discovered proofs of intelligence too great to easily gain belief : were I to write them, priests would rail, monks grumble, and such philosophers as suppose man alone endowed with the power of thought, allowing nothing but what they call instinct to animals, would proclaim me a fabulous writer, and my opinions heterodox to what they suppose sound philosophy. Should I live, I may hereafter publish an essay on this subject, in which this my mouse, and a spider, will appear as remarkable characters." This intelligent mouse, which was wont to come at his whistle, jump on his shoulder, and caper on a trencher, was barbarously, though fortunately for him, as appeared in the event, taken from him, presented to a lady, and put into a cage, where it pined, refused sustenance, and died. How the spider amused him, I have not ascertained ; but we may readily believe that it was not in the same mode as that enjoyed by the Count de Lauzun, who, "when imprisoned in the castle of Pignerol, amused himself during a long time with catching flies, and delivering them to be devoured by a rapacious spider ; "an amusement," says Perceval, from whom the story is taken, "equally singular and cruel, and contrary to his former character." To what then shall we impute such conduct ? He wanted something to excite him and break the distressing monotony of imprisonment. He probably thought he was doing a kindness to the spider ; never considering that though it had a just right to all the game it could immesh in its own net, it was merciless to the poor flies to employ human dexterity in their capture, to gratify the gluttonous appetite of their inveterate foe. In a closer state of confinement, he might have rejoiced in the friendship even of a fly, and deprecated the cruelty that would have given it the least molestation. Dufavel, one of the labourers employed in sinking a well near Lyons, in France, was buried alive from the beginning till the middle of September, 1836, by the falling in of the supports, which happily fell in such a position as to form an arch and prevent him from being crushed. " In the utter

darkness of his melancholy prison-house, Dufavel was
enabled, in a curious enough manner, to keep a reckoning
of the progress of time. A large fly found its way into
his cell, and continued to keep him company all the time
that he remained there. When he heard this insect buzzing about, he understood that it was day; and when it
went to sleep, he concluded that night had arrived. This
winged time-keeper boarded as well as lodged with him,
as he was made aware by the circumstance, that in lifting
his food, he frequently disturbed the fly, which had been
seated upon it helping itself without ceremony, and which,
when thus interrupted in its repast, flew away buzzing,
as if intending to reproach him for his unkindness in re-
fusing it a share. He afterwards confessed that the company of this fly had been a great consolation to him
during his sufferings, and that he had often envied the
facility with which it could pass and repass through the
narrow opening between his dark dungeon and the upper
world."

To animals man stands indebted for not only numberless physical gratifications, but for instruction in the
mechanical arts, and the practice of moral duty. Many
are the useful lessons which philosophers and divines
have drawn from observation of their habits and instincts.
" They," says Bacon, (vol. ii. p. 448) "who discourse of
the inventions and originals of things, refer them rather
to chance than to art; and rather to beasts, birds, fishes,
serpents, than to men." Much may be said in proof
or illustration of this hypothesis. The swallow's clay-
built nest, it is said, suggested to Doxius the son of Cœlius
the art of building; and to him is attributed the renown
of having erected the first house of Athens, and taught men
that houses are superior to holes and caverns in the ground.
According to Ovid, the spine of a fish first suggested that
most useful instrument, the saw.—*Met.* lib. viii. l. 244.
The philosophic poet, Lucretius, affirms that from the
zephyrs whispering among the reeds, men first learned to
form the rural pipe; and that the liquid voice of birds
gave them their first lessons in vocal music.—*Rer. Nat.*
lib. v. l. 1378. And it is conjectured that the American

I 2

savage learned the use of hammocks from the hanging nests of some of his magnificent birds.

Pope has caught and amplified the idea with his usual felicity :—

" Go : from the creatures thy instruction take ;
Learn from the birds what food the thickets yield ;
Learn from the beasts the physic of the field ;
Thy arts of building from the bee receive ,
Learn of the mole to plough, the worm to weave ;
Learn of the little Nautilus to sail,
Spread the thin oar, and catch the driving gale."

Though imagination may lead farther in illustration of this topic than experience or fact will warrant, it will scarcely be doubted that from animals many a useful hint has been taken that led to important results. Nature is often our best instructor, and reason may profit by the tuition of instinct. The twisted roots of the oak suggested to the able architect of the Eddystone Lighthouse, the mode of laying its foundation as firm as the rock on which it stands, with a strength and tenacity that can resist the fury of the tempest and the breaker. As much may yet remain to be learned from animals, it would be well if we were more in the habit of observing their habits and profiting by their instruction. The lower as well as the upper world displays the power and wisdom of the divine Architect; and the creatures of the earth may give us lectures in theology and morality not less edifying than the constellations of heaven.

That animals, engaged in the service, and for the use and benefit of man, are entitled to protection, to security from abuse, and to all the kind treatment necessary to their comfort, appears so self-evident a proposition as to require no argument for its support. Those which have been domesticated, and which live only, it may be said, for man's profit and gratification, do often enjoy such protection and security, even from possessors who have little claim to the character of benevolent or merciful. They are well fed, well housed, and judiciously treated, when attacked by disease; from the strongest of all motives in selfish minds, the fear of a reduction or loss of profit when they are maltreated or neglected. But we would have them well treated from a higher motive—from a feeling of gratitude for their services—from sympathy in their pains, when they suffer—and finally, from considering them as creatures of God, formed by the same Almighty hand that formed ourselves, and though subject to man's dominion, still retaining their peculiar rights. Many of the productions of the vegetable world were formed for their special use, and the most common and copious of them all, grass, as has been already stated, which mantles the face of the whole earth.

Though the dairy-man, the horse-dealer, and the shepherd will not allow the animals under their care to experience such treatment as would injure their appearance or diminish their value in the market, they too often treat them with such roughness as no one being should ever deal to another susceptible of pain. We do not sufficiently consider that brute animals have as keen sensations as man himself, of hunger and thirst, of heat and cold, of confinement, of blows, and stripes, and wounds inflicted by the club, the whip, and the goad. In fact, it is from our conviction of their sensibility to pain that it is inflicted. A human brute may allege that the horse, the ass, or the dog, on which he practices his cruel gymnastics, has as little feeling in one sense as he proves himself to have in another. Wherefore then does he belabour them? His practise gives the lie to his assertion. No man of common sense can suppose it possible that the skin can be cut through by the lash, welts and swellings raised by the strokes of a rod, or the back and chest excoriated by an ill-adjusted harness—much less that limbs can be fractured, sinews lacerated, and nerves twisted and rent asunder without excruciating agony. And though animals cannot tell, in articulate sounds what they feel, no man of common understanding can question their sense of pain. They may be, to a certain extent, and in many instances no doubt are sensible even of the indignity of receiving a blow; as sensible at least as the ruffian who deals it. But their mute imploring looks, their groans and cries, their wincing, starting, and contortions, too plainly indicate the intensity of their suffering.

A remarkable proof of a dog's sensibility, even under merited chastisement, occurred recently in Hull, as the

Hull Times informs us. " Mr. Burnell Ward, druggist, of English-street, in this town, had a favourite little dog, and a few days since, for some infringement of good breeding of which it had been guilty, gave the animal a slight kick. The dog being unaccustomed to receive such treatment from its master, it is to be presumed took the punishment to heart, for it immediately trotted off to the foreshore of the Humber, opposite Bellevue-terrace, and was observed by some men who were at work near Mr. Medley's slip to walk into the water with great deliberation, and drown itself. We confess we were at first somewhat incredulous as to the correctness of this story, but on inquiry we have found it to be strictly true."

Were we to ask one of those demi-savages who are in the habit of treating their animals unmercifully, wherefore he was so cruel to his faithful and serviceable beasts, if we escaped an insulting answer, we should be told, perhaps, that they were *his own*, and that he had a right to use them as he pleased. That they are his own, as the term is commonly understood, may be admitted; that he has a right to maltreat and abuse them is an egregious error. A man may say that his wife, children, servants, are his own; and none will dispute his right to call them in a certain sense his property. But does it follow that he may, without a crime, treat them in a manner unbecoming a husband, father, and master? Are there not in all such relations some reciprocal duties? If a servant gives his labour, he is entitled to his wages. He does not bargain to receive kicks and blows instead of proper sustenance and pecuniary compensation. Neither does the brute, though unable to stipulate terms or to enter into any formal agreement. A man holds his property in cattle on certain implied conditions—conditions imposed by the laws of God, though so little regarded by man. In these are included such treatment as is befitting the animal in question, suitable food in the field or the stall, proper attention to its comfort in the articles of housing and litter, and in cases of accident or disease, such remedies as experience shall have proved to be most efficacious; and where the evil is irremediable, so that protracted life is only protracted pain, humanity will dictate that a period should be put to its sufferings in the easiest and most expeditious manner, as by a musquet ball, or a dagger plunged into the spinal marrow. Thus the Carthagenians put their elephants to death when they proved refractory in battle—*celerrima via mortis*, as it is well expressed by Livy, lib. xxvii. c. 49. " The rein-deer is killed by piercing the spinal marrow near one of the first vertebræ, by which it immediately falls."—*Amæn. Acad.* p. 201. On this point even some animals will teach a lesson of mercy. When beasts and birds of prey seize on their victim, except in cases where it is necessary that it should be kept sound to feed their young, they strike it in a vital part, generally in the neck, and death instantly ensues. The pole-cat kills its prey at a single spring; and one blow of the lion is mortal. The rabbit does not languish under the sharp incisors of the ferret or the fox, as under the knife of the vivisector; nor has the grouse any time to lament her fate beneath the sharp talon or dissecting beak of the falcon.

When animals which have served their period faithfully, are disabled by age and long service, it is a plain dictate of justice, not to say humanity, to make them as comfortable as possible for the residue of their lives. Montaigne truly observes that " there is a certain respect and general duty of humanity that ties us not only to beasts that have life and sense, but even to trees and plants. We owe justice to men, and grace and benignity to other creatures that are capable of it. There is a certain natural commerce and mutual obligation betwixt them and us: neither shall I be afraid to discover the tenderness of my nature so childish, that I cannot well refuse to play with my dog when he most unseasonably importunes me so to do." He then gives us several examples of the kindness shown to animals by different nations and individuals, whom, though not Christian, it would be well if those who profess Christianity would in this respect imitate. " The Turks have alms and hospitals for beasts." The Athenians, in the time of Pericles, ordered a mule that had exhausted its strength in drawing stones to build the temple Hecatompedon, to be supported at the public expense, as if it had been one of their superanuated wrestlers. The Agrigentines raised sumptuous monuments over their favourite horses, and the dogs and birds that had been kept for the amusement of their children. "Simon gave an honourable sepulture to the mares with which he had three times gained the prize of the course at the Olympic games. The ancient Xantippus caused his dog to be interred on an eminence near the sea, which has ever since retained the name; and Plutarch says, " That he made conscience of selling to the slaughter an ox that had been long in his service."

► The most recent fact of a similar nature that has come to the author's knowledge, is contained in the will of the late Lord Eldon, in which he " bequeaths his coach-horses to Lady Frances Jane Bankes, with the direction that they are to have a free run of the grass at Encombe. The earl also bequeaths his favourite dog Pincher to the same lady, with a clear annual allowance of £8 to buy him food."

It is most gratifying to have a few such facts as these to record. They vindicate the character of human nature, and show that though there is much cruelty to be deplored, gratitude and humanity are still to be found in the breast of man.

CHAPTER IX.

CAUSES OF CRUELTY TO ANIMALS.

I dare not maintain that man is by nature cruel. We often charge upon nature those evils which spring from the unnatural indulgence and abuse of propensities originally good. Admitting, according to the phrenologist, that we have the organs of combativeness and destructiveness given, as all the other gifts of a kind Creator, for wise and beneficant purposes, it will be admitted on the other hand, that we have also the organs of benevolence and conscientiousness; and that it is as natural and as gratifying to obey the impulses of the latter as the former. But in all well constituted and well regulated minds, the latter, as they ought, must have the predominance ; and the most violent propensities in such minds are subject to the control of the higher principles of mercy and compassion, aided, as these are, by veneration, or a sense of the reverence and devotion due to the Deity.

With respect to the indulgence of any propensity, or the cultivation of any of the moral sentiments, man is very much the creature of circumstances and education. Some nations are cruel and ferocious ; others, gentle and humane ; though " God made of one blood all the nations of the earth." This diversity originating partly in climate, and partly in food, is increased and perpetuated by manners and customs political and religious.

Among the causes of cruelty to animals in civilized nations, the following may be enumerated as the principal :

1. *Gambling and the love of gain*—whence cock-fighting, horse-racing, or the running and trotting of horses against time.

2. *The mere gratification of brutal passions, and the love of sport*—whence bull-baiting, bull-running, dog-fighting, the tying of kettles to dogs' tails, hunting cats, houghing kine, maiming and slaughtering sheep clandestinely, from hatred or revenge of their owner.

3. *Luxury and gluttony*—whence the painfully unnatural modes of fattening and preparing animals for the table, and of putting them to death, the bleeding of calves, capon-making, enormous slaughter of birds, beasts, fishes, for some high festival, putting out the eyes of birds that they may the better sing.

4. *Ignorance, and false pretences*—whence the torturing of hedgehogs, and the destruction of rooks, woodpeckers, and other birds, under the erroneous idea that they are more injurious than useful to the farmer and horticulturist.

5. *Antipathies, or unjust and illfounded dislikes*—of which cats, mice, spiders, beetles, frogs, are the victims.

6. *Love of science perverted, vivisection, natural history.*

On each of these causes of cruelty, the following sections will contain some observations.

CAUSES OF CRUELTY.

SECTION FIRST.

GAMBLING AND THE LOVE OF GAIN.

"Quid non mortalia pectora cogis,
Auri sacra fames !"—VIRG.

"Can it be true that an English nobleman, in the eighteenth century,
won a bet by procuring a man to eat a cat alive ?"—MISS EDGEWORTH.

" Can it be true ?" Well might a humane mind like
Miss Edgeworth's question the truth of so monstrous an
atrocity. It seems incredible ; but what is the crime to
which a rage for betting will not stimulate ? An apostle
has said, that " the love of money is the root of all evil."
That it is the root of much evil to the animal tribes, all
who have paid the least attention to the subject will admit. The reader of this essay is already aware that the
author does not object to fishing and hunting, as pursuits
of commercial profit. They are necessary to human subsistance, and may be carried on without meriting the
charge of cruelty. But he objects to animals being subjected to any pain which can be avoided, still more to
their being made the destroyers of each other, and above
all, to their mutual destruction in mercenary games.
Gambling in any form, though with the inanimate instruments of cards and dice, is a most pernicious and destructive vice, the cause of frequent suicides, and the ruin
of whole families. But it is attended with still greater
criminality, it is adding iniquity to iniquity, to make a
gambling sport of the battles and carnage of animals—
animals which a bounteous Providence bestows for man's
comfort, and which he is expected to treat with humanity.
To cause them to turn against one another, and to their
own destruction, the very arms which God gave them for
their defence and protection, is a crying sin, compared
with which the seething of a kid in the milk of its dam
would, even in the belief of a disciple of Moses, be as innocence itself. Such a sin is the practice of cock-fighting,

of all low and vulgar sports, the most cruel and demo-
ralizing. No scene can be more shocking to a mind of
any feeling and refinement than a cock-pit, around which
one may think he sees, without any great effort of imagination, every evil passion of the human heart personified;
such aspects of cut-throat villains as cause an involuntary
shudder. Then to see those noble birds so shorn of their
beautiful plumage, so deformed, so armed with spurs of
steel, brought into the bloody arena, and slaughtered by
mutual wounds, amidst the curses and blasphemies of the
ruthless dastardly ruffians, who seem to want the power
more than the inclination, to have men and beasts instead
of birds to revive the infamous gladiatorial games ! Of
all species of gambling, this is the most detestable; it
calls loudly for the strong arm of the law to put it down
summarily and effectually. That it should receive any
countenance from men pretending to the name of gentlemen, not to say Christians, may seem incredible. Christians ! no; Christianity loathes and denounces such
practices as sinful abominations, meriting the severity of
divine chastisement.

The author of the article " Cock," in the Encyclo-
pædia Britannica, Dub. ed. 1791, after an able description
of this noble animal, justly animadverts on the barbarity
of cockfighting, on " the noise and nonsense, the profane
cursing and swearing of those who have the effrontery to
call themselves, with all these bloody doings about them,
Christians, nay, what with many is a superior and dis-
tinct character, men of benevolence and morality. But
let the benevolence and morality of such be appreciated
from the following instance, recorded as authentic in the
obituary of the Gentleman's Magazine for April, 1789.
' Died, April 4, at Tottenham, John Ardesoif, Esq. a
young man of large fortune, and in the splendour of his
carriages and horses rivalled by few gentlemen. His
table was that of hospitality, where it may be said he sacrificed too much to conviviality; but if he had his foibles,
he had his merits also that far outweighed them. Mr.
Ardesoif was very fond of cock-fighting, and had a favourite cock upon which he had won many matches. The
last bet he laid upon this cock, he lost; which so enraged

K

him, that he had the bird tied to a spit and roasted alive before a large fire. The screams of the miserable animal were so affecting, that some gentlemen who were present attempted to interfere, which so enraged Mr. Ardesoif, that he seized a poker, and with the most furious vehemence, declared that he would kill the first man who interposed ; but in the midst of his passionate asseverations he fell down dead upon the spot. Such, we are assured, were the circumstances which attended the death of this great pillar of humanity.' "

As to matches against space and time for the sake of lucre, in which horses are lashed and spurred till their strength is exhausted, and they fall the victims of their exertion, they deserve the stigma of every friend of humanity. What were the strokes given by Balaam to his ass, in comparison of the tortures inflicted on these noble animals ? Let their gory sides, their excoriated flanks, their broken hoofs, and disjointed fetlocks declare. Sometimes they fall down, and, happily for themselves, expire in the violence of their exertions ; for if they survive, it is only to experience a more miserable fate in the end. The well known song of the high-mettled racer, is a picture taken from the life, a too real representation of facts frequently repeated :—

"With neck like a rainbow, erecting his crest,
Pampered, prancing, and pleased, his head touching his breast,
Scarcely snuffing the air, he's so proud and elate,
The high-mettled racer first starts for the plate."

After being the favorite of the race-course, the most extolled of hunters, whose value was not to be estimated, " By the mass, my Lord, it is not all Bedford level would purchase him ;" as he advances in age, and declines in strength and fleetness, he gradually descends from his elevation ; and instead of being rewarded for his past services, with a free pasture and exemption from farther labour, for the plates he has won and the honours he has brought his ungrateful master, he is sold for whatever he may bring, and becomes a " hack upon the road." Whence descending to a still lower grade, he is harnessed to a dung-cart, or sent to trace his weary round in a mill. Behold him at last worn to a mere skeleton, tottering, and scarcely able to sustain his own weight, broken-winded, spavined, lame, and blind :—

> " And now, cold and lifeless, expos'd to the view,
> In the very same cart which he yesterday drew,
> While a pitying crowd his sad relics surrounds,
> The high-mettled racer is sold for the hounds."

Such histories as this among the animal tribes are too common in this Christian land to call forth animadversion, unless from some sentimental song-writer like Dibdin, whose lines have just been quoted. The Turks, (of whom we are in the habit of speaking with a contempt which they might justly retort with interest,) infidels as they are, could teach us Christians, both by precept and example, some lessons on this topic, that breathe far more of the genuine spirit of our religion, than many that are delivered from the pulpits even of eloquent divines. Busbequius, who has been already quoted, a learned and intelligent traveller into Turkey and the neighbouring countries, as ambassador from the court of Vienna to Solyman the Great, had the best opportunities of observing the manners and customs of the subjects of the Turkish dominion; and he gives us repeated proofs of their great humanity to animals, and particularly to horses. " I myself," says he, " saw when I was in Pontus, how indulgent the countrymen were to young colts, and how kindly they used them soon after they were foaled; they would stroke them, bring them into their parlours, and almost to their tables, and use them even like children. They hung something about their necks like a jewel, even a garter which was full of amulets against poison, which they are most afraid of; and the grooms that are to dress them are as indulgent as their masters; they frequently sleek them down with their hands, and never use any cudgel to bang their sides, but in case of great necessity. This makes their horses great lovers of mankind; and they are so far from kicking, wincing, or growing untractable by this gentle usage, that you shall hardly find a masterless horse among them."

" But, alas! our Christian grooms treat horses at quite another rate; they never think them rightly curried, till they thunder at them with their voice, and let their club or horse-whip dwell as it were on their sides. This makes some horses even to tremble when their keepers come into the stable, so that they hate and fear them too; but the Turks love to have their horses very gentle, that at a word of command they may fall down on their knees, and in this posture receive their riders. I saw some horses, when their master had fallen from the saddle, that would stand stock still without wagging a foot till he got up again. Another time I saw a groom standing at a distance in the midst of a whole ring of horses, and at a word of command they would either go round, or stand still. Once I saw some horses, when their master was with me in an upper room, prick up their ears to hear his voice; and when they did so, they neighed for joy."

The consequence of this kind treatment is that the Turkish horses not only enjoy life, but " do also live longer than ours. I have seen a horse of theirs as lusty at twenty years old, as ours are at eight; yea, they say, in the stables of the Emperor there are horses of fifty years old; and which for some great merit, are exempt from labour, and feed daily at the Grand Seignior's charge."

Such relations as this are as instructive as they are gratifying. Nor is the humanity of the Turks confined to horses. Other animals are equally the objects of their affection. The above mentioned writer informs us that a Venetian goldsmith, settled at Constantinople, was, for his supposed bad treatment of a bird, dragged by the people before the judge, and narrowly escaped being sentenced to the bastinado. A modern learned and interesting traveller, the Rev. R. Walsh, in his journey to Constantinople, confirms the testimony of Busbequius as to the humanity of Turks to the feathered creation. The sea of Marmora, he tells us, is frequented by a species of *Alcedo*, a bird not quite so large as a pigeon, in such numbers that he counted fifteen large flocks of them in his passage from Pera to Therapia. " I have often wished," says he, " to shoot one, to examine it; but the Turks have such a tender and conscientious regard for the life of every animal but man, that no person is permitted to kill any bird upon the Bosphorus without incurring their displeasure."—p. 87.

From the Africans, another race, whom many take pride
in degrading as an inferior species of mankind, Christians
may learn the advantages of kind usage of cattle. Park,
after informing us that the industry of the Foulahs in
pasturage and agriculture is everywhere remarkable, and
that their herds and flocks are numerous and in fine condition, says, " They display great skill in the management of their cattle, making them extremely gentle by
kindness and familiarity." Vaillant testifies the same of
the Hottentots : " Their cows, as they never beat or torment them, are surprisingly tractable; it is never necessary to tie them. The inhabitant of Caffraria lives so
familiarly amidst his cattle, and speaks to them with so
much mildness, that they pay the most perfect obedience
to his voice." To these authorities may be added that of
a distinguished naturalist, Buffon: " Patience, gentleness and caresses are the only methods to be used in
making the ox submit to the yoke willingly. Violence
and ill usage only serve to make him sullen and intractable for ever." The same eloquent writer gives us the
following well-merited eulogy on the ass. " He is naturally as humble, patient, and quiet as the horse is proud,
ardent, and impetuous ; he suffers with constancy, and
perhaps with courage, chastisement and blows ; he is moderate both in the quantity and quality of his food ; he is
contented with the hardest and most disagreeable herbs,
which the horse and other animals will leave with disdain.
The ass has, like all other animals, his family, his species,
and his rank; his blood is pure, and although his nobility is less illustrious, it is equally good, equally ancient
with that of the horse." But notwithstanding the numerous excellencies of this useful animal, and his laborious
services, (which to the poor man especially are inestimable,) he is oftentimes most cruelly abused by men and
boys. His humility, patience and non-resistance are
stigmatized as stubbornness and ill-nature ; incentives to
the brutal to whip and cudgel him as if he had no more
feeling than a bag of sand. Would that the barbarians

who so abuse him, were tried for a short time in his harness under the discipline of their own scourge, that they might learn what it is to be welted, excoriated, and flayed alive!

Some persons contrive to earn a livelihood by the exhibition of dogs, monkeys, and bears, that have been taught to dance, to go through military manœuvres, and perform various feats of dexterity. To this there could be no reasonable objection, provided no cruelties were practised to get up such exhibitions; and to prohibit them might seem an infringement of the rights of those who are fond of seeing themselves caricatured, and the human species so abominably imitated. But we must condemn the horrible discipline by which such violence is offered to the natural habits and instincts of the performers; for illustration of which it may suffice to give Bewick's account of the barbarities by which the bear is disciplined to the will of his master. *Ex uno disce omnes.* " The excessive cruelties practised on this poor animal in teaching it to walk upright, and to regulate its motions to the sound of the pipe, are such as make sensibility shudder. Its eyes are frequently put out, and an iron ring being passed through the cartilage of the nose to lead it by, it is kept from food, and beaten till it yields obedience to the will of its savage tutors. Some of them are taught to perform by setting their feet upon heated iron plates, and then playing music to them while in this uneasy situation. It is truly shocking to every feeling mind to reflect that such cruelties should be practised upon any part of the brute creation by our fellow men, and much to be wished that the timely interference of the magistrate would prevent every exhibition of this kind, that in Britain at least we might not be reproached with tolerating practices so disgraceful to humanity."

But exhibitions of this kind are not of a sufficiently stimulating nature, especially as they furnish no opportunity for betting. Sporters of true blood—*scires e sanguine natos*—must have something more piquant. Nothing less than a combat with the king of the beasts will content them. Accordingly, a few years ago, they were gratified. But the innocence of *Nero*, the first lion brought to the " scratch," having disappointed many savage expectations, (for he suffered himself to be beaten by two leashes of dogs,) on the third of August, in the year of our Lord eighteen hundred and twenty-five, in the town of Warwick, Mr. Wombwell decided a bet of one hundred sovereigns on the issue of a fight with *Wallace*. This lion proved himself a true son of the forest, though whelped in the capital of Scotland, and punished the two first dogs that assailed him in less than a minute. " He clapped his paw upon poor Ball, took Tinker in his teeth, and deliberately walked round the cage with him, as a cat would do with a mouse." In the *second bout* " Wallace fancied Billy, grasped him by the loins, and when shaking him, Tiger ran away. Billy was not exactly killed, but bit an inch or two deep in the loins only; Turk died of his wounds. Captain, Billy, and Sweep all recovered ; but it required a great deal of nursing to preserve their lives."

Thus, for the indulgence of the lowest and meanest propensities, were these poor dogs that would readily have sacrificed their lives in their ungrateful master's service, barbarously exposed to the lacerating jaws of a lion ! Happily lions are scarce and expensive, as well as dangerous, and such exhibitions cannot be of frequent occurrence. But dogs are numerous, and these are often matched against each other in battle to gratify the brutal and mercenary taste of their owners. Two of these useful creatures may be seen leaping and playing with each other in a most amusive frolicksome mood, till they are seized by the ears, irritated by the pain, and instigated to fight till one or both be unable to wage the contest any longer. The author was once an accidental witness of such a scene. One of the dogs was of the bull kind, and so tenacious was his hold, that the effort to separate him from his antagonist was like tearing him limb from limb. But what was this to the cool-blooded atrocity of the young man mentioned by Bewick, who laid some trifling wager at a bull-bait " that he would, at separate times, cut off all the four feet of his dog, and that after every amputation it would attack the bull. The cruel experiment was tried, and the dog continued to seize the bull as eagerly as if he had been perfectly whole."

What dogs and lions can achieve in the arena of combat, and what bull-dogs are capable of enduring, having now been ascertained, let us hope that no closer approximation to the sanguinary games of the Roman amphitheatre may ever be attempted in Great Britain, nor her soil again polluted by a repetition of such spectacles.

CAUSES OF CRUELTY.

SECTION SECOND.

BRUTAL PASSIONS AND THE LOVE OF SPORT.

"Mala gaudia mentis."—VIRG.

"Sport to you is death to us."—ÆSOP'S FROGS.

Many species of cruelty are practised, which have not even the vulgar motive of money-making to plead in their excuse, nor aught but the mere gratification of brutal passions. Such, I suppose, were those of bull-baiting and bull-running, for I know not if any betting took place at the perpetration of such enormities. Happily they are now nearly every where abandoned. That they should have been tolerated so long in a Christian land would seem incredible, were there not so many unquestionable proofs of their frequency. The following quotation from Taplin's Sporting Dictionary, will give us some idea of such detestable exhibitions.

"Without enlarging much upon the 'hellish practice' of the *sport itself*, it cannot be inapplicable to advert one moment to the effect a scene of so much insatiate cruelty must inevitably produce upon the growing offspring of the lower classes, in towns where a custom so generally execrated is so shamefully carried on. Previous to the commencement 'every heart beats high with the coming joy,' not a window but is crowded with women and children, not a street or an avenue but is crowded with *brutes*, the very scum and refuse of society from every part of the surrounding country; and then begins a scene of the most cruel and infernal practice that ever entered the heart of man, under the appellation of *sporting mirth* to the multitude.

" In the church of this town, on Sunday, the 20th day of December, (being the day previous to the baiting of the bull,) 1801, a sermon was preached by the Rev. Dr. Barry, which sermon is since published, and in which the following passages may be found:—

" Gracious God ! benevolent parent of the universe, what a prodigy must he be in a Christian land who could thus disgrace his nature by such gigantic infamy, at which the blood of a heathen—of a very Hottentot might curdle! Two useful animals, the bull and the faithful dog, to be thus tormented, and for what purpose ? Does it tend as some have said, (Windham) to keep alive the spirit of the English character ? In answer to this we must remark, that the barbarous sport (if sport it can be called) was unknown to the ancient bravery of our ancestors, was introduced into this country in the reign of a *bad king;* and earnestly do I pray to Almighty God, that in the reign of a most pious and benevolent Prince, it may be *for ever set aside!* Cowards, of all men the least un-moved, can both inflict and witness cruelties. The heroes of a bull-bait, the patrons of mercenary pugilists, and the champions of a cock-fight can produce, I should think, but few, if any, disciples brought up under their tuition, who have done service to their country, either as warriors or citizens ; but abundant are the testimonies which have been registered at the *gallows* of her devoted victims, trained up to these pursuits of bull-baiting."

Would that all clergymen would reprobate cruelty from their pulpits with such honest indignation as this ! The worthy Doctor acted as became a Christian minister in denouncing such barbarous sports, and as a high-minded generous Briton, in repudiating the idea that they are useful to keep alive the spirit of Englishmen. Shame to a British senate that could suffer their ears to be profaned by such a false and unfounded assertion ! There could not be a more audacious libel and foul calumny on the courage of Britons, than to affirm that such sports are necessary to its preservation. No argument could betray more ignorance of the nature of that genuine courage which comes from moral principle, and not brutal instinct. It is proverbially true that cowards are cruel, and nothing great, nothing good in any sense can come from cruelty. It skulks from the pains it is so ready to inflict, and shows a craven soul at the time when resolution and bravery are most required. The heroes of a cock-pit or bull-bait would shrink, as snails in their shells, into their own despicable cowardice, if marched to the front of battle, and commanded to try the game of life or death with men. If proofs of this were wanted, enough might be produced: but it may suffice to give the testimony of one whose *ipse dixit* was once deemed infallible, and decisive as proof from holy writ. Aristotle, in the eighth book and fourth chapter of his Treatise on Government, when speaking of the education of children, says that the Lacedæmonians fell into a great mistake in supposing that "to make their children fierce by painful labour was chiefly . useful to inspire them with courage; though this is neither the only thing nor the principal thing necessary to attend to; and even with respect to this they may not thus attain their end; for we do not find either in other animals, or other nations, that courage necessarily attends the most cruel, but rather the milder, and those who have the dispositions of lions; for there are many people who are eager both to kill men and to devour human flesh, as the Achæans and Heniochi in Pontus, and many others in Asia, some of whom are as bad, others worse than these, who indeed live by tyranny, but are men of no courage." * * * "What is fair and honourable ought to take place in education of what is fierce and cruel; for it is not a wolf nor any other wild beast which will brave any noble danger, but rather a good man."—*(Ellis's Translation.)*

With the bull-baiting of the English may be classed the bull-fights of the Spaniards, the progeny of the ancient *Taurilia;* games instituted to their most appropriate patrons, the infernal Gods. But I shall not shock the reader's feelings by repeating any of the numerous descriptions given by travellers, who have witnessed these horrible exhibitions. Captain Basil Hall, after describing one at which he was present in Lima, informs us that " the greater number of the company, although females, seemed enchanted with the brutal scene. It was melancholy to see a great proportion of children amongst the spectators, from one of whom, a little girl only eight years old, I learned that she had been present at three bull-fights, the details of which she gave with great animation and pleasure, dwelling especially on the most horrid circumstances. It would shock and disgust to no purpose to give a minute account of other instances of wanton cruelty, which, however, appeared to be the principal recommendation of these exhibitions."

" I heard a Chilian gentleman," continues our author, " offer a curious theory on this subject. He declared that the Spaniards had systematically sought by these cruel shows, and other similar means, to degrade the taste of the colonies, and thereby more easily to tyrannize over the inhabitants. The people, he said, first rendered utterly insensible to the feelings of others, by a constant familiarity with cruelty and injustice, soon became indifferent to the wrongs of their country, and in the end lost all motive to generous exertion in themselves."— *Extracts from a Journal*, &c. vol. 1. pp. 104, 105.

The theory may be "curious," it is also philosophical, and founded on observation and experience. The love of cruel sports is a sure indication of the absence of all the nobler virtues. Well did the satirist describe the degeneracy and slavery of the Roman people, when he said they cared for nothing but " *panem et Circenses*," for which words we may find an English equivalent in porter and cock-fighting.

Badger-beating, another infernal sport which some perchance might call manly, was once exceedingly prevalent in London and its vicinity. The metropolis, as Taplin informs us, had a constant supply of badgers from the woods of Essex, Kent, and Surry. " The most abandoned miscreants, with their bull-dogs and terriers, from every extremity of the town" crowded to the exhibition. " To the dreadful and inhuman scene of baiting bears and badgers with the most ferocious dogs, till nature was quite exhausted, succeeded dog fights, boxing matches, and every species of the most incredible infamy, under sanction of the *knights of the cleaver*, till by the persevering efforts of the more humane inhabitants, and the spirited determination of the magistracy, the practice seems totally abolished, and likely to be buried in a much wished-for oblivion."

Though we must rejoice that any steps have been taken towards a reformation, there is still room to fear that the taste for such exhibitions is far from being extinct. The baiting of bears and badgers has been followed by other sports not less exciting; as by that of the dog "Billy" and the rats, of which he was to destroy some scores in a given time; and that of a certain biped in the shape of a man, who contested the palm of superiority with the quadruped in the same fascinating entertainment. Dogs, and monkeys too, have afforded excellent sport. In a London newspaper, 1820, we read, "A monkey weighing only twelve pounds, has within the last few days encountered several of the best bred dogs of twenty-four pounds weight. The odds in the first instance were against the monkey two to one; but, strange to relate, the monkey in these combats, with his tusks seized upon the dogs, and cut their throats as if done with a razor. In the short space of a minute most of the dogs have been disabled from loss of blood, and died within a few hours after the battle. This circumstance has quite astonished the sporting world. There is little doubt but the best dogs of thirty pounds weight must, in combat with the above monkey, fall a sacrifice."

The encouragers and spectators of such sports are not all of plebeian rank. Some of them can boast of patrician blood, and of a nobler scutcheon than the "knights of the cleaver." What should we say if not only senators, but knights of the cross, were to be discovered among them ?

The "wholesale slaughter," as it has been justly denominated, which, for the mere sake of killing, is sometimes perpetrated by the privileged few among the feathered tribes, should not be suffered to escape animadversion. We occasionally read of sportsmen in the highlands of Scotland, and elsewhere, who, like the dog Billy of whom honourable mention has been made, can boast of the almost incredible number of lives that have fallen before them in a very limited period of time. Thus in October, 1836, we were informed that "Lord Cranstoun, and a large party had just left Ross-hall, Sutherlandshire, where they had a most successful campaign (massacre) against the game; having bagged no less than 900 brace of grouse and black game, 89 of ptarmigans, 17 deer, and 43 roes. The Honourable Misses Cranstoun and their female friends also bagged 13 salmon."

Much of the game massacred in such "campaigns" is entirely lost as an article of human sustenance. Sportsmen would rather kill than eat game, and though they had the keenest appetite they could not possibly devour all they slaughter. Much is given to the dogs; much becomes putrid before it can find a market, or reach the friends for whom it is designed as a present. If destined for home consumption, there must be extravagant waste, or a fearful gluttony, to get a clear riddance of it. Lord Cranstoun must have had a regiment of hungry grenadiers—hungry by a long march and the keen mountain air—to consume his 900 brace of grouse and black-game, 89 of ptarmigans, 17 deer, and 43 roes; and their wives and daughters should have been invited to assist the honourable ladies to bag the 13 salmon into the reticule of their stomach.

Such sportsmen as his lordship should have some moderation in their sports, and consider with Lord Bacon that "that which is for exercise and sport and courtesy, should not be turned to gluttony and sale-victual."— (Works, iv. p. 251.)

We read of a certain Marchioness, who "took the field a few days ago, and in one *battu* brought down twelve brace of birds." How far it is consistent with the female character to take an active part in these murderous sports the reader may determine. For our own part we prefer the attar of roses to the smell of gunpowder, and think a needle, a thimble, and a crow-quill pen more ornamental to the delicate fingers of a lady than pistols, blunderbusses, and double-barrelled guns. The "virtuous woman" of holy writ "seeketh (not snipes and partridges, but)

L

wool and flax. She layeth her hands on the spindle, and
her hands hold the distaff. Her husband (whom she
delighteth to honor) is known in the gates, when he sit-
teth among the elders of the land," not by his ardor in
the chase or his rank in the jockey club, but by his
deliberative wisdom in the senate of his country : and
he is distinguished by other trophies than foxes' tails
appended to his wife's robes, and paraded at a public
assembly.

> "But if the rougher sex by this fierce sport
> Is hurried wild, let not such horrid joy
> E'er stain the bosom of the British fair."—THOMSON.

Birds are often unmercifully slaughtered where not even
the hope of a meal, of profit by " sale-victual," nor the
pretext of injury, nor aught but the simple love of *sport*,
operates as a motive for their destruction. Thus we read
in the *Kentish Chronicle* :—

" A countryman, one day last week, in three shots
killed 54 sea gulls on the lands of Milestone farm, near
Bridge. The first shot he brought down 12, at the second
15, and at the third 27."

This was an act of wanton barbarity ; and such acts, we
fear, are often perpetrated as glorious. Those poor birds
had, probably, retired to the glebe-lands for shelter from
the storms of their native element ; and if they rendered
no service to the farmer, assuredly they did him no injury. The Chronicle which records the above achievement should also have stigmatized it with reprobation.

If Mrs. Hemans, when she wrote " *The Sea-bird
wandering inland*," had seen or thought of this act of
the countryman, she would not have sung that the sea-
bird " did well" to leave her native shores, to visit the
hills and the mountain heath :—

> " Thou hast done well, oh ! thou bright sea-bird ;
> There is joy where the song of the lark is heard.
> With the dancing of waters through copse and dell,
> And the bee's low tune in the fox-glove's bell."

She would have strung her lyre to another tune :—

> Thou hast done ill, oh ! thou bright sea-bird ;
> There is wo where the gunner's fell voice is heard,
> Where the murderous hind lies concealed in the heath,
> To greet thee with brimstone volleys of death.

Thou hast done ill to come to the glen ;
There the hound lies couched by the bird-killer's den :
Ne'er more on thy cliff shalt thou perch o'er the flood ;
But thy silvery plumes shall be crimsoned with blood.

Fishes, and other inhabitants of the deep, are in like manner slaughtered for mere *sport!*

" During this voyage we saw numerous herds of porpoises playing in the water; but their gambols were disturbed. They were fired at with musketry and large guns; but none of them were taken. Indeed I do not know whether the object was capture for the sake of their oil or blubber, or the mischievous and cruel one of having *sport*. The animal man has degenerated, I believe, more than all other animals in acquiring this disposition. The porpoises, in their flight, made great splashing in the water, and sunk themselves for a time under its surface. We saw flocks of flying fish which were pursued by dolphins, not for sport, I suppose, but for food."—WALKER's *Fragments, &c.* pp. 256, 257.

On the subject of man's right to hunting and fishing, enough has been said in a former section of this essay; but while we admit the privilege, we protest against all the cruelties that attend those pursuits, and against all unnecessary expenditure of life, of which there is great reason to complain. Sometimes, as was actually the case this winter, (1837-1838,) shoals of fishes appear in incredible numbers on the sea shores, presenting a bounteous provision for the poor of the land, when they can be properly cured. But it not unfrequently happens that they are seen in regions where there is no supply of salt; and then they are taken and drawn off to manure the ground. This the author cannot help considering as a cruel and prodigal waste of life. Better to let the fishes live and enjoy their brief existence, than for so paltry a gain to be their destroyer. It never could be the design of providence that they should be taken from their native element for the purposes of manure. If circumstances prevent the enjoyment of an offered blessing, it should not be abused, nor converted to a curse. Wiser, and better, and more conformable to the divine plan, to let the wanderers of the deep pass on their way, and fulfil the end of their being, as God may appoint, than to deform the soil, pollute the atmosphere, and generate a plague by their putrescence.

The training of hounds for the chace is accompanied by many dreadful cruelties to the hounds themselves, as well as to other creatures, in order to reduce them to perfect obedience. They must be severely lashed, and initiated to their office by various barbarous rites. "I know an old sportsman," says Beckford, "who enters his young hounds first at a cat, which he drags along the ground for a mile or two, at the end of which he turns out a badger, first taking care to break his teeth"—(p. 80.) "Huntsmen flog their hounds while they feed them; and if they have not always a bellyfull one way, they seldom fail to have it in the other;" and as the Monthly Reviewer (Sept. 1781,) observes, "eat or not eat, work or play, whipping is always in season." The huntsman's nomenclature is highly characteristic; his favourites are designated by such amiable appellations as the following: *Arsenic, Barbarous, Cerberus, Dragon, Firebrand, Fury, Havoc, Lictor, Lacerate, Myrmidon, Miscreant, Pillager, Ravenous, Ruffian, Screecher, Spitfire, Torturer, Vagabond, Viper.*

Angling is a sport in which many flagrant cruelties are committed without the slightest compunction. Nay, some who have described them, are among the most popular writers in our language; for instance, Isaac Walton, surnamed the "HONEST," an epithet to which he is well entitled, were it only for the minute and circumstantial detail which he gives, of the various barbarous modes of baiting the angler's hooks with living animals. His book, entitled "The Complete Angler," has received its full meed of celebrity, not only for the pleasing familiarity and amenity of its style, but for the descriptions of rural scenery with which it is interspersed. In the reader's admiration of these, the cruelties with which it abounds seem to be altogether overlooked. He tells of a thousand plans for taking the various kinds of river fish, and shows his skill in the culinary art, by teaching how they are best prepared for the table. As for the "poor fish," he expresses great pity for them when they are taken by an otter or a cormorant, "with whom any honest man may make just cause of quarrel ;" but when he captures them himself, it is the " choicest sport !"

"' Puss is a cruel rogue,' says Nan,
Frying live lobsters in a pan."

But "honest" Isaac is all humanity. In the character of Piscator he says, " I am not of a cruel nature ; I love to kill nothing but fish." He forgets the otter and her cubs, at the slaughter of which he was recently present, and his wish or prayer that God would grant that his friends, Venator and Auceps, may " meet this day another bitch-otter, and kill her *merrily*, and all her young ones too !" As if the all merciful Creator had formed these animals only for the gratification of man's destructive propensities ! He thought there was nothing cruel in subjecting to the torture many thousands of worms and of ant-flies, and flesh-flies, and wall-flies, and the humble bee, and the black bee that builds in clay walls, and grasshoppers, and snails slit open to show the white, and beetles with their legs and wings chopped off, and sticklebacks and minnows shorn of their fins and tails, and thrust through with the barbed hook, in such a mode as not to kill, but to keep alive in torture as long as possible. Honest Isaac thought nothing of all this ; it was the " choicest sport !" He instructs his pupil how to prepare a dace or a perch, " which is the longest lived on the hook," as bait for the pike ; a most painful operation which he describes with the skill of an anatomist, the great object being to pass the wire through it without the merciful act of causing its death. He is equally minute in telling how to put the arming wire through the mouth of a frog and out at his gills, and with a needle and silk sew the upper part of his leg to the arming wire, " and in so doing, use him as though you loved him, that is, harm him as little as you may possibly, that he may live longer." Well may it be said, that " the tender mercies of the wicked are cruel." After informing us that the mouth of the frog grows up when the hook is put into it, and that he continues so for at least six months without eating, the author adds in pious admiration, " and is sustained, none but he whose name is Wonderful knows how."

L 2

Thus piously does he introduce the name of the Creator, as the ruffians of a cock-pit introduce it profanely, in connexion with such deeds as the least reflection would show to be most abhorrent from the divine nature. His book is a compound of contradictions, of wisdom and folly, of compassion and cruelty. In one page he quotes, " Blessed are the merciful," and in the next he teaches to impale flies and grass-hoppers! He admires the beauty and cheerfulness of the landscape, and hastens to destroy the beings by which its beauty and cheerfulness are enhanced! He speaks with reverence and devotion of the Creator, and yet inflicts such tortures on his creatures as if he were a rebel against his sovereignty, and sought for vengeance on the Maker by the destruction of the things that are made!

On the infamous crimes of houghing and mutilating cattle, to be avenged of their owner for some personal offence, or to gratify a spirit of political or religious animosity, it would be superfluous to expatiate. Such crimes, dastardly as they are barbarous, are confined to the lowest and most degraded of our species. Their perpetrators are not within the reach of the moralist. The legislature alone can deal with them, when detected, in a way that may be so effectual as to prevent their repetition.

CAUSES OF CRUELTY.

SECTION THIRD.

LUXURY AND GLUTTONY.

" O, could the Samian sage these horrors see,
What would he say, or to what deserts flee !
Who animal, like human, flesh declined,
And scarce indulged in pulse—of every kind."
GIFFORD's *Juvenal.*

Luxury and gluttony are prolific sources of cruelty to animals. A thorough epicure who eats not to live, but lives only to eat, never hesitates to inflict any pain, or cause an animal to undergo any operation, however tedious and cruel, by which he thinks the flavour of its flesh may be improved. Hence a thousand and ten thousand enormities practised in the art of cookery, to gratify appetite, and a foolish, often criminal ostentation. The degenerate Romans, in many of their feasts displayed such pomp and extravagance as might seem incredible, accompanied with an ambitiously prodigal waste of animal life. Their gorgeous palaces and costly furniture—their massy gold and silver plate—their curtains of cloth of gold and embroidery—their perfumes, and their beverage of melted pearls, would have wanted their proper accompaniment, had there not been tables also furnished with the rarest and most costly viands. Accordingly all the kingdoms of nature were ransacked for whatever could contribute to satiate the demands of Roman luxury. Clodius Æsopus, the tragedian, had a huge platter, in which were served up all manner of singing birds, and such as could imitate the voice of man, at enormous expense, not merely to gratify the palate, but for the foolish boast that he had eaten the imitators of the human voice. But this dish of the tragedian was surpassed by that of Vitellius, dignified by the name of " Minerva's buckler," on account of its magnitude. " In this he blended together the livers of gilt-heads, the brains of pheasants, the tongues of phenicopters (flamingos), and the milts of lampreys brought from the Spanish and Carpathian seas by the masters of his ships and galleys." Heliogabalus had the heads taken off 600 ostriches to make a dish of their brains. Nor were the Romans the only people remarkable for such extravagancies. The English, centuries ago, might contest the palm with them. The feast given by George Neville, brother to the great Earl of Warwick, at his instalment into the Archbishoprick of York, in 1470, was prodigal beyond example. The quantities of wild fowl slaughtered seem to have been enough to cause a scarcity for ages to come.—See FULLER's *Church History*, lib. 4, cent. 15, p. 193.

Of the number of animals slain for great festivals, or on other occasions, there may be no just reason to complain, provided they are necessary; but the manner in which many of them are prepared for the butcher, before they are brought to the table, is a subject of grave reprehension. No food is so palatable as that to which hunger gives a relish; but when the appetite has been pampered and glutted to satiety, it requires to be stimulated by artificial means. Then the simple meals which nature provides—the fish fresh from its native stream, or the fowl from the stubble or barn-door, is found to be far too simple. The animal must be fed, tortured, put to death, and cooked, not as unsophisticated nature would dictate, but in some refined mode that will impart a flavor and richness which nature in her parsimony has denied. Some Vidius Pollio must have the lampreys in his fishponds fattened on human flesh; and a cook must be found who can "strike a lancet into the jugular of a carp, and stew it in its own blood." Let your salmon be crimped, your eels skinned, and your lobsters fried alive; make capons of your poultry, and cram them by force till they are ready to burst. For example:—"An unfortunate goose is bound in a hot, close situation, debarred all motion, its eyes put out to prevent the entrance of any excitement from without, then crammed with food; under these unnatural circumstances the liver becomes diseased,* it swells, a rich oily fat is deposited around and in its substance, and it forms that delicacy so highly esteemed by the gourmand, but which should be abhorred by every man of humane feelings, the far-famed *foie gras de Strasbourg*."—LORD's *Popular Physiology*, p. 198.

Plutarch in his second treatise on the eating of flesh, to which he was decidedly adverse, expatiates on this subject with great strength and feeling. "If we are not ashamed," says he, "by reason of custom, to live unblamably, let us at least sin with discretion; let us eat flesh, but let it be for hunger, and not for wantonness. Let us kill an animal, but let us do it with sorrow and pity, and not abusing and tormenting it, as many now-a-days are used to do, while some run red-hot spits through the

* The Roman epicures were not ignorant of this luxury.—See JUV. v. 114. MART. lib. xiii. 5, 8, and PLINY, lib. x. c. 22. The latter says, "Good canse it is that there be some question and controversie about the first inventor of this great, good, and singular commoditie to mankind."

bodies of swine, that by the tincture of the quenched iron, the blood may be to that degree mortified, that it may sweeten and soften the flesh in its circulation." Plutarch mentions other instances of the cruelties of luxury still more disgusting and revolting, perpetrated "not for nourishment or want, but for mere gluttony, wantonness, and expensiveness, that they may make a pleasure of villainy."

Again he says, "We are nothing put out of countenance either by the beauteous gayety of the colours, or by the charmingness of the musical voices, or by the rare sagacity of the intellects, or by the cleanness and neatness of diet, or by the rare discretion and prudence of these poor unfortunate animals; but for the sake of some little mouthful of flesh, deprive a soul of the sun and light, and of that proportion of life it has been born into the world to enjoy. And then we fancy that the voices it utters and screams forth to us are nothing else but certain inarticulate sounds and noises, and not the several deprecations, entreaties, and pleadings of each of them, as it were saying thus to us: 'I deprecate not thy necessity (if such there be) but thy wantonness. Kill me for thy feeding; but do not take me off for thy better feeding. O horrible cruelty!'"—See PLUTARCH's *Morals Translated*, Lond. 1704, vol. v.

Thunberg, in his second journey into Caffraria, notices a merciless mode of preparing the tortoise for the table. "The *Testudo pusilla* was the most common species here: it was this which was now laid upon the fire for our eating. I slipped into the kitchen on purpose to see the mode of dressing it, and found that the girls were cruel enough to lay the poor animal wide open on the live coals, where, sprawling with its head and feet, it was broiled alive, till at length it burst to pieces with the heat."

Nothing living that can be eaten escapes man's devouring jaws. That an animal *can* be eaten is deemed a sufficient reason for putting it to death. The improvement of its flesh in size or flavor is also deemed a sufficient reason for subjecting it to any process, however cruel, by which that object may be attained. The excuse for baiting bulls is that it renders them more edible. Dr.

James L. Drummond, in his letters to a young Naturalist, says, "It was once, and I fear still is the practice in some places, to whip pigs to death, because their flesh was thought to be improved by it. In these countries calves are drained of their blood, and made to feel, by repeated operations, all the miseries of exhaustion, merely to make the veal of a whiter colour."—(*Let*. xviii.) In another letter (viii.) he suspects there are grounds for supposing that the myriads of flies which infest some provinces of Spain, may be owing to the destruction of the swallows. "In Andalusia," says he, "I have repeatedly seen Spaniards shooting every little bird they could find, for the market, and carrying them strung in form of festoons over their shoulders. I have also seen them take many small birds by limed twigs, which, when caught, they killed by a squeeze in the hand. Too often, indeed, the squeeze did not produce instant death, and it was pitiful to see the beautiful little creatures gasping and panting on the ground, the blood oozing from their bills. * * Buffon mentions that in France the domestic swallow roosts at the close of summer, in great quantities, on alders by the banks of rivers, and great numbers are caught, which are eaten in some countries, as in Valencia in Spain, and Lignitz in Silesia. I find in the same author that the martin is caught in Alsace in nets; he states that Professor Hermann assures him, 'that the white-rumps or martins grow fat in autumn, and are then *very good to eat.*' Of the sand-martin, another of the swallow tribe, the same author states that the young ones grow very fat, and may be compared for delicacy to the ortolans; and also that in some countries, as in Valencia in Spain, there is a *great consumption* of sand-martins. He says also of the swift, that 'this bird, like all the rest of its kind, (that is, all the swallow tribe,) is excellent for the table when fat; the young ones, especially those taken out of the nest, are reckoned in Savoy and Piedmont *'delicate morsels.'* A young bird taken out of the nest, a delicate morsel! I hope the heartless epicures may be eaten up by flies, till they become of a different opinion."

Insects, like birds, are the victims of man's epicurean rapacity.

"Hark! the bee winds her small but mellow horn,
Blithe to salute the sunny smile of morn."

Yes—blithe in the enjoyment of the munificence of nature,
and happily unconscious that she is soon to be sacrificed
on the altar of cruelty. What mind that is not "dull as
the fat weed that grows on Lethe's wharf," but must
admire this exquisitely beautiful little creature in her
raiment of sable velvet, belted with gold, and borne on
filmy wings transparent as the dew-drop; furnished with
her fine pneumatic apparatus, which no science could improve, to exhaust the honey lodged in the nectary of
flowers; and armed for her defence with a keen barb, which
when provoked she wields with a power that a giant might
dread, and a courage that the self-devoted champion of
liberty might admire? But what are her external beauties,
her furniture, her arms, compared to her mind, that par-
ticle, as some of the ancients thought, of the divine intelligence—*esse apibus partem divinæ mentis*—that leads
her to build her hexagonal ambrosial domes—a true El
Dorado or city of gold, with a geometric skill which no
Newton or La Place could excel—with a strength which,
considering the fragility or tenuity of her materials, Vitru-
vius or Palladio might envy; and to form a government
which no Lycurgus, Solon, or Numa could match—so
perfect in its economy as never to require reformation—
perpetuated from generation to generation, and amidst
all the revolutions of empire unchanged? What shall
we say of her care in elaborating a peculiar nutriment
for her young—her providence in collecting the honied
store in the season of plenty for consumption in the
season of want—her unremitting toil from morn till eve
—her prescience and avoidance of the coming storm—
her regular return to her well-remembered home, after
far wanderings over the trackless mountain heath, a feat
worthy of the mellifluous song of the Bard of Memory—
her allegiance to the constituted authorities of her mon-
archy, for which she is ready to combat and to die? While
pursuing her innocent occupation from flower to flower,
and, as my Milesian countryman has sung, in a strain of
originality all his own, "perfuming the fields with music,"*

---

* Is not this a fine exemplification of Horace's *callida junctura?* The
Quarterly Reviewers, perhaps, will have the kindness to inform me.

she is rudely struck down by the callous hand of a clown —callous as the hoof of the ass which he drives to watering; or by some vicious loggerhead of a school-boy who has played truant, and for the chance of finding a tiny drop of honey which she has laboriously collected, squeezed as in a vice, and deliberated mangled, and torn limb from limb! For such paltry indulgence of appetite are deeds of cruelty perpetrated, at which humanity stands aghast.

The destruction of whole hives of bees for their honey, has long been a subject of regret to the humane, and different modes have been devised for committing the robbery without the murder; but none with such success as to ensure general adoption. "If man's convenience, health, or safety" requires the sacrifice, let it be made, but with as much expedition, and as little pain as possible. "*Convenience*," by the way, is a *word* of great latitude, and multifarious application. Is it not often used when arbitrary pleasure, luxurious taste, or gluttonous appetite, would be more german to the subject?

"O man! tyrannic lord, how long, how long,
Shall prostrate nature groan beneath your rage,
Awaiting renovation? When obliged,
Must you destroy? Of their ambrosial food
Can you not borrow, and in just return,
Afford them shelter from the wintry winds?"—Thomson.

The poor cockchaffer impaled on a pin, tied to a thread, and made to "spin," has not even an atom of honey to suggest an excuse for doing it such wrong. No; but it utters its agonies in a whirring sound which tingles as sweet music in the ear of the torturer!

Not only the "lusts of the flesh," and the pomp and the "pride of life," seek and find gratification in cruelty, but also the desires of the eye and the ear. It is recorded of Parrhasius that he put a man to the torture, that he might more truly depict the agonies of his Prometheus. The Romans had mullets brought alive to their table that they might enjoy the beautiful variety of colours exhibited in their expiring moments. Among the moderns, many animals are robbed of their fair proportions, to correct nature, forsooth, and create beauty where she erred, from bad taste, in making them deformed! Some have their ears cropped, others their tails nicked and seared; and the

eyes of birds are put out to increase the strength and
sweetness of their song. Mr. Waterton, whom we have
had occasion to quote more than once, deplores the fate
of the poor chaffinch that has suffered this grievous deprivation, in a style which is honourable to his feelings.
" Sad and mournful is the fate which awaits this harmless
songster in Belgium and Holland, and in other kingdoms
of the continent. In your visit to the towns in these
countries you see it, outside the window, a lonely prisoner
in a wooden cage, which is scarcely large enough to allow
it to turn round upon its perch. It no longer enjoys the
light of day. Its eyes have been seared with a red-hot
iron, in order to increase its powers of song, which, unfor-
tunately for the cause of humanity, are supposed to be
heightened and prolonged far beyond their ordinary dura-
tion by this barbarous process."
  * * * "O that the potentate, in whose dominions
this little bird is doomed to such a cruel fate, would pass
an edict to forbid the perpetration of this barbarous deed!
Then would I exclaim, O king of men, thy act is worthy
of a royal heart. That kind Being, who is a friend to
the friendless, will recompense thee for this."—WATER-
TON's *Essays on Natural History.*
  Since all creatures delight in liberty, and none more
than birds accustomed to have the whole amplitude of
the heavens for their range, their confinement in cages,
unless of such as have been brought forth and reared in
that state, must appear to every mind of common sensibility a grievous hardship. But what is this to the loss
of the most delightful of the senses, and what must we
think of those who have the heart to perpetrate or permit it?
  Many, it may be feared, who are among the last to
whom cruelty in any form can be imputed directly, must,
notwithstanding, be implicated in the charge of blamable
inattention to a subject of such importance as this. If
we hear or know of any existing cruelties, are we blameless
if we do not endeavour to effect their extinction? Can
our kitchens, our larders, our festive boards testify nothing
against us? We know them not—we hear them not.
No; we take care to shut out from our eyes and our ears

M

whatever would offend. We dread the pain of having our
sensibility wounded, and hence the evils we should be
instrumental in redressing are allowed to grow and multiply. They who, in the days of the Prophet Amos, "lay
on beds of ivory, and stretched themselves upon their
couches, and eat of the lambs out of the flock, and the
calves out of the midst of the stall, that chanted to the
sound of the viol, * * and drank wine in bowls, and
anointed themselves with the choicest unguents, grieved
not for the affliction of Joseph." While we "eat the fat
and drink the sweet," we never, for an instant, reflect on
the animal sufferings which precede the banquet;—the
barbed hook, the lacerating shot, the shrieks, the groans,
and the dying agony. Such reflections would embitter
the taste; therefore they are excluded as enemies of our
peace; and cruelties continue to be perpetrated, not because we approve of them, but because we allow ourselves
to become even unconscious of their existence.

CAUSES OF CRUELTY.

SECTION FOURTH.

IGNORANCE AND FALSE PRETENCES.

"While man exclaims, ' See all things for my use !'
' See man for mine !' replies a pamper'd goose."—POPE.

"Man scruples not to say that he enjoyeth the heavens and the elements, as if all had been made, and still move only for him. In this sense,
a gosling may say as much, and perhaps with more truth and justness."—
CHARRON.

"The *gasterophilus equi* can subsist no where but in the stomach of the
horse or ass; which animals, therefore, this insect might boast, with some
show of reason, to have been created for its use rather than for ours,
being to us useful only, but to it indispensable."—KIRBY's and SPENCE's
Entomology, vol. I. p. 387.

MUCH cruelty is committed through ignorance, and under false pretences. Though nothing is held so cheap
as the lives of animals, yet, as if there were still some
suspicion lurking in the mind, that they should not be
gratuitously slaughtered, or without some sufficient reason, you may hear various motives assigned to excuse or

justify the putting to death numberless creatures, that are harmless in their lives, and of little or no use when dead. Thus one creature is killed because it is beautiful, and its skin or its feathers may be ornamental to some trashery collection; a second is impaled or crushed to atoms under foot because it is ugly; a third is doomed to the same fate because it is neither beautiful nor ugly; a fourth because it is a cruel creature, and likes an insect or a bird for dinner, as much as an alderman loves a lobster and grouse; a fifth is not worthy to live, because the Creator in his infinite wisdom made it good for nothing! and a sixth must be destroyed—"for any other reason why"—*qualibet altera causa*. The wolf in the fable alleging impossible causes of quarrel with the lamb that he was determined to devour, is no bad representative of many an impaler of insects, of canicides and zootomists.

To the admirer of beauty, and the connoisseur in ugliness, I would say, there is nothing so beautiful as clemency, and, in the whole range of existence, nothing so ugly as a cruel man or woman. But who constituted you a judge of beauty and deformity, or allowed you to assume that either the one or the other is a sufficient cause for putting a creature to death? Whatever be its form and dress, God gave them, and you have no right to make his gifts a plea for its destruction. A wise man has said, "Whoso mocketh the poor reproacheth his Maker." And we may add, agreeably to this sentiment, that he who destroys an animal because he deems it ugly, casts a reproach on the Creator who gave it the russet plumage or the coarse fur, the black shard, or the spiny shell, which he calls ugly. What would he think should some being of superior order, of superior taste too, and other ideas of beauty than his, insist on slicing off his nose, because it is not formed after the Grecian model, or on crushing his frame to jelly, because it cannot boast of the same grace and symmetry as the Apollo Belvidere? There would be as much reason in the one case as in the other. But suppose the creature to be formed according to his own standard of beauty, with all the elegance of shape and magnificence of dress that he admires, would it be safe from injury? By no means. Whatever chance of protection or escape it might hope from his contempt, it would have none from his admiration. Its beauty seals its fate, and at all events it must be captured or shot. We need not, therefore, be surprised to see frequent announcements like the following in the public journals:—

"RARÆ AVES.—A few days ago, a beautiful milk-white jay was shot at Woodlands, near this town, and a rose-coloured thrush was also killed at Bawtry. They may be seen at Mr. Reid's, French-gate."—*Doncaster Chronicle.*

Some writers lessen the estimation in which many animals should be held by stigmatizing them with epithets as degrading as they are unjust. Thus, Hildrop, a humane writer, and a friend of animals, calls insects "vile and contemptible." Some of them are deemed so on account of certain unpleasant associations, though nothing that comes from the Creator's hand can with propriety be denominated contemptible; much less should be recklessly destroyed. Many species of insects are among the most beautiful objects in creation, exhibiting such an endless variety of forms, colours, motions, instincts, as excites the astonishment of every observer. Who does not admire the bee, the dragon-fly, the moth, and the butterfly?

> "The velvet nap which on his wings doth lie,
> The silken down with which his back is dight,
> His broad outstretched horns, his hairy thighs,
> His glorious colours, and his glistening eyes."—SPENCER.

The common domestic fly, 'busy, curious, thirsty,' is a beautiful creature; a specimen of such exquisite workmanship as no hands on earth can rival. See, if no Domitian be nigh, how he comes to court your friendship, to partake with the easy familiarity of an old friend of the sweets of your table, and how he protrudes his little trunk to taste the sugary drop that has fallen on your board. Now he is brushing his eyes and head with the furred extremities of his fore legs, which he employs as hands; and now with his hinder legs he is rubbing his filmy transparent wings, as if he would give them a new polish, and invest them with a brighter iridescence.— Wary and circumspect he surveys all around him, and the slightest movement escapes not the rapidity of his glance. In a moment he is gone and vanished; but anon he will return, and give you another opportunity of observing what beauty, what inimitable skill, what vigilance are combined in a creature so diminutive. Hurt him not; should you injure him in a leg or wing, the injury is irreparable. Crush him; and all the wealth and all the science in the world could do nothing to restore him.

Multitudes of animals are most unmercifully destroyed from ignorance of their uses; from an idea that they are noxious or injurious to some petty concern of a field or garden; and at the very time they are rendering important services to man, they are mowed down as if they were his sworn enemies, and had conspired against his life. Hence the rooks, in some parts of England, were at one time in danger of being extirpated, as we learn from the author of "A Philosophical Survey of the Animal Creation." "The rook," says he, "is a species of crow that feeds upon worms produced from the eggs of the May-bug. As these and all the winged insects in general, are to be supported by the roots of plants, they deposit their eggs pretty deep in the earth, in a hole they dig for that purpose. The worms and caterpillars upon which the rook feeds, are not exposed to the mercy of this bird till the earth is thrown up. Hence it is that rooks always frequent lands recently cultivated, that the sight of the husbandman with his plough puts them in action, and that they search with so much assiduity about furrows newly formed."

"Some years ago the farmers in one of the principal counties of England, entertained a notion that these birds were prejudicial to their grain; and they determined, as if with one accord, to extirpate the race. The rooks were every where persecuted; their nests demolished; their young ones destroyed. But in proportion to the decrease of this animal, they found themselves overrun with swarms of worms, caterpillars, butterflies, and bugs; which attached themselves to the grain, trees, and fruits, and occasioned greater desolation in one day than the rooks would have done in the space of a twelvemonth. Many farmers were ruined. At length the persecution ceased ; and they found that in proportion as this race of animals was restored, the scourge which their destruction had occasioned ceased likewise."

To this authority may be added that of Selby, who, in his *Illustrations of British Ornithology*, p. 73, affirms that " wherever the banishing or extirpating of rooks has been carried into effect, the most serious injury to the corn and other crops has invariably followed, from the unchecked devastations of the grub and the caterpillar. In Northumberland I have witnessed their usefulness in feeding on the larvæ of the insect commonly known by the name of *Harry-long-legs, (Tipula oleracea,)* which is particularly destructive to the roots of grain and young clover."

This is a very instructive history. It should be made universally known; and at the same time it should induce men to examine well whether many of the creatures against which they wage an exterminating war, may not be among their benefactors. Notwithstanding, crows still continue to be the objects of remorseless persecution. Will it be believed that in the month of June, in the year of our Lord 1838, " William Evans, of Trefargoed, in company with another farmer, on Monday sen'night, killed 1915 crows in Pantyderi-wood, Pembrokeshire, from three to six o'clock in the evening ?" Of the motive to this massacre we are not informed, but it was probably from the mistaken idea that these birds were enemies to agriculture; an idea of which some minds seem incapable of being dispossessed. The American farmers of New England once offered a reward of three-pence per head for the heads of the purple grackle, because it took a little of the grain to which it had an equitable claim, for its services in preventing the depredation of insects When, in consequence of this cruel and impolitic act, the birds were " nearly extirpated, insects increased to such a degree as to cause a total loss of the herbage, and the inhabitants were obliged to obtain hay for their cattle, not only from Pennsylvania, but even from Great Britain."— KIRBY, vol. i. p. 289.—*Linn. Trans.* v. 105, note.

Many birds, besides rooks, are destroyed, under the mistaken idea that they are injurious to the garden or earhard, at the very time they are most useful to both in feeding themselves and their nestlings on grubs and caterpillars.

"The common sparrow, though proscribed as a most mischievous bird, destroys a vast number of insects. Bradley has calculated that a single pair, having young to maintain, will destroy 3360 caterpillars in a week."[*] The blue tit-mouse (*parus cæruleus*, LINN.) often falls a victim to ignorance in this country (Ireland,) as it does in England, in consequence of the injury it is supposed to do to fruit trees. Mr. Selby most justly pleads in favour of its being a friend rather than an enemy to the horticulturist."[†] A. De Capell Brooke, in his "Travels to the North Cape," says that "the surprising number and tameness of the common magpie, both in Sweden and Norway, cannot fail to strike the traveller. It invariably builds on some low bushy tree, just before the cottage door. In England, (and in Ireland,) their eggs would soon be borne off in triumph by some mischievous boy, but here they remain in perfect safety." Not only would their eggs be borne off, but themselves, if they came within reach of gun-shot, be probably destroyed. A pair of these lively interesting birds had their nest for several successive seasons in the garden of Tyrone-house, now occupied by the Board of National Education, in the rear of the author's dwelling in Gardiner-street, Dublin. One of them came frequently at an early hour in the morning, and tapped with her beak at a window in the gable of a contiguous out-house, having seen, as I conjectured, her own reflection in the glass, and mistaken it for another bird of her own species. It was amusing to observe her quick motions, her vigilant eye, and intelligent look, as she hopped from place to place, suggesting, in the midst of a great city, images of rural scenery, *rus in urbe*. She sometimes ventured into the yard in search of forage, and I began to entertain for her a friendship, and hoped by a little attention to her comforts to inspire her with a confidence that might lead to

* Kirby, I. 291. Reaum. II. 468. † Mr. Thompson on the Birds of Ireland. Annals of Natural History, No. 3, p. 190.

a more familiar intimacy. At last she brought out her young, three in number ; full-fledged and beautiful in their white and black glossy plumage. Under her guidance they were practising their first lessons in flying; and in a few days more would probably have been ready to seek some new locality for themselves. It was not, therefore, without a thrill of indignation and horror, that I beheld them one afternoon lying on the ground, fluttering in the blood of their death wounds, having been shot from a neighbouring back window by some idle ruffian, who could have no object in destroying them, but to shew his skill in hitting a mark, or to gratify a diabolical spirit of cruelty. If asked wherefore he shot them, he would probably have said, that they robbed birds' nests, or took chickens from the farm-yard. What then ? Who dignified him with the office of judge and avenger ? A magpie has as good a right to live as her ruthless destroyer. But birds' eggs and young chicks are not always in season, nor easy to be procured. What does she feed on then ? In the present instance it is not likely that she had either. Magpies, like rooks, render good service to the field, and it argues as great a want of sense as of humanity to destroy them. If at the day of judgment we must give an account of every idle word we speak, how much more awful must be the reckoning for every cruel deed we commit ?

Sometimes a prejudice is found to exist against a particular species of bird for being unlucky or ill-omened, and then it is deemed as meritorious to destroy it as to get rid of a nuisance. The lapwing once suffered much from such a prejudice in Scotland, having on some occasions been the cause of unwittingly discovering the haunts of men who fled from persecution; it being the nature of this bird in the breeding season, to fly screaming near those who approach its nest, to lure them away. Mr. Waterton has given us two striking illustrations of the evil of ignorance, in treating the woodpecker and goatsucker* with cruel hostility, at the very time too when

* Both of these names are unfortunate; the latter particularly as tending to perpetuate the very error in which its name originated.

they are acting as industrious and sagacious friends to
man ; the former in searching for " a hidden and unsuspected foe which had been devouring his wood," the latter
in preying on the flies that were annoying the herd.
" The vultures, like the goatsucker and woodpecker, seem
to be in disgrace with man.   They are generally termed
a voracious, stinking, cruel, and ignoble tribe.   Under
these impressions the fowler discharges his gun at them,
and probably thinks he has done well in ridding the earth
of such vermin.

" Some governments impose a fine on him who kills a
vulture.   This is a salutary law, and it were to be wished
that other governments would follow so good an example.
I would fain say here a word or two in favour of this
valuable scavenger.

" Kind Providence has conferred a blessing on hot
countries in giving them the vulture ; he (it) has ordered
it to consume that which, if left to dissolve in putrefac-
tion, would infect the air and produce a pestilence. * * *
In 1808 I saw the vultures in Angustura as tame as
domestic fowls ; a person who had never seen a vulture
would have taken them for turkies.   They were very useful to the Spaniards ; had it not been for them, the refuse
of the slaughter-house in Angustura would have caused
an intolerable nuisance." p. 210.

Quadrupeds, as well as birds, suffer much under slan-
derous imputations, as can be attested by the badger and
the hedgehog.   The former, a harmless inoffensive animal,
is baited and worried by dogs, because he destroys lambs
and rabbits !   This charge, however, has not been sub-
stantiated ; and it is known that he feeds on roots, fruits,
insects, frogs, and such small game.   But he is strong
and powerful, and can repel his assailants, when fairly
matched, with great dexterity.   He is, therefore, capable
of affording an " inhuman diversion," as Bewick states, " to
the idle and the vicious, who take a cruel pleasure in seeing this harmless animal surrounded by its enemies, and
defending itself from their attacks, which it does with
astonishing agility and success."   The hedgehog also is
assailed by dogs, torn in pieces, drowned, or burned, because he sucks cows ! whereas he might as well be ac-

cused of sucking the great northern bear. He also climbs apple-trees, and carries off the fruit sticking to the spines on his back! Such a dexterous feat would merit the apples; and should he eat the fruits that fall in his way, they would be but a small compensation for his services to the horticulturist in gnawing the roots of the plantain, a troublesome weed, and in destroying worms, beetles, and various species of insects. If taken to the kitchen, he will soon clear it of cock-roaches, and ably discharge the duties of a turn-spit dog.

That God has created nothing in vain should be considered as an axiom both in philosophy and religion; though there may be some things of which we cannot see the immediate use, and others, in certain localities, positively injurious. Animals the most feeble, and apparently insignificant, even those which escape unassisted vision, as the *infusoria* and other animalcules, serve the most beneficial purposes. They supply nutriment to creatures larger and stronger; and these in their turn become the prey of a still stronger race; and these again, of birds, fishes, quadrupeds, and man. Buffon says, "Insects do more harm than good;" a strange assertion from so distinguished a naturalist! The entire genus of swallows, the woodpeckers, and the young of almost the whole feathered creation, and the tribes of fishes, would contradict his assertion. The ant-eater, the chameleon, the mole, the bat, the hedgehog, and the badger, will testify against him, as will also the bee-master, the silk-manufacturer, and the physician.

Insects are teazing, sometimes destructive; but they labour industriously to provide us with food and raiment, with dyestuffs and medicine.* Innumerable myriads of gnats, *(culex pipiens,)* in the northern regions, supply food for shoals of fishes and millions of game, and may be considered as the proximate cause of the annual migrations of the finny and the feathered tribes, which afford

---

* " The quantity of the cochineal insect at present annually exported from South America, is said by Humboldt to be 32,000 arrobas, there worth 500,000l. sterling; a vast amount to arise from so small an insect, and well calculated to shew us the absurdity of despising any animals on account of their minuteness."—KIRBY, vol. i. p. 323.

such an abundant supply of nutriment, not only to the Laplander and Esquimaux, but to the inhabitants of every shore which they visit. Were insects annihilated, how many species of other animals would languish and die; and man himself would be among the greatest sufferers. For it is with the animal kingdom, as with the body politic, or the microcosm of the human frame, if " one member suffer, all the members suffer with it," and the loss of one class or order would involve that of another, till all would perish. If some species are injurious to the garden and the orchard, the wardrobe and the museum, they are beneficial in some other department, and the mischief of which we complain is amply compensated by the greater good of which they are the ministers. The *dermestes*, the *cerambyx*, and the *cantharis navalis* prey upon wood. They injure the water-pipe, reduce the fallen trees of the forest to powder, and bore through the war-ship's ribs; but while busied in these operations, they are furnishing employment to the pump-borer, the sawyer, and the carpenter. St. Pierre has beautifully observed, that " the weevel and the moth oblige the wealthy monopolizer to bring his goods to market, and by destroying the wardrobes of the opulent,* they give bread to the industrious. Were grain as incorruptible as gold, it would be soon as scarce; and we ought to bless the hand that created the insect that *obliges* them to sift, turn, and ultimately to bring the grain to public sale."

How often do men betray their ignorance and folly in making assertions destructive of this fundamental principle, that all things have their use ? When animals cannot be fairly put to death because they are injurious to the interests of man, having pecked a pear or made free with a cherry, it is easy to allege that they are *good for nothing*, and therefore should not be suffered to live. But though the premises here were true, the conclusion would be false. Both, however, are erroneous. Whenever a man affirms that any production of nature is good

---

* Queen Elizabeth is said to have left above 3000 suits, of various shapes and colours, in her wardrobe when she died.—(SINCLAIR *on Revenue*, p. 177.) Would they not have been better employed in clothing 3000 of her naked subjects?

for nothing, he not only makes a clear confession of his ignorance, but he impugns the wisdom of the Creator, by imagining it possible that he could create aught, however insignificant it may appear, that is not of use in the general system. It would become him better to say, 'It must have its uses, for God made it, though I cannot at present perceive them.' Time and experience have often proved how men may be mistaken in their views of utility, and may condemn as worthless the mine which a deeper search has proved to be of inestimable value. Had some such reflections as these passed through the mind of our quondam friend, "Honest Isaak," he would not have spoken of the stickleback (*gasterosteus aculeatus*) in the following strain : "There is also a little fish called a sticklebag, a fish without scales, but hath his body fenced with several prickles. I know not where he dwells in winter; nor what he is good for in summer, but *only to make sport for boys and women anglers."* He then instructs his pupils how to " put the hook in at the mouth and out at the tail, and to *sew* his mouth to the line in such a way that he may turn quick and tempt any trout ?" It seems strange that a religious mind like Isaak's did not think this beautiful little fish created for some other end, than to furnish boys and women anglers with a subject for the exercise of their cruelty.* But ' Isaak' was not singular in this notion. Men may still be found who seem so thoroughly convinced of its truth, that they wonder how it should be questioned. It is entertaining to see some of these gentlemen pluming themselves on their superiority, and at the same time distressing to see how they abuse it. It might have a salutary effect, were any one who is a chief among them seriously to consider in how many respects animals are superior to himself. Most of them can live more independently, and fulfil the design of their creation much better than he. Of what can he boast, to place him above rivalship or competition ? Can he match the elephant in strength, the horse in fleetness, the lynx or the eagle in vision, the spider in deli-

---

* The reader may see a very interesting account of this little fish, in the third of Dr. J. L. Drummond's *" Letters to a Young Naturalist."*

cacy of touch, or the hound in scent ? Can he elaborate
any article like the honey of the bee, or concoct a poison
like the rattle-snake's ? Even in intelligence he is ex-
celled by them, for they make use of that portion of understanding which God has given them, as God designed,
and " know and reason not contemptibly ;" but he abuses
his intellect and the gifts of God, and reasons, if reasoning it may be called, in a way which even they, if they
could speak, would call contemptible. It might become
some tyrant like Commodus, to affirm that the tall necks
of the ostriches were formed only to be a mark to shew
the certainty with which his moon-headed arrows could
mow them off in the bloody circus. But what is a cruel
man good for ? Certainly not for so much as Walton's
" sticklebag ;" for he affords sport neither to " boys nor
women anglers." It is monstrous to hear an unfeathered
brute, in the shape of a man, boasting of his superiority
on account of his shape, and because he has the power,
alleging that he has the right, to maim, wound, and
slaughter God's creatures, for sport, whim, or savage curiosity. Superior ! no ; the least of his victims is better
than he ; for it obeys better the laws of its constitution,
and cannot be taxed with the guilt of their violation. It
is as valuable too in the sphere where God has placed it,
as he in his ; and when he dies, his loss will be as little
felt as that of the gnat or the fly which he crushes between his fingers. To die, indeed, it may be said, is the
only thing he is good for, since it may afford some pleasure to " boys and women" to think that he is for ever
gone, and that the world is disburthened of a monster.

The cruelties perpetrated upon animals, for only following those instincts which an all-wise Creator has given
for their preservation, are of a most truculent description,
and demand not only the severest reprehension of the
moralist, but the castigation of the laws. Some of them
are so shocking, that they would seem incredible, were
they not too well attested to be considered as inventions.
The lashings, mutilations, dissections, and various other
tortures, are beyond expression horrible. Sailors and
fishers put out the eyes of dog-fish and sharks, and send
them adrift to perish of famine in darkness and agony ;

N

and this for no reason but that of the unfortunate animals yielding to the irresistible force of appetite, in devouring whatever edible substance they find on the baited hook, or that has fallen by accident overboard. The fisher may think he does an act of justice in torturing the enemy of his trade; and the seaman that he is authorized to inflict on the devourer of his companion, a punishment commensurate to the wrong. But what shall we say of such parsons as him of Pentlow, of whom Lawrence gives the following anecdote :—" The worthy priest had lost a chicken, and soon after taking a poor hawk, the *supposed* offender, he put the animal to the torture of a slow and lingering death, for doing his duty by following the instinct of his nature. The poor bird was turned adrift, with a label affixed to his neck, containing these quaint and inhuman lines :—

> " The parson of Pentlow he did this,
> For killing one poor chicken of his ;
> He put out his eyes, and sewed up *** ***,
> And so let him fly 'till the day of his doom."

One would suppose that wretches like this sought to level their impotent revenge against the God of nature himself."—LAWRENCE *on the Horse*, vol. i. p. 152.

White of Selborne presents us with a similar instance of merciless atrocity, but without the stigma of his merited animadversion. "A neighbouring gentleman one summer had lost most of his chickens by a sparrow-hawk. * * The owner, inwardly vexed to see his flock diminishing, hung a setting net adroitly between the pile and the house, into which the caitiff dashed and was entangled. Resentment suggested the law of retaliation; he therefore clipped the hawk's wings, cut off his talons, and fixing a cork on his bill, threw him down among the brood-hens. Imagination cannot paint the scene that ensued; the expressions that fear, rage, and revenge inspired, were new, or at least such as were unnoticed before. The exasperated matrons upbraided—they execrated —they insulted—they triumphed. In a word, they never desisted from buffetting their adversary, till they had torn him in a hundred pieces."—*Letter* lxxxv.

Thus to injure and destroy animals for obeying the
instincts of their nature, is not only a violation of their
rights, and a demonstration of ignorance and barbarism, but
an act of rebellion against God: and yet there is nothing
which causes them to be more frequently visited with
vengeance, than their obedience to laws which they have no
power to resist. It is as natural for the fox to seize on
the poultry of the farm-yard, as for man to eat of the
fruits of the earth; and it would be as reasonable and just
to break a man's bones for eating partridge, as to torture
a bird of prey for partaking of the same fare.

In nothing is some men's inconsistency more striking
than in their mode of treating animals. They value or
abuse bird or beast, just as its instincts happen to accord
or disagree with their own wishes or convenience. A cat
is prized for vigilance and activity in clearing the house
of vermin; but if, in obedience to the same instinct which
makes her a good hunter, she seizes on a goldfinch or
canary bird, she is in no small danger of being worried
to death.

FOTHERGILL, in his *Philosophy of Natural History,*
pp. 172, 173, justly observes that " Nothing can be more
childish and unphilosophical than to call the tiger cruel, the
eagle inexorable, or the crocodile merciless, attaching any
peculiar malignity to those terms; since in allaying their
imperious appetites, such animals are but fulfilling, in
their various capacities, the word of Him who commanded
the one to roam the forests, another to haunt the inaccessible heights of craggy mountains, and the third to dwell
amidst the solitary waters of a desert land; each to mitigate evils that would soon become fatal and universal
without the use of such agency. In the sight of Omnipotence and of unlimited benevolence, the lion is not less
innocent in the destruction of his prey, even though that
prey should be the proud lord of the creation himself,
than the bleating lamb, while browsing on the tender
grass allotted for its food: nor is the gaunt wolf, smeared
with gore, and warm from the carnage, more guilty than
the plaintive dove that picks up the scattered grain of the
field. To the God of nature the scream of the vulture,
echoing from the awful solitude of the Andes, is not more

frightful than the melodious strains of the nightingale, rising in full chorus from the groves of Italy. Man alone is cruel; he alone is oppressive and inexorable; and he alone bears the tremendous responsibility."

"The moth that eats into our clothes has something to plead for our pity; for he came, like us, naked into the world, and he has destroyed our garments, not in malice or wantonness, but that he may clothe himself with the same wool which we have stripped from the sheep."— *Insect Architecture*, p. 2.

May not something be pleaded in behalf even of the book-worm? When Parnel hunted and sacrificed this creature, which he denominates a " ravening beast of prey," he should have spared it for the services which it sometimes renders to religion, by reducing to powder the worthless tomes of scholastic divinity and theological jargon, which have tended only to cloud the understanding, and obstruct the pure and holy influences of Gospel truth.

To a mind accustomed to meditate on the works and ways of God, nothing affords such a subject of admiration as the various arts practised by animals to obtain their food; their stratagems, their contrivances, their labours, patience, perseverance, and courage afford an inexhaustible source of curious and gratifying research. An eminent naturalist, with some of whose observations these pages have already been enriched, after giving a detailed account of the marvellous ingenuity of spiders in capturing their prey, thus proceeds:—

"Instead of considering them (spiders) as repulsive compounds of cruelty and ferocity, you will henceforward see in their procedures only the ingenious contrivance of patient and industrious hunters, who, while obeying the great law of nature in procuring their sustenance, are actively serviceable to the human race in destroying noxious insects. You will allow the poet to stigmatize them as

"——— cunning and fierce,
Mixture abhorred;"

but you will see that these epithets are in reality as unjustly applied to them, (at least with reference to the mode in which they procure their necessary subsistence) as to the patient sportsman who lays snares for the birds that are to serve for the dinner of his family; and when you hear

> "—— the fluttering wing
> And shriller sound declare extreme distress,"

you will as little think it the part of true mercy to stretch forth " the helping hospitable hand" to the entrapped fly, as to the captive birds. The spider requires his meal as well as the Indian; and however to our weak capacity the great law of creation "eat or be eaten" may seem cruel or unnecessary, knowing, as we do, that it is the ordinance of a beneficent Being who does all things well, and that in fact the sum of happiness is greatly augmented by it, no man who does not let a morbid sensibility get the better of his judgment, will, on account of their subjection to this rule, look upon predaceous animals with abhorrence." —vol. i. pp. 424, 425.

CAUSES OF CRUELTY.

SECTION FIFTH.

ANTIPATHIES.

> " Some men there are love not a gaping pig ;
> Some that are mad if they behold a cat."—SHAKSPEARE.

NATURE has kindly and wisely given certain instinctive feelings to animals, by which they immediately become conscious of the presence of an enemy. Thus a hen recognizes the hawk as the foe of her downy brood, and clucks them under her wing, whenever the bird of prey makes its appearance. The hare flees from the hound; the horse shudders at the growl of a lion; and the cock has more dread of the weasel than of all the wild beasts of Africa. Some animals have a mutual dislike, which we call ANTIPATHY, to each other; as the dog and the cat, the elephant and the rhinoceros, the horse and the ass, until they become reconciled by custom.

Man seems to partake of these feelings, as is evident from the dislike which he manifests for certain creatures, and his eagerness to destroy them wherever they are to be found. Many, so far from thinking it an inhuman act, make it their pride and boast to tell how they have killed ear-wigs, spiders, beetles, caterpillars, and rats, not because these creatures are injurious to them or their property, but simply from an unaccountable dislike. Some delicate ladies shout and scream till the welkin rings, at the sight of a mouse or a cock-roach. This may often be imputed to affectation and childish folly; but sometimes, we doubt not, to an unaffected apprehension of a bite or a sting.

Why animals that are formidable for their strength and ferocity, their poisonous fangs and retractile claws, should be dreaded, may be easily understood. Few would choose to hug a porcupine or hedgehog, or suffer a scorpion to nestle in their bosom. But wherefore should the most harmless and timid of creatures excite apprehension and disgust? One is frightened from his propriety by a death's-head-moth, and another thrown into convulsions by a fork-tailed reptile. Germanicus, a high-spirited Roman soldier, could not endure the sight or the voice of a cock, an antipathy of which Beattie the poet and philosopher partook, and which he has expressed in the most merciless malediction ever uttered by a "minstrel" on a noble bird.

> "Fell chanticleer! who oft hath reft away
> My fancied good, and brought substantial ill!
> O, to thy cursed scream, discordant still,
> Let harmony aye shut her gentle ear;
> Thy boastful mirth let jealous rivals spill,
> Insult thy crest, and glossy pinions tear,
> And ever in thy dreams the ruthless fox appear!"

This curse, like the false prophet's, must be reversed:—

> Kind chanticleer! who oft hath scared away
> The night-mare's horrors with thy clarion shrill;
> O, to thy jocund voice, harmonious still,
> May sage and poet lend a grateful ear;
> Thy gallant breast may love's pure transports thrill;
> Proud be thy crest unshorn—thy watch-cry clear;
> May plenty gloss thy plumes, and joy thy spirit cheer!

Man's antipathies are not limited to animals; they extend to various other objects, to fruits, flowers, and various kinds of viands. Some cannot endure the flesh of an eel, others abhor pork, though not from any religious motive. Vaillant could not bear the tongue of an elephant, though he relished the hoof when stewed in Hottentot fashion, as an unparalleled luxury.

Many have a marvellous antipathy to rats. These unfortunate animals indeed have no friends; they are worried by dogs; devoured by cats; pounced on by birds of prey; poisoned, entrapped, hunted wherever they are found; and destroyed even by their own species. Were they not prodigiously prolific, they must become extinct. The humane man, who should venture to say a word in behalf of a rat, would only encounter the sneers and the scoffs of the little world around him; and yet at the hazard of this, though without invoking the powers of song, and saying with Grainger, " Muse, sing of rats;" one may dare to affirm that it is an act of gratuitous cruelty to take the life even of a rat, when it is doing us no harm. Should I meet it on the sandy beach, or among sterile rocks, wherefore should I assail it ? By what right molest it in its native hereditary province ? Because it is in many situations a troublesome and destructive animal, is that any reason for annoying it in a situation where it is inoffensive ? The old plea may be alleged, that it is " good for nothing." Well—what then ? If all creatures that are good for nothing were to be exterminated, how many cockney sporters must perish ? But who has proved that a rat is good for nothing ? It was created by a power infinite in wisdom, and therefore it must be good for something. You cannot see for what. Then blame your own blindness and ignorance, and investigate whether you may not discover that it has some uses ? Is it not a useful scavenger ? Does it not devour meats that would putrify and taint the atmosphere ? Does it not supply an occasional meal to birds and beasts of prey ? Nay, has it not sometimes sustained the life of the famishing mariner; and been purchased for its weight of silver or gold during the straitness of a siege ?*

* " The Chinese bring to market rats which are drawn quite clean, and like pigs in our country, hung up by the hind legs; and they look very nice."—*Quarterly Review*, April, 1838.

Thunberg says that he travelled through a scorching desert of Caffraria, so destitute of water that even a sparrow could not subsist in it, and so devoid of every living creature that only a few rats were to be seen here and there in holes of the earth. Here we might suppose if they had not plenty, they had, at least, peace and freedom from annoyance. But no—"We tried," says our traveller, "to shoot some of them as they popped their heads out; but found them, to our great surprise as well as disappointment, inexpressibly quick in withdrawing into their holes, as soon as they saw the flash of the pan. I tried several times with an excellent gun to hit one of them, but found it impracticable, till I fell upon the method of putting a piece of paper before the pan, which prevented them from seeing the flash of the prime." Shooting the rats was an act of mercy, in comparison of another mode of putting them to death, mentioned by Lawrence in his treatise on the horse. An "infernal hag," says he, "the housekeeper of a boarding-school, caused a miserable rat to be roasted alive over a slow fire in presence of all the boys; and this, I was informed, was the constant practice of a certain post-master in the neighbourhood." p. 151.

The cat, like the rat, is the object of some people's antipathy, though a beautiful, graceful, and most useful animal. To justify the bad treatment with which she is visited, she is maligned as spiteful and treacherous, for no very apparent reason, but that she sometimes shews a proper resentment of injurious usage, and will not suffer herself to be handled as if she were totally destitute of feeling. She is also accused of being more attached to places than to persons, as if this were a crime, and not a constitutional affection. She is however capable of lasting attachment to her master or mistress; and instances are not wanting of her accompanying them in their excursions to the field, as if she delighted to bear a part in their amusement. But notwithstanding her beauty and utility, she is often the object of cruel persecution; hunted and pelted with stones by evil-minded men and boys; put into a bowl, set afloat upon the waters, and pursued by dogs; dragged for a mile or two along the ground, to irritate young hounds, as we have seen in page 112; sometimes she is flayed alive to enhance the value of her fur; and extensive districts have been robbed of their whole feline race for the paltry gain of their skins.

Frogs and toads, both harmless, are to many the objects of special dislike, and are destroyed as malefactors. The toad has even been baked alive as a specific for some disease in horses. It is the first ingredient thrown by the witches of Shakspeare into their infernal caldron.

> "Toad that under coldest stone
> Days and nights hast thirty-one
> Swelter'd venom sleeping got,
> Boil thou first i' the charmed pot."

The following observations from the Rev. Rowland Hill, in behalf of this creature, indicate an amiability of disposition worthy of commendation :—" An uncommon degree of odium is fixed to the existence of a toad. They are supposed to be poisonous ; this is quite a vulgar error. They are useful reptiles; and are even capable of the knowledge of our attention and humanity. It is wanton cruelty to destroy them. In my country abode I even attempted to make them a place of retirement, and called it a *toadery*. Every creature that God has sent we should protect, and, in a subordinate degree, they demand our attention. * * It is no disgrace to the Christian character to plead the persecuted cause of the harmless toad."— [Disgrace! no, verily!] *Journey of a Tour through the North of England, &c.* by ROWLAND HILL, A. M., p.p. 86, 87. Shakspeare, in accordance with the popular error, has denominated the toad "ugly and venomous;" but yet it " wears a precious jewel in its head :"

> " A jewel not to draw the stupid stare
> Of gold's idolaters; but wisdom's gaze,
> Which there, as in the heaven-constructed brain
> Of Plato or the Stagyrite, may trace
> Th' impressions of a hand in plastic skill
> Consummate, and in power omnipotent."
> *W. H. D's Pleasures of Benevolence.*

The water-newt *(lacerta aquatica,)* also suffers under an unmerited stigma. This harmless little creature is in some regions known by the name of *man-keeper* or *man-eater,* and is in consequence destroyed as the enemy of the human species. It is said to hasten down the throat of the man whom it happens to discover sleeping with his mouth open, and to prey on his vitals, till it be excluded by the following ingenious stratagem. The person possessed must eat a salt herring, and lying down by a murmuring stream feign himself asleep, with expanded jaws. His inmate, allured by the sound of the water, comes forth to quench the thirst which it participates with its host; but is, of course, suffered to return no more. The hairy caterpillar of the tiger moth, (*bombyx caja*,) with some others, has had the misfortune to obtain the name of *step-mother* or *grand-mother*, why I cannot tell; and whenever seen crossing the path, is seized and crushed by some idle urchin. A common appellation of that long and slender limbed insect, the *tipula oleracea* of Linnæus, is the *devil's-needle*, a title fatal to its existence, for it is crushed as if in despite of the author of ill, whereas the perpetration of such deeds is to him the most acceptable homage.

That some animals should be objects of antipathy, and consequently of injurious treatment, on account of their uninviting appearance, or their real or imaginary noxious properties, can be easily conceived. But that any of the most beautiful and inoffensive kind should be thus regarded, and persecuted to death from motives of political or religious bigotry, may seem to the humane reader a folly and wickedness too enormous to merit credit. When cattle are houghed and maimed, it is from animosity to their owner, not to the harmless beasts. What shall we think of the " most diminutive of birds" being hunted and stoned, for a supposed political offence of one or two of its progenitors above seven score years before it was born ? A tradition is prevalent in some parts both of the north and south of Ireland, that on one occasion James the Second's forces were on the point of surprising King William's army early in the morning, when some *wrens*, attracted probably by the fragments of the preceding night's meal, alighted on the head of a drum which had served for a table, and the noise of their bills in the act of picking awoke the drummer, who instantly beat to arms, and saved William's army from defeat. The wren accordingly has been, ever since, a prime favourite with

143

the Orange party, and an object of persecution to the friends of James, who on an appointed day have organised bands of ruffians, young and old, who go forth armed "with staves" to beat the hedges, and with stones to pelt this innocent and elegant little bird. St. Stephen's is the day preferred for this manly achievement; as if those engaged in it were ambitious of personating in a small way, the murderers of the first Christian martyr. Had the little birds that actually awoke the drummer been taken in the fact and executed, their punishment would have been sufficiently truculent; but to visit the offence, supposing it to be such, on all their race, is an enormity unmatched even by that of the amiable youth, who, in the insurrection of 1798, hanged a drake, because the hand of the Creator had adorned its beautiful neck and head with the national colour, the eye-refreshing green of the " emerald isle."

Superstition is a fertile source of cruelty to animals. Some of the Jewish laws, as we have already seen, were directed against certain superstitious rites of the heathen, that were accompanied with barbarous sacrifices, of which the witches in Horace furnish a proof and illustration. In countries where the light of Christianity has penetrated, we might suppose that this cause of cruelty, at least, should cease to exist. But facts demonstrate that this would be a rash and erroneous supposition ; and that deeds are perpetrated in our own day, which fully equal, if they do not surpass, Canidia's tearing the living lamb in pieces with her teeth. " The *Chelmsford Chronicle* of May, 1838, contains an account of the examination of a Mrs. Harris, at Witham petty sessions, on a charge of having boiled a cat alive. The cruelty arose from an ignorant and superstitious idea that it would enable her to find out some gipsies who had tricked her out of some property, on pretence of making her rich, if furnished with the means of working certain spells." White's account of the mode of making a " shrew ash," affords us farther illustration. The twig of a shrew ash was supposed to relieve the anguish said to be caused by the creeping of a shrew mouse on a horse, cow, or sheep, and it was made thus : " Into the body of the tree a deep hole was bored with an augur, and a poor devoted shrew mouse was thrust in alive, and plugged in, no doubt, with several quaint incantations, long since forgotten."—(Letter lxx.) Happily the vicar of the manor "stubbed and burnt" the last tree of the kind, and put an end to the practice in his locality.

It seems but fair to admit that if some animals are made to suffer as enemies, from antipathy and superstition, others are treated with kindness and affection from opposite causes, and from respect and gratitude for their virtues and services imaginary or real. Hence it is curious to find how, among almost every people, some animal is peculiarly favoured. Oppian informs us, that to kill a dolphin was deemed impious by the fishers of his day.

"The dolphin ne'er must bleed;
Detesting heaven resents th' inhuman deed."

The ibis was held sacred by the Egyptians. We learn from Sonnini that the Turks as well as the Greeks pay great respect to the weasel. It was formerly worshipped in the Thebais. "The Greek women carry their attention so far as not to disturb it; and they even treat it with a politeness truly whimsical. "*Welcome*," say they, when they perceive a weasel in their house; "*come in, my pretty wench; no harm shall happen to you here; you are quite at home; pray, make free*," &c. They affirm that, sensible of these civilities, the weasel does no mischief; whereas, every thing would be devoured, add they, if they did not behave to this animal in a courteous manner."

The pagan nations of Siberia also (the Jakhuti, for instance,) have their favourite animals, the goose, the swan, or the raven, which they treat as sacred, and forbid to be eaten by any of their tribe.—STRAHLENBERG's *Siberia*, p. 383. The *semnopithecus entellus* is held in such veneration by the Hindus, that they never destroy it, commit what ravages it may. The stork is a favourite in Holland, the magpie in the more northern states of Europe, and the red-breast is indebted to the well-known ballad, "The Babes in the Wood," as well as to its own confidence and familiarity, for the protection and friendship which it enjoys in the British islands.

The social affections must have an object on which they

can be indulged, and when men cannot find it in their own species, they seek it in another. Hence such caresses are often lavished on a bird or a beast, as excite ridicule or envy. Ladies have their lap-dogs, and men*their hobbies. We blame them not; on the contrary, we deem a fondness for animals the certain index of a philanthropic disposition.

CAUSES OF CRUELTY.

SECTION SIXTH.

LOVE OF SCIENCE PERVERTED.—VIVISECTION.

> "Ye who the mysteries of nature scan
> With microscopic vision, O forbear
> To purchase knowledge at the price, too dear,
> Of violated mercy ; nor the fane
> Of heaven-taught science to a den convert
> Of reeking slaughter, hung with horrid racks
> And implements of torture ! Spare the pangs
> Of the poor victim whose imploring eye
> Beseeches pity. On th' insensate frame,
> Whence life has fled, the useful search pursue ;
> And even there with reverence, as aware
> The vital spirit yet were hovering nigh,
> Its old abode solicitous to guard .
> From wanton jest and cold indignity."
>
> *W. H. D's Pleasures of Benevolence.*

Incidere autem vivorum. corpora et crudele et supervacuum est.
Celsus, p. 20.

It was maintained, prior to the age of Celsus, that in order to acquire an accurate knowledge of the human frame, it was necessary to inspect not only the internal structure of the dead, but to anatomize the living. Herophilus, a native of Carthage, born in the reign of Ptolemy Soter, and also Erasistratus, were stigmatized by some and eulogised by others, for having dissected criminals taken from the public prisons, and, while they were yet alive, inspected the position, colour, figure, magnitude of those parts which had before been concealed. It was strongly argued, that the knowledge thus acquired was absolutely necessary to those who would discriminate between a healthy and an unsound state of the internal

o

parts of the body, and apply the proper remedy to the parts diseased ; that the practice might be taxed with cruelty, but it was just that a few wicked men should expiate their crimes, and compensate the wrongs they had done to society, by suffering for the benefit of future generations.—CELSI *Opera, p. 7. Patavii,* 1750.

The natural and instinctive abhorrence which man feels for the dissection of his own species, even when dead, would cause him to revolt from its practice on the living. Accordingly, it does not appear ever to have come into extensive use; though a modern philosopher, M. de Maupertuis, has proved that it may not yet be without its advocates. In his letter to the King of Prussia on the advancement of science, he speaks " of the uses to be made of the punishment of criminals;" and says, " I should gladly see the lives of criminals made subservient to operations of this nature, even when there were but little hopes of success ; nay, I should even think that we ought to hazard them without scruple, even for improvements of more remote utility. Discoveries might be made with regard to the wonderful union of the soul and body, if we had the courage to look for the bonds of this union in the brains of a living man. Let us not be shocked at the air of cruelty which this carries with it : the life of a man is nothing when put in comparison with the whole human race; and the life of a criminal is less than nothing."

How would this sage have been pleased, had he been selected as the favoured subject for the experiment which was to shew the "wonderful union" of body and soul ? The experiment, to have ample justice, should by all means be made on a philosopher who felt an interest in the problem ; for if made on one of the οἱ πολλοι, the many, it might prove inconclusive. But such a sage as Maupertuis could reason on the different steps of the process; explain all his sensations ; indicate by expressive signs when " the bonds" were tightened or relaxed ; and if he felt a little pain, and began to tremble at dissolution, could draw consolation from the reflection that the life of a man is nothing, and the life even of a philosopher "less than nothing," in comparison of the pleasure that would be enjoyed by the whole human race in having the great mystery revealed !

Some of the contemporaries of Celsus, however, destitute of the light of the *Illuminati*, reasoned in a different strain. They reprobated the practice of anatomizing living men as cruel and unnecessary, and altogether unprofitable ; they contended that the medical art has for its object the preservation, not the destruction of life; that the parts of a subject dissected alive no longer retain their original function or appearance; that as, even when the frame suffers no violence, it undergoes great changes from fear, want, lassitude, and other affections, much greater must be the changes caused by painful incisions ; and, in short, that nothing can be more foolish than to suppose that the viscera, or members of a dying man, or of one who has just expired, are similar to those of a man in health. The dissection of some parts is attended by the immediate death of the subject, so that the dissector, after all, contemplates the parts not of a living but of a dead man, and he may be said to act cruelly the part of a cut-throat, rather than to inspect the intestines in their natural state of vitality. Accidents often furnish opportunities of seeing all that properly can be seen in living subjects, as when a gladiator falls wounded in the arena, a soldier on the field of battle, or a traveller has his limbs bruised and fractured by robbers. A prudent physician will, in such cases, inspect or examine the injured parts, and in prosecuting the means of saving life, not of inflicting death, he may learn from offices of mercy what others attempt to know by acts of dire cruelty. Nay, the laceration even of dead bodies is unnecessary; for though not cruel, it is indecent.

Such, according to Celsus, (pp. 11, 12.) were the opinions of two opposite classes of medical men. He says the question was discussed with much acrimony, and that many volumes were written upon it. For himself he steers a middle course ; being decided in his belief that the dissection of living bodies is cruel and superfluous; that of the dead necessary to all students of medicine ; a conclusion, I presume, in which all well-instructed physicians and surgeons will agree, so far at least as the human subject is in question. With respect to the vivisection of animals there still exists no small difference.

Our great Sir Francis Bacon observes, that " for the passages and pores it is true which was anciently noted, that the more subtle of them appear not in anatomies, because they are shut and latent in dead bodies, though they be open and manifest in life, which being supposed, though the inhumanity of *anatomia vivorum* was by Celsus justly reproved, yet in regard of the great use of this observation, the inquiry needed not by him so lightly to have been relinquished altogether, or referred to the casual practises of surgery, but might have been well diverted upon dissection of beasts alive, which, notwithstanding the dissimilitude of their parts, may sufficiently satisfy this inquiry."—Vol. ii. p. 482.

The writer of these pages is not such an enemy to science, as to affirm that no animal should in any case be brought a living victim to her shrine. He admits that some useful discoveries, as those of the Lacteals, and of the circulation of the blood, have been made, or most clearly illustrated by vivisection. When a great and valuable object is to be attained, some expence of pain and suffering must be allowed. The life of a human being is more to be prized than that of a brute, and if one can be saved by the death of the other, there can be no hesitation as to the latter. But what the friends of humanity may and do justly complain of, is not only a wanton sacrifice of life, but the infliction of cruel and lingering torment, for the gratification of a useless curiosity. When facts have been ascertained and established by men of acknowledged skill and merited reputation, wherefore is any sciolist to venture on a repetition of the experiments by which those facts have been demonstrated? Wherefore are boys, who have just commenced the study of anatomy, to make upon living creatures their incipient efforts in this difficult art ? Is it not enough to attend to the instructions of their teachers, and to practise upon inanimate creatures ? May they not rest assured that the knowledge of which they are in quest has been already gained, and can be imparted to them on much more certain grounds than they could ever lay for themselves ? Or, should they be exhorted to repeat all that has been already done, with Asellius to dissect living dogs to ascertain the existence and functions of the Lacteals, and with Haller employ a "hammer and chisel" to open the skulls of goats and cats, to see if there be any motion in the brain corresponding to the respiration? Is this the way to train them for treating their future patients with tenderness?

In a "Treatise on the Sensible and Irritable Parts of Animals," read by Dr. Haller in the Academy of Gottingen, April 22, 1752, translated from the Latin by M. Tissot, M.D. and published in London, 1755, he gives an account of several cruel experiments on living animals. In the passage alluded to above, he says, "I opened the skulls of several dogs with a hammer and a chisel, which is a more commodious way than with a trepan, and exposed to view a large part of the brain; and this experiment *I frequently repeated* upon dogs, goats, rats, frogs, cats, and other animals. The event was always the same, viz. I saw a manifest motion in the *dura mater*, or rather in the whole brain; * * but neither has any motion, unless the cranium is removed, which therefore in a living, sound animal is an effectual obstacle to it; * * wherefore this consent of the brain with respiration can never be applied to a sound healthy person." Unhappily for "dogs, goats, rats, frogs, cats, and other animals," a controversy arose upon this subject between Haller and M. Schlichting, and the numbers of those animals were thinned without pity or remorse, to bring it to a conclusion; and when at last Haller's opinion was confirmed, a new set of experiments had to be instituted, to discover the cause of the motion of the brain when stripped of the cranium, which keeps it immoveable. M. de Sauvage, in a letter to Haller, dated March 1, 1752, says, "The dog was trepanned, and we observed a very considerable motion of the brain exactly like that which you described in your letter to me. In order to be certain whether it is the reflux of the blood which causes the elevation during the time of expiration, M. La Mure *opened more than ten dogs.*"

The *Medico-Chirurgical Review* for Oct. 1819, (page 213), in reference to some observations of Charles Bell, F.R.S. &c. on the dissection of living animals, says,

"The death of a few rabbits for the purposes of useful science, is certainly not much calculated to call forth a rhapsodical anathema against the sin of 'torturing living animals,' while millions of them are weekly slaughtered to sate the appetite of pampered epicures. We have every reason to believe that strong sense far predominates over morbid sensibility in the profession."

To the "strong sense," nay more, to the benevolence and humanity of the profession, no one will bear more willing testimony than the author. Many members of the profession he honours and esteems as among the first and best benefactors of mankind. Notwithstanding, it must be admitted that there are exceptions, and that under the design of promoting science many cruelties are perpetrated. No man of even feeble sense will object to the *death* of " a few," nor of many animals, for purposes of real utility. It is not their death, but the *manner of their death* that is the subject of complaint ; the protracted and intense agony to which they are subjected before they expire. Now some of the experiments made on rabbits are of a revolting character, not only to minds of " morbid sensibility," but of common feeling and " strong sense." It might be enough here simply to refer to those made by Dr. Philip ; and those of some members of the Royal Society, who questioned the accuracy of Dr. Philip's statements ; but as they may not be generally known, the following notice of them, abridged from the Medico-Chirurgical Review, may prove not unacceptable to the reader.

Of four papers which Dr. Philip presented to the Royal Society, three were published in the Transactions : the facts stated in the other, containing an account of the action of galvanism on the stomach of rabbits, having been questioned by some members of the society, its publication was declined. On applying to the Vice-President to have the paper returned, he received a copy of it by the clerk, with a paper appended to it, in a different hand, describing an experiment made by some inquirer who chose to be anonymous, to put Dr. Philip's alleged discoveries to the test. This paper states, that two rabbits, which had no food for seventeen hours, were allowed to eat parsley. The nerves of the ———— were then divided in the neck of each. One of them was allowed to remain quiet. The stomach of the other was subjected to the action of a voltaic battery of twenty plates, in a mode which it is not necessary to describe. "The process was continued during five hours, at the end of which period both rabbits were killed." On examining and comparing their stomachs, the appearances were precisely the same.

Dr. Philip must have felt justly indignant at such a statement being presented to the Royal Society, and received as a fair repetition of his experiment, to which it conformed in no essential particular. "The inference afforded by his experiments is, that when the eighth pair of nerves is divided, and the digestive power of the stomach thus wholly suspended, it may be renewed and supported by passing a continued stream of galvanism through the stomach." In the experiment intended to confute him, neither the first nor the last condition was observed. The nerves of the eighth pair were not divided, neither was the stream of galvanism on the stomach continuous, but "occasional." Well therefore may he ask, "In what essential respect does this experiment resemble my galvanic experiments?"

Dr. Philip appealed in vindication of himself to the President and Council of the Royal Society, and in April, 1819, a paper appeared in the Quarterly Journal of the Royal Institution by way of reply, quoting Dr. Philip's own account of his experiments, and describing those of "three members of the Royal Society," all of which are marked by circumstances of great cruelty. In one of the former "the galvanic influence produced strong contraction of the muscles, particularly of the fore limbs, and frequently *the pain* it occasioned was such that the *animal cried out violently*, and made it necessary for a little to discontinue the process." After five hours, "the respiration began to be disordered. In a quarter of an hour it became so difficult that the animal appeared to be dying. It was gasping. *** The galvanic process was several times discontinued and renewed, so that we repeatedly saw the gasping and extreme dyspnœa return on discontinuing, and disappear on renewing it. The animal seemed how much exhausted, and could scarcely raise itself. It had been held down on its side during the whole experiment. It died in six hours after the division of the nerves." The galvanic experiments by three members of the Royal Society were made on two rabbits and a young cat. "They appear (says the Quarterly Journal) to set this inquiry at rest, and to disprove the experiments made by Dr. Wilson Philip. It was intended to have laid them before the Royal Society, but the morbid sensibility shewn by so many members on hearing the experiments detailed by Dr. Wilson Philip, deterred the author from running the risk of so soon again awakening these feelings."

To these observations Dr. Philip replied in a letter to W. T. Brande, Esq. in which he justifies the accuracy of his experiments, and shows that those of the "three members" were as different from his in their preliminaries as in their result. "The morbid sensibility," says he, "of many of the members of the Royal Society to some of my experiments, which were made on living animals, can neither be termed morbid nor unreasonable, if, as I was informed, reports were industriously circulated, that these experiments were not only useless, but that, from an erroneous choice of the animal on which they were made, it was impossible they should be otherwise."

Dr. Philip's experiments were again "repeated in the Royal Institution, in presence of Sir Humphry Davy, Mr. Knight, Mr. Brodie, Mr. Broughton, Mr. Darling, and many other medical gentlemen, among whom was the editor of this journal," (the Medico-Chirurgical, Sept. 1821, p. 310), who says, "We are in justice bound to state that Dr. Philip's statements were fully, unequivocally, and satisfactorily verified, without leaving the smallest doubt of their correctness on the mind of any one present."

This question being thus happily set at rest—in pace quiescat—and let us hope that rabbits, dogs, and young cats may never again be subjected to such a truculent inquisition.*

* Dr. Philip seems to have been fully aware of the painful nature of the investigation, and blames his opponents for not conducting their experiments with more lenity. "I cannot help remarking," says he, "that the

Since writing the above, the following passages in LORD's *Popular Physiology* struck the author as a farther illustration of the uncertainty of the conclusions drawn from the dissection of living animals.

Dr. Philip inferred that galvanic fluid and the nervous influence are the same, because he found them producing similar effects. "Now," says Lord, "if we consider this advanced as a strict logical proof, a fallacy is at once evident, though Dr. Philip has ingeniously kept it out of view, by making his syllogism an *enthymeme,* and placing the fallacy in the suppressed proposition. For his argument is this : Galvanism produces the same effects as the nervous influence sent from the brain; therefore galvanism *is* the nervous influence. The suppressed proposition is : ' sameness of effects infers identity of cause.' And the fallacy of this we can demonstrate without leaving the ground Dr. Philip has chosen ; for if he select the contraction of a muscle as the effect, we know it can be caused by pinching with the forceps the cut end of the nerve going to it, and it can also be caused by sending a galvanic shock through the nerve ; but it is evident that pinching with the forceps is not therefore a galvanic shock. We may therefore safely conclude, that the nature of the nervous influence is unknown : we may therefore safely conjecture that it is likely to remain so ; being like the vital principle, too recondite for the comprehension of our faculties in their present limited state." pp. 412—414.

It seldom happens, as we may learn from the preceding facts, that one set of experiments is found sufficient to satisfy the inquirer, or induce him to rest with confidence on the first result. A second set must be made to confirm or invalidate the first. After all, something has escaped observation ; the conditions of the first experiment were not fulfilled in the second; objections are started which must be removed; different conclusions are drawn from the same premises ; the animal selected for experiment, after its torture and death, is suspected to have been

introduction of the tinfoil under the skin, perhaps the most painful part of the experiment, is an instance of useless cruelty, the skin being a sufficiently good conductor of galvanism."

an " erroneous choice," and another must be procured :*
a controversy springs up ; different sides are taken by the
old and the young, by the practised anatomist and the
bungling blockhead, whom nature designed to be a butcher
and not a man of science.   New modes of conducting the
operation are contrived, and new varieties of torture inflicted.   Sometimes the experiments are microscopical,
and therefore " proverbially liable to error."   Others again
have no analogy to any thing in the human frame, and
therefore, so far as human anatomy is concerned, altogether useless.   Some are made without any plausible object, for mere curiosity ; and others with the ostensible
design of advancing science.   In either case, we too often
find as little regard for the sufferings of animals, as if they
were shrubs or vegetables, to be pruned and minced by
the knife of the gardener; or blocks of marble, on which it
would be meritorious to show with what dexterity some
new aspirant to the fame of Haller could employ the
" hammer and chisel."   Dr. Elliotson informs us that
Magendie, the most ruthless and truculent of vivisectors,
in one of his barbarous experiments, began by " cutting
out a large round piece from the back of a beautiful little
puppy, as he would from an apple dumpling."   And
again, that he " cuts living animals here and there, with
no definite object, but just to see what will happen !"
The distressing shrieks, the agonizing tortures of the poor
victim, are heard and seen with stoical apathy.   In the
false morality of empiricism, the end justifies the means ;
and for a prospective, imaginable, or possible good, myriads of enormous cruelties are perpetrated, as disgraceful
to the name of science, as they must be criminal in the
sight of that great Being, whose " tender mercies are over
all his works."

In corroboration of these sentiments, let me add some
just observations communicated by a friend, whose knowledge of anatomy and physiology entitles them to special

---

* Thus Asellius, having dissected a living dog, discovered the Lacteals.
To trace the connexion and uses of these vessels he dissected another;
but to his surprise, could discern no appearance of them.   He then remembered that the first dog had been dissected after a plentiful meal, and
so it became necessary to dissect a third under the same conditions.

consideration. " It often happens that the same vivisection gives different results to different experimentalists, and that after the deliberate butchery of hundreds of animals, no certain or useful fact is ascertained. Some light has been thrown on physiology by experiments on organs near the surface; but when the *ima penetralia* are laid open, accompanied, as such a process must be, by horror of mind and disarrangement of every natural function in the animal, the phenomena are no more truly indicative of physiological facts to the experimentalist, than of futurity to some aruspex; nay, such experiments often lead to gross misconceptions. Magendie, for example, the most cold-blooded and cruel of physiologists, conceives that the use of the *pancreas* is unknown, though from its structure and every thing relating to it, it had for centuries been considered by able anatomists and physiologists analogous in all respects to a salivary gland. His dissent he founded on this, that in animals *laid open* he could not observe that a liquid-like saliva flowed from it, but a viscid mucus, and that only in a very small quantity. Now consider what an accurate knowledge would be gained of the office of this gland, had the learned societies of Paris tied M. Magendie himself down on a table, laid him open, and dissected all clear, till they could fairly open the duodenum, and watch hour after hour the quantity of fluid which distilled from the mouth of his pancreatic duct. The learned bodies, I presume, would put little dependence on the proceeds of such an experiment. They would naturally conclude, that after such a shock, during so much torture, and the part being exposed in a way that nature never intended, it would be quite unphilosophical to expect that the gland would perform its office as it should do. Now this is a case of uncertainty that must attend all violent experiments on living animals; and therefore they should be discouraged *in toto*. They are cruel to an extreme that is little contemplated, and their results are of no practical, and very little speculative utility."

A professional gentleman, a surgeon and physician, who obtained his degree in the University of Edinburgh, and who has paid due attention to the subject under consideration, has kindly favoured the author with the following communication. His name would stamp value on his opinions; but let the facts he imparts speak for themselves.

"That experiments on living animals may, under some circumstances be justifiable, I will not deny; but what is chiefly to be objected to is their unnecessary and wanton repetition. I believe too, that in very few instances will they lead to any valuable result. They are often found contradictory to each other, and lead to different conclusions.

"But what is most to be deprecated is the practise of teachers ·recommending to their pupils to repeat these experiments, and teaching them to harden their hearts, by familiarizing them to the cruelest mutilation and mangling of animals at their lectures, to shew what can be perfectly understood by description, without any such exhibitions.

"During the first winter in which I attended Edinburgh University, and when I was a mere boy, I was a pupil of Dr. Monro's anatomy class; and also of that of Mr. Fyfe, his demonstrator. The latter gave a course of demonstrations, or lectures, at seven o'clock in the evening, and on several occasions such exhibitions were made as those to which I have alluded. On one of these a living pig was tied down to the table, and to prevent its screaming from annoying the class, an incision was made into its throat, (*Anglice*, its throat was cut) and· a part of its wind-pipe removed: and nothing could exceed the delight of most of those present, on perceiving that when the lecturer closed the opening of the wind-pipe with his thumb, and thus permitted the air to resume its natural passage through the glottis, the animal screamed; while, by removing his thumb, it was again rendered voiceless. This could be perfectly understood without any such inhuman experiment. The pig's belly was then ripped open in its whole length, and then from side to side, so that the skin and muscles could be thrown in four flaps from the surface of the intestines which they had previously covered; and· this for the purpose of shewing that the intestines have a vermicular motion for pushing on their contents, a fact which one minute's explanation could render perfectly clear, and which can be seen at any time, by simply looking at the intestines of a sheep recently killed. I do not recollect particularly any other objects intended to be shewn at this exhibition; but I have distinctly before my eyes the sufferings of the animal, as its intestines were cut out piece by piece, and cast on the lecture table, to shew how long the vermicular or peristaltic motion might remain after their separation.

"On another occasion, a beautiful spaniel dog was fastened down to the table with strong cords bound tight round each leg; and for the purpose of securing his head, and preventing motion, a thick piece of whip-cord had been passed (not without much violent resistance,) from the back part of the mouth through the nostrils, so that one end came out through each; these were carried round the extremity of the table, and fastened so that the animal could not move in the slightest degree. The former experiments (if they are to be called such) were repeated, and various others besides. An opening was made into the chest on one side, to show that the animal might live and breathe by the other; then both sides were opened, to show how long he might still breathe before he became insensible; then the openings were closed, to show that respiration would return, and the animal revive and again become sensible of his sufferings. The latter parts of the operation were done before the opening of the belly. The expression of torture, as the animal uncovered his ivory teeth, and tried to struggle as he felt every cut of the scalpel, was greater than any thing indicative of excruciating pain I ever witnessed before or since; but I believe the agony the creature must have suffered, by every attempt to move his head, from the cord cutting the septum of the nostrils, was greater even than that inflicted by the knife."

The kind author of this communication adds :—" Of the above facts I was an eye witness, and for the truth of them in every particular, I can conscientiously vouch. You can clothe them in proper languge, as my recollection of them is noted in the first words that occurred."

But they require no artificial decoration of style to ex-

P

pose their atrocity, and call down upon them the reprobation and abhorrence of every humane mind. It is disgraceful to the age, that students at the university of one
of the most enlightened cities in the world, " mere boys,"
at that period of life when they are most susceptible of
every impression, should be initiated into such scenes as
have been described ; and that teachers whom they have
been taught to regard with respect and veneration, should
recommend them to perpetrate such cruelties, under the
specious idea that they are prosecuting science ! Science
indeed ! *hoc prætexit nomine culpam.* Science ! to
mutilate poor animals, and subject them to such excruciating tortures as would shock a cannibal ! The American
savage who puts his enemy to death by all the torments
he can devise, has the passion of revenge, at least, to
plead in defence of his barbarity ; but what shall be
pleaded in extenuation of the passionless, cold-blooded,
unrelenting cruelty of a vividissector's slaughter-house ?
Science ! no ; her name is dishonoured and prostituted
by being even mentioned in connexion with scenes so abhorrent from her nature.

Another medical friend, whose name would be creditable to these pages, has favoured me with a letter on this
subject. He says that he readily admits that much unnecessary cruelty has been perpetrated, both from the
lingering torments which some experiments inflict, and
also from the culpable profusion of animals which are
sacrificed : at the same time he thinks that in some cases
experiments on living animals are required, and that without such experiments our knowledge of the physiology of
digestion, and of the circulation of the blood, would be far
from being so well-founded as it actually is. " In the
greater number of cases," says he, " vivisections are not
so useful in making discoveries, as in proving discoveries
suggested by other means ; in other words, mere random
experiments in quest of discoveries are both useless and
culpable. Thus, the structure of the heart, the position
and direction of the valves of the arteries and veins, were
of themselves quite sufficient to guide the genius of Har-
vey to the discovery of the circulation ; but this discovery
once made, required what Bacon calls an *experimentum*

crucis, and such a test was afforded by a few experiments on living animals. * * * * * * However, I fully allow that all random experiments ought to be severely censured ; and he who experiments on living creatures, merely in the vague hope of observing something new, is guilty both of cruelty and folly. He acts like the fool who enters a laboratory, and begins to mix every kind of substance, in the hope of forming some new chemical compound. Vivisections in any case can be useful only when conducted by men of sense and humanity."

To these testimonies let me add that of Dr. J. L. Drummond, Professor of Anatomy and Physiology in the Belfast Academical Institution. In the eighteenth of his instructive and entertaining "*Letters to a Young Naturalist*," he deprecates the practice of vivisection with becoming indignation, and shows that it is seldom, if ever, in any sense beneficial. "Experiments of this description," says he, "are unhallowed in their nature, and they will almost always be unsatisfactory in their result to a rigid investigator of truth ; for a conclusion can seldom be depended on, which is derived from observation of a mangled suffering creature, bleeding under the dissecting knife. * * I can find no excuse for any man who will dissect living dogs, rip up their bellies, (or, as the softened phrase is, lay open their abdomen,) cut out their stomach, or spleen, or kidneys, or perform other dreadful mutilations, merely to satisfy a feeling of curiosity ; and still less do I think that he can be excused for recommending such a practice." p. 287.

Cruel experiments, made solely for the sake of gratifying curiosity, are justly reprobated by the learned Doctor, as are also the "horrible excesses" and "savage reckless enthusiasm" with which they are conducted by the French physiologists. "They torture animals innumerable, without end or aim, farther than *hoping* to get at something ; like a child who breaks a watch in pieces, thinking to obtain thereby a knowlèdge of the reason why it ticks. Many hundred dogs have been dissected alive, to prove whether the stomach is active or passive in vomiting ; but I would ask, when an animal is writhing in agony, struck with dismay and astonishment, with its belly opened and

the bowels exposed to the atmosphere, are we to expect
that in all the horrors of this situation, the stomach will
exhibit itself, or perform its functions just as if nothing
had happened ? I cannot believe it ; and if ten thousand
such experiments were made, there still will and must be
a want of proof."

As skilful anatomists and physiologists are best qualified to give an opinion on this subject, I trust I shall be
excused not only for the length of the preceding quotations, but for others yet to come. It cannot be said that
their decisions are founded on ignorance, or on partial and
limited information. Many of those who have studied
physiology most profoundly, and devoted their whole lives
to its pursuit, are the most determined in their condemnation of vivisection. No one who has but glanced into
Dr. Elliotson's work on physiology, will deny that his
decision is based on a most extensive experimental knowledge, and entitled to the greatest respect and most im-
plicit confidence. After noticing some experiments of a
French dissector on living animals, so atrociously wicked
that they cannot be described in this place, he says, " I
do not think a physiologist would have ventured to di-
vulge such a disgusting experiment in this country, and
I cannot refrain from expressing my horror at the amount
of torture which Dr. Brachet inflicted upon so many unoffending brutes. Nearly or quite two hundred must
have suffered under his hands. I hardly think knowledge is worth having at such a purchase ; or that it was
ordained that we should obtain knowledge by cruelty.
I care nothing for killing a brute outright, without pain :
it is then but as before it was born, feels no loss, and
escapes all further chance of suffering. Vivisection may
be justifiable in some instances ; but before an inquirer
commences an experiment of torture, he ought to be satisfied of its absolute necessity ; that the investigation is
important, and the means indispensable ; and also, that
he is master of the existing knowledge on the subject,
and qualified to operate and to philosophise on the results.
He should proceed to the task with the deepest feelings
of regret. I do not wish to make a parade of feeling ;
but to torture animals unnecessarily is a most cowardly

161

and cold-blooded act, and in my opinion one of the utmost depravity and sin. A course of experimental physiology, in which brutes are agonised to exhibit facts already established, is a disgrace to the country which permits it."—*Human Physiology*, p. 449, note.

The following is an instance of the ruthless barbarity of French physiologists :—" I inspired," says Dr. Brachet, " a dog with the greatest aversion for me, by plaguing and inflicting some pain or other upon it as often as I saw it. When this feeling was carried to its height, so that the animal became furious as soon as it saw or heard me, I put out its eyes : I could then appear before it without its manifesting any aversion. I spoke, and immediately its barkings and furious movements proved the passion which animated it. I destroyed the drum of its ears, and disorganized the internal ear as much as I could ; when an intense inflammation which was excited had rendered it deaf, I filled up its ears with wax. It could no longer hear at all. Then I went to its side, spoke aloud, and even caressed it, without its falling into a rage ; it seemed even sensible to my caresses."

On this experiment, foolish and unmeaning as it was wicked, and which was repeated with the same result, Dr. Elliotson animadverts with laudable indignation. "What," he asks, "was all this to prove? Simply, that if one brute has an aversion to another, it does not feel nor shew that aversion, when it has no means of knowing that the other brute is present. If he had stood near the dog on the other side of a wall, he might have equally proved what common sense required not to be proved. After all, I do not understand how the poor dog did not scent him. I blush for human nature in detailing this experiment, and shall finish it by informing my readers that the Memoir containing this and all the other horrors, obtained the physiological prize from the French Institute in 1826."— *Human Physiology*, note, pp. 449, 450, (fifth edit.)

Dr. Elliotson says that the inquirer, in making a necessary experiment, should " proceed to the task with the deepest feelings of regret;" a sentiment with which every man of the least humanity must accord. But the French physiologists seem actually to take a pride in inventing

P 2

new torments, and to feel pleasure in contemplating the agonies into which they throw poor animals by their diabolical cruelty. "It is droll," says Magendie, "to see animals skip and jump about of their own accord, after you have taken out all their brains a little above the optic tubercles;" and as to new-born kittens, he says, " they tumble over in all directions, and walk so nimbly, if you cut out their hemispheres, that it is quite astonishing."

It would be an easy task to fill a volume with an account of these atrocities, perpetrated by this ruthless dissector. But wherefore weary the reader by the disgusting detail ?

Quid memorem infandas cædes ? quid facta tyranni
Effera ?—Virg. viii. 483.

The Anatomical Schools of Germany seem ambitious of rivalling the French in this department, as we learn from the following passage in "Impressions of a Tour," published in *Blackwood's Magazine* for January, 1838, p. 96. "The last thing I noticed about Bonn was the advertisement of a medical professor, affixed to the gate, and announcing experiments on the living animal, as a part of his regular course. In this there was something unblushing and disgusting; but a professor in the German colleges, unless he be opulent, must propose any thing, and do any thing, to stimulate curiosity, and tempt an audience." The American schools also promise to match the French and German, if we may judge from a passage in Harlam's *Medical and Physical Researches,* Phil. 1835, pp. 648, 649, in which he adopts the same fallacy as the *Medico-Chirurgical Review,* and speaks with surprise that man should "hesitate in sacrificing a few insignificant animals for the amelioration and elevation of the condition of his species." But he makes no difference between the extinction of life by an instantaneous shock, and the protracted horrors of dying by inches under the knife and the forceps of an anatomist! Again then it must be repeated, that *it is not the death, but the manner of the death* of a few insignificant animals, that is the subject of the moralist's complaint : the lingering, mer·ciless process, by which the condition of his species is neither meliorated nor raised, but deteriorated and degraded.

The Dublin schools of surgery have acquired a just and well-merited celebrity, which may they long continue to merit and enjoy; but assuredly it was not by such meretricious acts as those which have been noticed, and on which it would be a dereliction of duty not to animadvert. By careful investigation of the animal structure of the dead, not by mangling the living, they have extended the sphere of useful knowledge, and gained for themselves and their country an imperishable fame; a fame neither tarnished by the bloody sacrifice, nor desecrated by the cries and agonies of unoffending creatures; but honoured and exalted by genuine science, and approved by the voice of that humanity whose sufferings it is the office of anatomical skill to allay. Sydenham has well said, " I esteem any progress in that kind of knowledge, (how small soever it be,) though it teach no more than the cure of the toothache, or of corns upon the feet, to be of more value than the pomp of nice speculations."

Innumerable experiments have been made on the brains of animals; in the infamy of which the Edinburgh schools of anatomy are entitled to an ample portion. The Earl of Carnarvon, president of the Society for the Prevention of Cruelty to Animals, merits the eulogy of every friend of humanity, for having at the annual meeting, 1837, brought the subject before the public in an eloquent address, worthy of that presidency which he holds. After expressing a just detestation of the practise of dissecting living animals, he asks, " What will you say of that man who keeps a dog, not for hours, but for days under the torture of the dissecting knife, until the spectator, grown callous to suffering, becomes as savage as the operator himself? What will you say to him who could calmly for days prolong atrocities and sufferings, which no Christian eye can witness without horror, no Christian lip describe but in the most unmeasured language of indignation? I will state still further. What will a Christian audience say, when they hear that the revolting fact was perpetrated and recorded in the city of Edinburgh? That an iron was heated, and then forced into the brain of the unfortunate animal, which with fiendish skill was kept alive for the space of sixteen days. *(Cries of shame.)* By whom was this atrocity perpetrated ? By men who pride themselves on their science and their civilization, but who, in fact, are more benighted in point of civilization and Christianity than the benighted savages of Scythia. Will you be able to restrain your indignation then, when you are calmly told that it is better to leave such matters to the " *discretion*" of individuals ? In other cases, the law of outraged morals steps in to protect and avenge ; but against these cases, offensive to the light, outraging decency, repugnant to generous sympathy and to the Christian faith, the law deals not its thunders. The young and inexperienced, who are attracted to these charnel-houses, where horrors not to be described are permitted under the name of science, must in time have all feelings of compassion for suffering entirely obliterated."

The utter *inutility* of such experiments as the noble earl reprobates, independently of their atrocity, should be a valid reason, with all men of sense, against their performance. They lead to no useful conclusion; they are often deceptive, often contradictory. Dr. Elliotson, speaking of cerebral mutilations, says that "attempts to mutilate artificially are not calculated to afford much information. Brutes can generally give no opportunity of minutely observing what mental change has been produced by the removal. * * When various portions of brain are removed, how can any inference be drawn, during the short existence of the poor animal, as to the state of its various faculties and inclinations? * * It is difficult, if not generally impossible, to remove one cerebral organ entirely and alone. Other parts of the encephalon, &c. are almost certain to be injured; and if others should not be injured, they may be influenced by the extension of the irritation from the injury, and by sympathy with the injured parts; just, for example, as we see epilepsy from exciting causes in every part of the encephalon, and from exciting causes even in distant organs; amaurosis is frequently induced by wounds of the supra-orbital nerve, sometimes by wounds of the infra-orbital nerve, and of the *portio dura*. M. Fleurens declares that in cutting the semi-circular canals, in which the acoustic nerves only are spread, peculiar motions occurred. If the horizontal canal on each side was divided, horizontal movement of the head took place from side to side, and rotation of the whole body. Division of the inferior vertical canals on each side produced vertical movements of the head, and caused the animal to lie on its back. Division of the superior vertical canals caused vertical movements of the head, but the animal lay forwards. The direction of the inferior vertical canal is backwards, and of the superior forwards. If all the canals were divided, all sorts of violent motions took place." Our learned physiologist proceeds to show that the injury of different portions of the same organ may have the same effect. "We may have blindness from wounding the optic nerves, the *tractus optici*, or the *corpora quadrigemina*." Hence, he observes, "the contradictory and strange observations and inferences of most experimenters on the brain of living brutes. The same effects, moreover, do not occur in the same experiments upon different species of animals. The observation of nature's own mutilation in brutes which have no developement of parts is therefore preferable, and next to this comes the observation of morbid changes in different parts. M. Relando says that he made innumerable experiments upon goats, lambs, pigs, deer, dogs, cats, and guinea-pigs, to ascertain the results of the lesion of the tubercles and parts near the *optic thalami,* but rarely obtained the same results."—*Note,* p. 426. Of mutilations by nature the Doctor gives instances, which he says "are conclusive, and render all vivisections on this point unnecessary." He quotes a case from the works of Magendie, the arch-vivisector himself, in proof of his assertion : "A girl lived to the age of eleven years with the use of her senses, and with voluntary motion, weak, it is true, but sufficient for her wants, and even for progression. After death no cerebellum, no mesocephalon could be found." MAGENDIE, *Precis.* tom. i. p. 414, *and Journal,* tom. xi. "Here," says Dr. Elliotson, "was one of nature's own mutilations, without mechanical injury, or disturbance of other parts; and with patience till it occurred, a multitude of innocent animals would have escaped cruel and disgusting vivisections; and an attempt would not have been made to prove that the cerebellum was necessary to motion or secretion, or to prevent involuntary motion backwards."

The curious reader is referred to the work from which these quotations are taken, for much more information on this subject. Enough, it is presumed, has been said to expose the ineffable cruelty and generally total uselessness of dissecting living animals, and to fire the breast of every friend of virtue with indignation against the abominable practice. Let us hope that it will soon cease to be patronized by every one who wishes to merit and obtain the rewards of an honourable profession. Now that it has been ascertained by the experiments of John Hunter, that " birds can breathe through an opening in the thigh bone, the shoulder bone, and the cells of the belly after the wind-pipe was completely tied up ;" since the action of the abdominal muscles in the lungs of living frogs has been witnessed ; since Spallanzani, in prosecution of his experiments on the nature of reproduction, has dissected above two thousand of these animals, and blunted needles and lancets innumerable by forcing them down the throats of turkies and other fowls, to prove the strength of the grinding power of the gizzard ; since Dr. Brachet has found that the respiration of cats can be continued or made to cease artificially after the division of the spinal chord, and M. Bourdon has shewn that it is impossible for poor brutes either to leap or swim, if a tube be inserted into a wound made in the trachea ; since Swammerdam, and his rival De Graef, learned, by flagitious proofs, that certain unmentionable phenomena in the animal economy are produced by true blood, ἀτρικις ἀιμα, and not by spirit or flatulency ; since the great " Canicide," " by sticking pins in the chorda oblongata of pigeons, proved that the birds thus ornamented would walk and fly backwards for above a month ;" since the carotid arteries of sheep and foxes have been cut in sufficient number to see how nature renovates or regenerates the tubes and the circulation ; and since it has been proved that a fox will not become a spaniel, nor a spaniel a fox, by the mutual transfusion of their blood ; an experiment of the redoubtable Magendie, as one of his pupils informed the author—let us deprecate the repetition of these and all similar cruelties. To men of true science they can yield no gratification, nor bring any increase of really useful knowledge. Any man possessed of common understanding, though altogether ignorant of anatomy, might justly suppose that operations performed on the organs of living animals, could never answer the purpose of revealing to us the proper functions of those organs, in their natural healthy state. A beast or bird tied or nailed down to a dissecting table, and cut open by a knife, mutilated by a saw, or cauterized with a red-hot iron; its nerves and sinews stretched by pincers, and the whole put into such dreadful torture as to draw from it lamentable cries, is not in a fit state to make revelations to the eye of science. An injury sustained by a single wheel; nay, in a single tooth of a wheel in a chronometer, or any other delicately constructed machine, deranges its whole movements. If a screw be loose in the most potent enginery, it turns all to confusion. A single string, if drawn too tight, or if it be too much relaxed in a musical instrument, takes away its power of discoursing such " eloquent music" as pleases the ear of a skilful musician. Much more may we suppose, that the derangement of a single wheel in the animal machine, or the unnatural tension or relaxation of a single chord, in the " harp of a thousand strings," must disorder the whole of its economy. The torture does not always elicit a true confession. We may witness the contortions without hearing the inspiration of the sibyl. The responses of a creature on the rack to the interrogatories of the inquisitor, must be always dark and disjointed, deceptive and unsatisfactory.*

If we can imagine some unfortunate animal, when brought to the dissecting-room for experiment, to be for the occasion endowed with speech and " sanctity of reason," we might farther imagine it to address the sacrificer in terms like these : " Your power, I admit, is not to be resisted. The Almighty has given you dominion over me; but it is a dominion of justice and mercy, not of cruelty and wrong. If you require such services as I can perform, I am ready to yield them; if my life be neces-

* It was long since remarked by Aristotle, that men when subjected to torture, will speak falsehood in preference to truth, if it serve their purpose better. Torture, therefore, is no test of truth. See his *Rhetoric*, lib. i. c. 15.

sary or advantageous to you, take it. If the dissection of my lifeless members will extend your knowledge of the divine wisdom, or in any mode contribute to the improvement of the medical and surgical art, and the consequent benefit of man, do with them whatever your ingenuity suggests to accomplish so laudable a design. But spare me the excruciating tortures that must be inflicted, by laying open those parts of my frame which nature never designed to be exposed to man's inspection, while they are yet palpitating with life. Transgress not the legitimate bounds of inquiry, nor hope to add to your honour and reputation, or to extend the sphere of science, by means which nature abhors. Suppose yourself, for a moment, in the power of a being as much superior to you, as you to me, and that he was preparing to subject you to the same process of investigation as you have prepared for me, what would be your feelings ? You are filled with indignation and horror when you read of the cruelties sometimes practised by men on each other; for you think them more sensibly alive to pain than other creatures, and your sympathies are more strongly excited for beings like yourself. Notwithstanding, it is happy for them that you dare not dissect living men with impunity, since the step from one degree of wickedness to another is not always difficult. But are not the inferior creatures, as you call them, capable of acute sensation ? Are they not composed of the same materials as man ? Do they not exhibit as much delicacy of construction; are not their muscles as tender; their nerves as finely strung ? And do not their writhings and contortions under the knife and the saw, the hammer and chisel, their lamentable cries, and groans, and shrieks, which send a shudder even to the demonstrator's iron heart, declare their sufferings in language sufficiently intelligible ? You hope to make some new discovery, forsooth, and you care not at what expense. Egregious vanity ! You would penetrate into the secret things which belong only to Jehovah; you would force your way into the Holy of Holies, which the law of God prohibits. Beware lest you perish in the attempt. But how are you qualified for this ambitious enterprize ? Have you learned all that has been already taught ? Have you so tho-

roughly investigated and found all that the inanimate frame
is capable of unfolding, that nothing remains to be achieved ;
and to gratify a preposterous ambition, and a criminal
curiosity, must you commence a course of diabolical experiments on living creatures, in hope of discovering
something new ? And suppose this as yet undiscovered
something to be found, what will be its real use in the
medical profession, and what will atone for the guilt you
must incur in prosecuting the inquiry ? You are desirous
of celebrity. Well, let it be an honest celebrity, and
pursue it in such paths as virtue will approve. Never let
the genius of evil be your conductor to the temple of
fame. Though all the kingdoms of the world and the
glory of them, were to be the reward of your falling down
and worshipping the enemy of God and man, what would
you be profited ? You are now preparing to immolate
me, by horrible tortures, on the blood-stained altar that he
loves ; and what will you gain by the sacrifice, but the
harrowing reflection of having perpetrated an enormous
atrocity, against which I protest, and make my final appeal
to heaven ?"

CAUSES OF CRUELTY.

SECTION SEVENTH.

SCIENCE PERVERTED.—NATURAL HISTORY.

" Every degree of unnecessary pain becomes cruelty, which, I need not
assure you, I abhor ; and from my own observations, however ruthlessly
the entomologist may seem to devote the few specimens wanted for scien-
tific purposes to destruction, no one, in ordinary circumstances, is less
prodigal of insect life. For my own part, I question whether the drowning individuals which I have saved from destruction, would not far out-
number all that I ever sacrificed to science."—KIRBY.

The advocates of vivisection, as we have seen, maintain that if animals may be killed for food, or to protect
ourselves from harm, they may be killed for intellectual
nutriment; to promote the advancement of science and
elucidate our knowledge of nature. The naturalist may

Q

urge a similar plea, and contend that those who have no objection to see their table loaded with every variety of game, should not grudge him the indulgence of his more refined taste. May the epicure slaughter thousands of beasts and of birds for his appetite, and the lovers of nature be censured for rescuing a few from the kitchen or the kennel ? We answer decidedly, No. You may kill what your necessities require ; but you must not torture. You are not to imagine that even a love of science will justify the application of the wedge and the screw, the needle and the dissecting knife, to living creatures. Naturalists, as well as vividissectors, have been accused of great cruelty. We wish we could, in all instances, repel the charge, but we must be contented with expressing our condemnation of every act by which animals are wantonly destroyed, or subjected to any pain that can possibly be prevented.

The desire of possessing new and rare specimens, or the most beautiful of the kind, sometimes tempts to a profligate expenditure of life. Vaillant ensconsed himself in the hollow of a tree, and "from this sacred niche," says he, " I brought down *without mercy* everything that presented itself before me :" and on another occasion, not contented with obtaining one specimen of an elephant, he shot four of these noble animals in one day ; a day which he afterwards regarded with as much pride as a conqueror regards that of his greatest victory.* His achievements, however, were trifling in comparison of those of Captain Rogers, of the Ceylon Rifle Corps. " During a sojourn of fifteen years in the island of Ceylon, he destroyed upwards of 600 of these gigantic quadrupeds, and has become eminently notorious for his skill in this particular description of sport." Audubon, in a letter which is prefixed to the " Natural history of Parrots, by Lander and Brown," has the following confession : " I shot sixteen birds on the passage, (to America,) which I got through the kind attention of our commander. I

* Thunberg, in his second journey into Caffraria, met with a man who "twice in his life had destroyed with his gun twenty-two elephants each day." But he shot them for their ivory, not for *sport*; it was his trade.

killed fifty more, when the Columbia was going too fast
for the purpose of picking them up. My young man is
now closely engaged in skinning, and killed a *bag-full
of warblers* yesterday. Vive la joie ! no taxes on shooting or fishing." No ; humanity only is taxed, and the
rights violated of creatures, that can make no appeal,
except to heaven, against such useless and profligate
slaughter. Adanson records an anecdote of himself
equally reprehensible. After describing a woody district
very full of green monkeys, and informing us how much
he was entertained, after he had killed two or three of
them, by the agility of the rest in endeavouring to escape
from his murderous shots, " I continued," says he, " still
to shoot at them, and though I killed no less than *three
and twenty* in less than an hour, and within the space of
twenty fathoms, yet not one of them screeched the whole
time." Our traveller prefaces this account by saying,
" What struck me most was the shooting of monkeys,
which *I enjoyed,* *** and I do not think there ever was
better *sport !*"

These, it must be admitted, are merciless achievements. But let us not judge of all naturalists by a few
such examples ; they form the exception, not the rule.
Examples of a contrary character may be adduced. When
three sea-swallows came on board Lieutenant Kotzebue's
vessel, and suffered themselves to be caught, so far from
acting as Audubon would have done, he liberated two,
and kept but one of them for the collection of natural
history ; and when a land bird paid him a visit far at sea,
instead of killing, he gave it a hearty meal of mill-beetles,
and set it at liberty. A. Capell Brooke, too, acted as became a humane man, when sailing among the islands on
the coast of Norway, where the slayer of the green monkeys would have found *excellent sport* in the destruction
of wild geese, eider ducks, and other birds congregated
on the rocks. These were in such numbers that he could
soon have filled his boat with them. But says he, " The
happy state of peace, which every description of the
feathered tribe seemed to enjoy, and the confidence they
placed in us, quite disarmed me of any murderous intention towards them, though I had come out well provided

with guns. I therefore determined not to molest them, at least till the breeding season was over; and the pleasure experienced at being daily in the midst of such an infinite variety, and observing their habits and the diversity of their plumage, amply repaid me."

The best friends of animals, I am persuaded, are found among men devoted to the study of natural history. They have no wish to exchange the delight which they enjoy, in the contemplation of animated nature, for the tyrannical exercise of a power to kill. But this is a delight which cannot always be enjoyed. Many of the chief objects of their curiosity can neither be preserved nor obtained without a sacrifice of life; and they may with reason ask if they are more to be blamed for choosing the most beautiful to adorn a collection, than a cook or a butcher the fattest and best for the table? They may be deemed the friends of humanity, inasmuch as they gratify by the exhibition of dead specimens, that curiosity which would otherwise seek gratification in other captures and in other deaths. As it is desirable to have the creature which they wish to obtain for a specimen as perfect as possible, they put it to death in the easiest and most expeditious mode, *celerrima via mortis*; and having gained their object, they are content. They may expatiate on the beauty of their prize, but they make no boast of the numbers they destroy. Who have pleaded against barbarity to beasts and birds with so much eloquence, as naturalists; or so successfully exposed the ignorance and the prejudices to which such multitudes of various species are sacrificed? Who but naturalists have shewn the folly as well as cruelty of extirpating rooks, woodpeckers, and goat-suckers? Who becomes the friend and advocate of swallows, by telling us that "they are the most inoffensive, harmless, entertaining, social, and useful of birds; they touch no fruit in our gardens; delight, all except one species, in attaching themselves to our houses; amuse us with their migrations, songs, and marvellous agility, and clear our outlets from the annoyances of gnats and other troublesome insects?" Kirby and Spence are not the only entomologists who have saved more insects from drowning than they ever sacrificed to science. Many birds and quadrupeds have found with naturalists protection, and an asylum from persecution and death ; and many too have received ample compensation in kind treatment, for the temporary sufferings to which they may have been subjected. Mr. Waterton, a naturalist, who every where expresses himself as a man of humanity, gives us the following interesting anecdote : having made an experiment on a she ass, of the effects of the Wourali poison, from which she recovered, he says, "The kind-hearted reader will rejoice on learning that Earl Percy, pitying her misfortunes, sent her down from London to Walton-hall, near Wakefield. There she goes by the name of Wouralia. Wouralia shall be sheltered from the wintry storm ; and when summer comes, she shall feed in the finest pasture. No burden shall be placed upon her, and she shall end her days in peace."—pp. 81, 82.

The learned and amiable Sir William Jones has touched on this subject in a way that merits consideration. He says, " Could the figure, instincts, and qualities of birds, beasts, insects, reptiles, and fish, be ascertained, either on the plan of Buffon or on that of Linnæus, without giving pain to the objects of our examination, few studies would afford us more solid instruction, or more exquisite delight ; but I never could learn by what right, nor conceive with what feelings a naturalist can occasion the misery of an innocent bird, and leave its young, perhaps, to perish in a cold nest, because it has gay plumage, and has never been accurately delineated ; or deprive even a butterfly of its natural enjoyments, because it has the misfortune to be rare or beautiful ; nor shall I ever forget the couplet of Firdausi, for which Sadi, who cites it with applause, pours blessings on his departed spirit :—

" Ah ! spare yon emmet, rich in hoarded grain,
He lives with pleasure, and he dies with pain."

" This may be only a confession of weakness, and it certainly is not meant as a boast of peculiar sensibility ; but whatever name may be given to my opinions, it has such an effect on my conduct, that I would never suffer the *cocila*, whose *wild native wood-notes* announce the approach of spring, to be caught in my garden, for the sake of comparing it with Buffon's description; though I have often examined the domestic and engaging *Mayana*, which *bids us good-morrow* at our windows, and expects as its reward little more than security : even when a fine young *manis* or *pangolin* was brought me against my wish, from the mountains, I solicited his restoration to his beloved rocks, because I found it impossible to preserve him in comfort at a distance from them."—Sir W. Jones's Works, vol. iii. pp. 221, 222.

The author's attention was first directed to this passage by a distinguished naturalist, by whom it was approved and admired. All genuine lovers of natural history must commend the humane and tender feelings which dictated such sentiments; most of them, it may be hoped, would follow the example of Sir William Jones, if placed in a situation where they could enjoy the beauty and the song of those interesting birds; and none of them could be guilty of the cruelty he imagines, in leaving the young of a captured bird to perish in a cold nest. No bird should be molested in the season of nursing or incubation. Such outrages against humanity are perpetrated in a Christian land, but not by those who "look through nature up to nature's God." However much they might desire to enrich their cabinet of curiosities with rare and valuable specimens, they would not, most assuredly they should not, purchase them by an inhuman deed, nor gratify their cupidity at the expense of their compassion.

Every genuine naturalist will admit, that while we study and admire the works of the God of mercy and truth, we should imitate his perfections, else our knowledge is profitless and vain. The poet says, "an undevout astronomer is mad." The same may be predicated of every undevout naturalist; for there is no object in nature that does not, to the reflecting mind, inculcate a lesson on the wisdom, power, and beneficence of the Creator. Humanity is allied to devotion. The lover of natural history, therefore, should be humane; and to make him so, is the proper tendency of his pursuits. We know it is not without great reluctance, that many of its cultivators consent to sacrifice the lives of such insects and reptiles, as would be exterminated in legions by the mass of mankind without the least pity or remorse. They are actuated by no wanton spirit of destruction. On the contrary, they grieve to be the ministers of suffering and death, and seek a solace to their compassionate feelings in the belief, that the inferior animals have less sensibility to pain than those of a higher order; and that as we descend in the scale of being, the sense of pain diminishes till it altogether ceases. It is quite notorious that many animals suffer mutilation and dismemberment, without apparent evidence of their sustaining any great loss. The tortoise walks about after decapitation; caterpillars live till they are eaten away by the ichneumon fly, and nothing left of them but the skin. Some insects seem to have the power of shaking off a limb, with as much facility as if it formed no integral part of their structure. The leech continues to draw blood when its caudal extremity is cut away. Collison, in No. 478 of the Transactions of the Royal Society, states that the larger species of crab, *cancer major*, "has a power in itself voluntarily to crack and break its own legs or claws and drop them off; a mucus or jelly is then discharged on the remaining part of the joint next the body, which, as a natural styptic, instantly stops the bleeding, and gradually hardens and grows callous, and forms a leg in miniature, which by degrees shoots forth, and attains to its natural size, to supply the place of that which was lost. This wonderful faculty is given to the crab for wise ends. Crabs are very quarrelsome, and with their great claws fight and kill one another. Whatever they seize they strongly retain for a long while. There is no escaping but by voluntarily leaving a part of the leg that has been seized, behind, in token of victory; the principal end is the saving the life of the conquered." The carving which the polypus can undergo, not only without a loss, but with an extension of its vitality, has long been a subject of admiration. Dr. George Johnston, in his recent history of British Zoophytes, says, "You may slit the animal (Hydra) up, and lay it out flat like a membrane with impunity; nay, it may be turned inside out, so that the stomachal surface may become the epidermous, and yet the creature will continue to live and enjoy itself; and even suffers very little by these cruel operations.

> "Scarce seems to feel, or know
> His wound."

For before the lapse of many minutes the upper half of a cross section will expand its tentacula, and catch prey as usual; and the two portions of a longitudinal division will, after an hour or two, take food and retain it." Lamark considers the lowest classes of the animal kingdom as destitute even of a consciousness of their existence, and capable of being moved only by external exciting causes acting on their *irritability*, whence he designates them by the appellation of APATHIQUES.*

A passage in Shakspeare's Measure for Measure, quoted by every writer on the subject of humanity to animals, from being greatly misunderstood, has favoured an opinion entirely opposed to that of our naturalists. Isabella, wishing to dissuade Claudio from fearing death, says,

> "Dar'st thou die?
> The sense of death is most in apprehension;
> And the poor beetle that we tread upon,
> In corporal sufferance feels a pang as great
> As when a giant dies."

The meaning of these lines is not that a beetle suffers as much bodily pain in dying as a giant, but that a giant suffers as little as a beetle, whose life is extinguished in an instant by being trod on. In the popular sense, the argument would tend directly to efface the conviction which Isabella was most anxious to impress. Why should you fear death? The pain of dying exists only in the mind; the corporal suffering is nothing. A man, nay a giant, notwithstanding his great strength and huge dimensions, feels no more agony in death than the feeblest insect that is crushed to atoms in a moment beneath your heel. Whether this be so or not, is another question. No doubt, the fear of death is one of the greatest pains with which it is often accompanied; and from this fear most animals are happily exempt. The humane mind rejoices in a belief so accordant to her ideas of the di-

---

* Etant dépourvus du sentiment, n'ayant pas meme de leur existence, &c.—LAMARK, *Hist. Nat.* 1. 335, Paris, 1835.

vine benevolence, that creatures destined for the support
of each other, insects especially that are subject to so
many casualties, have a less acute sense of pain than
reasoning man. But the least degree of pain is still an
evil, and therefore we should be exceedingly cautious how
we inflict it; cautious how we act on the presumption that
any animated being can be injured or put out of its natural state without suffering. Whatever may be the
insensibility of the lowest orders, of polypi, crustacea,
testacea, and insects, the argument does not apply to those
of a superior class. We have no *pathometer* by which
we can measure the degrees of any creature's sufferings.
Analogy would lead us to conclude that in parallel cases
they cannot differ much in intensity from our own ;
the cries and groans uttered by them when maimed or
wounded are not less expressive of agony. And if some
creatures, under such inflictions, have no faculty of giving
similar indications of suffering, it would be wrong thence
to conclude that none is undergone. Because the green
monkeys did not screech while being massacred by Adanson, did they suffer nothing ? They were too much overcome by terror to give utterance to what they felt. Ex-
tremes of grief and pain take away all power of expression
even from rational beings. We are too ready to transfer
our own apathy to the tortured animal, merely because it
can utter no complaint. But is it to be imagined possible
for joints to be dislocated, members dissevered, viscera
laid open, in any animated being whatever, without excruciating pangs ? The more delicate the structure the
more susceptible of injury, and the more acute may be
the perception of pain. The very silence of a dumb
animal seems to reproach the barbarity of its destroyer,
and "the voice of its blood crying from the ground,"
though unheard by the gross organs of man, is audible
to the Eternal.

The desire of naturalists to obtain new or rare specimens, sometimes leads them, it may be feared, to transgress the limits of humanity. No sooner does a bird
appear in a district where it was not before observed, being
driven thither, from its native climate probably, by severity
of weather, than a pursuit is commenced, and in order to

destroy it, all the guns in the neighbourhood are put into requisition. Woe to the confiding stranger that thus comes to claim the hospitality of a warmer region ! A prudent naturalist must deprecate the hostility with which it is assailed. Robert Ball, Esquire, of Dublin, to whom the Natural History of Ireland owes much, (and to whom it will one day be more largely indebted,) in a Lecture upon the Ornithology of his country, delivered to the Royal Society of Dublin, as wisely as humanely recommended that all such visitors should be spared. If suffered to escape unmolested, they would probably return in the ensuing season with more of their fraternity.

Some naturalists console themselves with the belief, that let them destroy what number they may of individuals, nature will take due care to preserve the species. But in this they fall into an egregious fallacy. All species are made up of individuals, and the destruction of the one is involved in that of the other.* Some species indeed are so amazingly prolific, as to set all the arts of destruction at defiance. This is the case especially among the finny tribes. But in other species it is different, insomuch that in regions where certain animals were once numerous, they are now altogether extinct. The beaver, the wolf, and the bear were once inhabitants of England, as were the wolf and the wolf dog of Ireland ; but not an individual of these animals is now to be found. Is there no danger of some species of birds sharing a similar fate, both abroad and at home ? What has become of the *dodo ?* The *spoon-bill* was once a native of Britain, and the *capercaille (tetrao urogallus,* LINN.) of Scotland, and of some parts of Ireland ; but now they are gone. The *bustard*, too, and the *bittern* will probably, ere long, have to be classed with the things that were.

As far as the author's knowledge of naturalists extends, he can give his honest testimony that no class of men are more humane or tender of the lives of animals, though

* " Itaque genera bestiarum conservari videmus, quod sine singularium sustentatione fieri non potest, cum in singulis rebus consistat generis cujusque universitas. Egregie Plato, De Legibus decimo, medici et nautæ exemplo demonstrat, totius partem non consistere sine partium etiam minimarum cura."—GROTIUS, *in Matt.* x. 29.

holding themselves fully justified for taking such as tend to increase or illustrate our knowledge of God and his works. At the same time, it is a grand object to gratify their taste at as little expense of pain to the creature as possible, and to put them to instantaneous death. The most eminent naturalist for many years in the north of Ireland, was John Templeton, Esquire, of Orange-grove, near Belfast. Botany was his favourite study, but he left no department of nature unexplored :—

> " Well could he speak of all the flowers of spring,
> Of fish of every fin and bird of every wing."

The Rev. Dr. Hincks, in a memoir of his life, in the *Magazine of Natural History*, vol. 1, p. 404, truly observes that " he was remarkable for his kind attention to every part of the animal creation. In this he set an excellent example to naturalists, for he always contrived to gratify his curiosity without pain to the subject of it, and would, at any time, have lost the opportunity of acquiring knowledge, rather than be the cause of suffering to a living creature. When circumstances justified the deprivation of life, he considered how it might take place with the least pain."

The author had the honour of ranking Mr. Templeton among his friends, and enjoyed frequent opportunities of hearing his humane sentiments, and witnessing the exercise of those virtues by which he was characterised. His example, it is to be hoped, has not been without its due influence. The members of the Belfast Natural History Society will honour the memory of their deceased friend, by following him, not only in the walks of science, but in the more estimable paths of philanthropy and mercy. Some of them are among the most ardent and successful investigators of nature, as may be attested by the names of Thompson, Haliday, and Paterson, to say nothing of their founder. A similar society has recently been formed in Dublin, and among its members are many young men who are pursuing the same high and honourable career ; and fast hastening, not only to rescue their country from the reproach to which she was so long liable, of total igno-

rance and neglect of Natural History,* but, as we trust,
to give her a name among the nations for her devotion to
that noble science. Would that similar societies were
formed in every city and county of Ireland, and that both
young and old of all sects and denominations constituted
their members! How much would their co-operation in
the studies of nature tend to promote their common good,
to neutralize the baneful influences of political and religious bigotry, and foster those principles of benevolence
in the exercise of which man finds his purest enjoyment?
Such studies both at home and abroad afford a healthful
recreation to youth, a cheerful amusement to age, a con-
stantly new and inexhaustible variety of pleasures not
confined to time or place, but perennial and universal;
springing exuberant in every clime and in every season,
in the torrid and the frozen zone, in the peopled city and
the desolate wilderness; never disgusting by excess nor
cloying by repetition; and while they familiarize the
mind to converse with the works of God, and imbue it
with a love of the beautiful and the grand, create or improve a taste for the good and the true, and elevate it to
contemplate, to adore, and to imitate the infinitely glorious
perfections of that Great Being, whose name is LOVE,
and whose " tender mercies are over all his works."

CHAPTER X.

HUMANITY TO ANIMALS CONSIDERED AS A SUBJECT OF EDUCATION.

"When the judges of the Areopagus condemned to death a boy for picking out the eyes of live quails, they must have considered that barbarity
as a presumption, or symptom of a disposition horribly cruel, and which,
should the boy grow up, would do infinite mischief in society."
QUINTILIAN, v. 9. Guthrie's translation, vol. i. p. 292.

IT has been observed by phrenologists, and particularly by Spurzheim, that there is no part of education

* See some curious and amusing illustrations of this in a little volume
entitled " *Thoughts on the Study of Natural History*," addressed to the

more shamefully neglected than the cultivation of conscientiousness, or the moral principle. While no pains, expense, or assiduity are spared in promoting the intellectual culture of the young, or in teaching them what are called *accomplishments*—to dance, to fence, and to ride—there is comparatively little or nothing done to improve the best part of the constitution—the moral sense—the benevolent affections. On the contrary, we often see the animal propensities indulged—a spirit of cruelty fostered—acquisitiveness, combativeness, destructiveness, and a taste for luxury, the great instigators of cruelty, called into fearful action. That children who have the misfortune to be so ill instructed should become tyrannical and inhuman men, is only what is to be expected. The fruit will be the genuine product of the seed sown. " Do men gather grapes of thorns, or figs of thistles ?"

Every parent who wishes to see his children become wise and virtuous men, will take care to imbue their minds with principles of humanity.* But if he suffers them to practise every species of cruelty of which they are capable, and prevents them not;—if he allows them to kill flies, spiders, and beetles; to teaze cats, dogs, and donkeys; to search for birds' nests; to destroy the eggs or the young with impunity; and, as soon as they can fling a stone, handle a bow and arrow, or fire a pistol or gun, to carry on the work of destruction; what is he to expect of them in their riper years, when every malignant passion has been strengthened by indulgence? He may consider the life of an insect or a bird as a thing of no value, and care not how dogs are lashed, cats hunted, and flies impaled. But these trifles, if such they seem, may lead to serious, and even appaling results. While a child is permitted to torture a poor animal, he is in training to become an executioner. The tyrant of the woods may become the

---

proprietors of the Belfast Academical Institution, 1820. This work is not so well known as it merits. It led to the foundation of the Belfast Museum of Natural History, an institution creditable to the taste and liberality of the inhabitants of that public-spirited town, and which has contributed in no small degree to promote a taste for the studies which it recommends.

* " Immanitas certe erga bestias est veluti tyrocinium scelestioris crudelitatis, et qui sustinent male habere pecudes, earumque malis videntur delectari, ii sæpe haud multo misericordiores erga homines evadunt."— CLERICUS *in Gen.* ix. 4.

R

tyrant of the city, and the killer of flies the scourge of his own family,

"Antiphates trepidi laris, ac Polyphemus."

It has been said that children are naturally cruel, that they have an instinctive pleasure in torturing flies, and treading upon worms. To affirm this is to malign their character, and impeach the wisdom and goodness of the Creator. If they are cruel it is not by nature, but a bad education; and there would be much greater cause of complaint, were it not for the benignant counteracting influence of that very nature which is so foully misrepresented. But human folly, having wrought all the evil of which it is capable, deformed what was fair, and perverted what was good, lays the blame on infinite wisdom and goodness! "The Saga relates, that in order to alter the mild disposition of Ingiald Illrada, he was fed with wolves' hearts. Judging from his future actions, this regimen appears to have had the desired effect." As wolves are extinct in this country, a different regimen is employed to "alter the mild disposition" of children—a regimen that operates directly on the mind, and freezes the "genial current of the soul." Kirby remarks, that "the first knowledge we get of insects is as tormentors; they are usually pointed out to those about us as ugly, filthy, and noxious creatures; and the whole insect world, butterflies and some few others excepted, are devoted by one universal ban to proscription and execration, as fit only to be trodden under our feet and crushed."

Young people are naturally active, turbulent, curious. They must be in motion, and hence they pursue animals, and in the ardour of pursuit, rudely seize, strike, sometimes kill them, not from cruelty, but to make sure of their capture. Curiosity also leads to minute examination, which terminates in dismemberment and death. All such practices should be discouraged, both by precept and example. If properly taught humanity, they will be humane. "Just as the twig is bent, the tree's inclined." The experience of all ages and countries bears testimony to the truth of the observation,

"Quo semel est imbuta recens, servabit odorem Testa diu."—Hor.

> "The odours of the wine that first shall stain
> The virgin vessel, it shall long retain."—FRANCIS.

The sensibilities and sympathies of children can be easily excited by kind admonition, and by expressions of pity and condolence for such animals as suffer injury or wrong. There is no great difficulty in shewing them the analogy between the affections, the wants, and the sufferings of a man and those of a brute. Should a child be detected in killing a fly, you may remonstrate or reason with him in a style similar to that of Titus with Marcus :—

Tit.—What dost thou strike at, Marcus, with thy knife?
Mar.—At that that I have killed, my lord; a fly.
Tit.—Out on thee, murderer! thou kill'st my heart;
Mine eyes are cloy'd with view of tyranny:
A deed of death done on the innocent
Becomes not Titus' brother; get thee gone;
I see, thou art not for my company.
Mar.—Alas, my lord, I have but kill'd a fly.
Tit.—But how, if that fly had a father and mother?
How would he hang his slender gilded wings,
And buzz lamenting doings in the air?
Poor harmless fly!
That with his pretty buzzing melody
Came here to make us merry; and thou hast kill'd him.
SHAKSPEARE.

If, instead of accosting a child thus, and leading him to participate in the wrongs and sufferings of an insect, some injudicious friend or domestic were to laud him for his dexterity and perseverance in catching and destroying one, as the Lady Valeria lauds the son of Coriolanus, how would his killing propensities, with his love of approbation, be stimulated into fearful activity! Valeria says to Volumnia :—

"O' my word, the father's son: I'll swear 'tis a very pretty boy. O' my troth, I look'd upon him o' Wednesday half an hour together: he has such a confirm'd countenance. I saw him run after a gilded butterfly; and when he caught it, he let it go again; and after it again; and over and over he comes and up again; catch'd it again: or whether his fall enraged him, or how 'twas, he did so set his teeth, and tear it; O, I warrant, how he mammock'd it!"
Vol.—One of his father's mood.
Val.—Indeed la, 'tis a noble child.

Such acts as are here eulogized were highly characteristic of the child of the warrior, who said that

"Like an eagle in a dove-cot, I
Fluttered your Volces in Corioli;"

but to praise them was only to foster the seeds of cruelty in the heart. If children be encouraged or permitted to vent their passions on unoffending brutes; and if, instead of being shamed and mortified, they are applauded, can we be surprised should they become cruel and tyrannical men? Let us not say that nature is in fault: bad example, improper indulgence, neglected education, these are in fault. These lay the foundation of a character that will reflect disgrace on the memory of parents, and work misery for generations unborn. Therefore crush the incipient evil. The moral like the physical pestilence gathers strength and virulence as long as it is unopposed—*viresque acquirit eundo*—and the cruelty which at first is contented with tormenting brutes, at length seeks gratification in a nobler quarry :—

> " On dogs and mules th' infection first began;
> At length the vengeful arrows fixed in man."

The author of a review of Elton's poems in Blackwood's Magazine for December, 1835, has too truly observed that the " vice of cruelty is often taught in infancy, by an unaccountable carelessness of parents on this point, and by inculcating a ferocious horror of some of God's creatures, even the most innocent. We well remember a scene that, in our mere boyhood, made an impression upon us that will never be effaced. A boy at school had stolen some of our books. The fact being ascertained, we took another boy with us, and went to his parents with whom he then was, and demanded the books. The father and the mother were sitting in the parlour; a younger child about five or six years of age, brought in a half-fledged bird, delighted with his prize. His amusement was to pluck off feather by feather from the creature, and throw it to the ceiling, bidding it fly, whilst the parents were looking on, and smilingly enjoying his animation. Could those parents with reason complain, if that child lived to break their hearts? But hearts they had none. But these lovely boys (the brothers, theme of the poet's song) had learned a different lesson.

> " They saw the gracious Father in his works,
> For they would listen to the book of life

With solemn, gladden'd aspect : him they loved
Ev'n in his meanest creatures; reverenc'd him
In the rook's instinct and the emmet's craft ;
The soothed familiar reptile fled them not ;
The speckled toad beneath the bramble lay,
His bright eye shining like a gem, nor shunn'd
Their footstep ; and the brutal urchin shrank
Rebuked, who, in their presence, sought to harm
One creature that had life. The most opprest
Or scorn'd to them were dearest ; nor their mind
Endured the dainty sophistry that deem'd
" The chamber or refectory" a shrine
Which no intruding worm may violate,
But that his life was forfeit: they had learnt
Another lesson from their gentle hearts :
And what their heart had taught them, no tame fear
Of mocks from the unfeeling, nor the sight
Of bold and base example, could repress :
But with an Abdiel pride, retorting scorn
Of unintimidated innocence,
They turned from the seducer, or withstood."

Different were the lessons taught to the youth who is supposed to repeat the following lines, which, whether written in sober seriousness or satiric ridicule, contain but too faithful a description of the modes in which children are taught to be cruel :—

" Who gave me a huge corking pin,
That I the cock-chafer might spin,
And laughed to see my childish grin ?
My granny.

" Who put me on a donkey's back,
And gave me whip to lash and smack
'Till its poor bones did almost crack ?
My granny."

The criminality of the parent who tolerates cruelty in his children will appear more flagrant, when we reflect how easy and how pleasing a task it is to render them gentle and humane. It is no difficult matter to make them understand that all living creatures are as sensible of pain as themselves, and that it is impossible to wound, mutilate, or crush the tiniest insect, without causing it an agony similar to what they would themselves experience from the extraction of a tooth, the tearing of their hair, or the dislocation or fracture of a limb. Admonition properly timed will seldom prove ineffectual ; but if it should, there are other modes of enforcing obedience. It may be salutary to let them feel a little of the pain they would inflict. Here Solomon's observation becomes peculiarly applicable: " He that spareth the rod hateth the child." To permit him to do wrong for fear of giving him a momentary pain, is a dangerous and mistaken fondness. It is letting the gangrene spread that will issue in death, rather than submit to a brief surgical operation. The gangrene of the mind is more to be dreaded than that of the body, and if not timely arrested, the end may be fatal. When flies became scarce, the Roman tyrant wreaked his passion for cruelty in the blood of his subjects. From the exhibition of the battles of wild beasts in the arena, it was found to be but a step to the more poignant sports of gladiators, in which hundreds of human beings lay massacred by mutual wounds, for the entertainment of a barbarous populace.

To teach humanity to children is only to second the designs of a benignant nature.

> Mollissima corda
> Humano generi dare se natura fatetur
> Quæ lachrymas dedit. Hæc nostri pars optima sensus.—Juv.

> " Nature, who gave us tears, by that alone
> Proclaims she made the feeling heart our own;
> And 'tis our noblest sense."—Gifford.

Miss Edgeworth remarks that, " Those who have not been habituated to the bloody form of cruelty, can never fix their eyes upon her without shuddering; even those to whom she may have in some instances been early familiarised, recoil from her appearance in any shape to which they have not been accustomed. At one of the magnificent shows, with which Pompey entertained the Roman people for five days successively, the populace enjoyed in profusion the death of wild beasts; no less than five hundred lions were killed; but on the last day, when twenty elephants were put to death, the people, unused to the sight, and to the lamentable howling of these animals, were seized with sudden compassion; and execrated Pompey himself for being the author of so much cruelty."

Aristotle blames the Lacedemonians for devoting so much of their children's time to gymnastics, with a view to encrease their strength and inspire them with courage; in both of which objects they failed, insomuch that among the candidates at the Olympic games, " we can scarcely find two or three who have gained a victory both when boys and men ; because the exercises they went through when young, deprived them of their strength." The same philosopher recommends music as an object of education, on account of its influence over the passions and affections. We condemn not either gymnastics or music, when practised with moderation, but we prefer humanity. Many children can never learn music, as all phrenologists will bear witness, and as many a parent knows to his cost after an enormous loss of money, and of what is more valuable, *time*. With equal success might you attempt to make them orators and poets, to give the strength of Hercules to a puppet, or the grace and dignity of Apollo to a dwarf. Less difficult is the task to inculcate lessons of morality ; all may be taught to be gentle and humane. They can be drilled and disciplined to virtue ; to practise the duties if not to feel the sentiments of mercy and compassion. But it is distressing to reflect how much more attention is paid to the intellectual than to the moral part of the constitution ; nay, that a posture-master shall be procured at great expense, and welcomed as the *magister morum*, while Æsop is treated with neglect and scorn. Among the wisest of the ancients morality was blended with mental instruction, and the effects of the latter on the former became so conspicuous, as to give rise to the proverb that learning renders all men gentle, απαντας παιδεια ημερους ποιει ; and a Latin poet testifies the same :—

> **Didicisse fideliter artes**
> **Emollit mores nec sinit esse feros.**
>
> The arts, well learned, the soul to peace incline,
> Tame the wild breast, and manners rude refine.

Wise teachers and legislators have justly considered humanity to animals as introductory of humanity to our fellow creatures. So thought Pythagoras, as Porphyry informs us, and all human experience demonstrates the fact. For what the Athenians thought upon the subject, it may suffice to refer to the anecdote quoted in the motto to this chapter. Triptolemus, the first Athenian legislator, made few laws or precepts; but three are recorded, which are so comprehensive as to embrace the sum of human duties, viz : " Honour your parents; worship the Gods; *hurt not animals.*"—PLUTARCH's LIVES, vol. 1. p. 218. note.

'The first law of the catechism of the Shamans is— " Thou shalt not kill any living creature;" " No living creature" shall be killed, whether it be of the higher class of beings, as a buddha, a perfect man, a teacher, a priest, or father or mother; or of the lower class of beings, as a grasshopper, or the smallest insect; in one word, whatever hath life thou shalt not kill."—*Translations from the Chinese and Armenian*, p. 48.

This law of the Shaman catechism might be borrowed with advantage by some parents and teachers, as an amplification of the sixth commandment. In their catechetical instructions they might shew, that if such sentiments are inculcated by the very heathen, how incumbent it is on those who are blessed with a purer faith, to act under their influence. Such laws and precepts are easily comprehended by the infant mind. Children of the tenderest age, even before they can articulate, may be taught to know and admire the forms of different animals by their pictures; and to take an interest in the sounds, colours, and movements of living creatures. They are generally fond of birds, cats, dogs, horses; and it requires but little skill to induce them to treat all such as are in their power with kindness. They soon learn to contemplate with delight the beauty of their figure, the glossy sleekness of their fur, the splendour of their plumage, the celerity of their course; and can easily be impressed with a sense of the cruelty of deforming what God made beautiful, or rendering wretched what God made happy. A judicious mother will teach her child the uses of the various domestic animals, and their claim to be treated kindly as profitable servants, companions, or friends. She will lead him in description through the animal kingdom, and explain how the power and wisdom of God are manifested in its formation; his goodness and mercy in its support. She will repeat to him many an anecdote of the lion, the crocodile, the whale, and the elephant. She will speak of the various feathered tribes, from the humming-bird nestling in a flower, to the eagle with sail-broad pinions soaring towards the sun, or the ostrich outstripping the horseman and his steed on the arid sands. She will present to his admiring view the changing hues of the pigeon's neck, the gold and silvery shades of the pheasant's wing, and the gorgeous sweep of the peacock's plumes. A single insect may furnish a copious theme for wonder and instruction; she will teach him to observe the supple play of its limbs, the quickness of its eye, the vivacity of its movements, the unfurling of its wings, the downy robe, or the steel-blue mail, the crest and the shield studded with amber and fringed with gold, sparkling in azure and crimson light, and surpassing in the richness of its decorations the drapery of queens, and mocking all the rivalry of art. She will expatiate on the various habits, clothing, and habitations of animals; their migratory, social, solitary instincts; their prognostic, geometric, textorial skill; their architectural contrivances; their long voyages; their care in providing for their young, their courage in defending them, and the arts by which they baffle or elude their enemy. Nor will she select those only which are deemed beautiful, as worthy of regard, but those which in vulgar apprehension are noxious or ugly. Instead of starting with feigned or real disgust at the sight of a spider, she will call her child to mark its racing speed, its thread most " exquisitely fine," and " its delicate web, which brilliantly glistens with dew." In the frog, the snail, the caterpillar, the chrysalis, and larva, she will lead him to discover something wonderful; and far from creating a false alarm, and an antipathy never afterwards to be overcome, she will induce him to take them gently in his hand, that he may inspect them more closely; and to heighten his wonder still farther, she will reveal to him by the microscope, a thousand marvels which escape the unassisted vision, and which

> " Hid from ages past, God now displays
> To combat atheists with in modern days;"—Cowper.

as the crest of a gnat, or the eye of a libellula; and while she expatiates on their use and contrivance, she will take care to impress the conviction, that as the hand of God alone could so beautifully adorn them, they are not to be wantonly injured or destroyed. She will teach him to observe the distinction between power and right, and inform him that it is laudable to do not what he can, but what is becoming a human being—*laus est facere quod decet, non quod licet ;* and should she observe a tendency to maltreat any creature, she will correct it by remonstrance and advice, or by pointing a moral to the heart in some instructive tale, like that of the Sultan Amurath in the twentieth number of " *The Adventurer.*" Amurath, the Sultan of the East, in the fretfulness of displeasure, struck the little dog that was jumping round him to receive his caresses, so severe a blow with his foot, that it left him scarce power to crawl away and hide himself under a sofa. " At that moment," says he, " the magic ring pressed my finger, and I felt a surprise and regret which quickly gave way to disdain. ' Shall not the Sultan Amurath,' said I, ' to whom a thousand kings pay tribute, and in whose hand is the life of nations—shall not Amurath strike a dog that offends him without being reproached for having transgressed the rule of right ?' My ring again pressed my finger, and the ruby became more pale ; immediately the palace shook with a burst of thunder, and the genius Syndarac again stood before me. ' Amurath,' said he, ' thou hast offended against thy brother of the dust ; a being who like thee, has received from the AL-MIGHTY a capacity of pleasure and pain : pleasure which caprice is not allowed to suspend, and pain which justice only has a right to inflict. If thou art justified by power in afflicting inferior beings, I should be justified in afflicting thee : but my power yet spares thee, because it is directed by the laws of sovereign goodness, and because thou mayest yet be reclaimed by admonition. But yield not to the impulse of quick resentment, nor indulge in cruelty the frowardness of disgust, lest by the laws of goodness I be compelled to afflict thee ; for he that scorns reproof must be reformed by punishment, or lost for ever."

Miss Edgeworth, a lady whose writings are always characterised by good sense and sound practical wisdom, in her work on Practical Education says, that " until young people have fixed *habits* of benevolence, and a taste for occupation, perhaps it is not prudent to trust them with the care or protection of animals. Even when they are enthusiastically fond of them, they cannot by their utmost ingenuity make the animals so happy in a state of captivity, as they would be in a state of liberty. They are apt to insist on doing animals good against their will, and they are often unjust in defence of their favourites. A boy of seven years old once knocked down his sister, to prevent her from squeezing his caterpillar." vol. ii. p. 28. Lond. 1801.

Yet we would not deny children, particularly in rural districts, the gratification of having a dog, a kitten, a pigeon, or domestic fowl, a kid, or a fawn for a pet, on certain conditions, as a reward for good conduct, and with the indispensable proviso that it should be treated judiciously, with a due regard to its habits and instincts, and injured neither by neglect nor too much fondness, since it is all one to a poor animal whether it be from love or hatred, if it must be tortured to death. The kind affections may be nourished and developed by such indulgence, transferred from brutes to man, and ultimately exalted into fixed principles of philanthropy. Against the confinement of any of our native birds in cages we absolutely protest.

A zoological garden or menagerie furnishes a fine theatre of entertainment and rational instruction, to the young as well as to the old. There they may learn from inspection of the real animals, to form more accurate notions of their figure, size, strength, and motions, than they could gather from pictures or verbal description, and at the same time to contemplate and admire the power, wisdom, and munificence of God, as manifested in their structure, clothing, habits, and instincts. Each animal contains a history of its own, and by a natural association, transports the mind to the country from which it came, and leads to an extension of our knowledge of the earth and of man. The reindeer conducts us in thought to the regions of eternal snow, to the sledge and the hut of the Laplander; while the elephant bears us to the wilds of Caffraria or the forests of Ceylon, to the palaces, the equipage, and the armies of oriental magnificence. Add to this, that such recreations promote the health of body and mind, and keep both in a state of vigorous activity and enjoyment.

Many useful lessons may be taught in the progress of a morning walk or rural excursion. Should a nest be found with eggs or with young, a leveret or a field mouse dislodged, by all means disturb them not, but expatiate on the cruelty that would injure or annoy them. Let the " Mouse's Petition" plead in its behalf. You may awaken kind feelings of sympathy by repeating Burns's moral and pathetic address to the " wee, sleekit, cow'rin, tim'rous beastie ;" and feelings of another kind, by the recital of some such facts as the following :—A gentleman of fortune in the neighbourhood of Dublin took pleasure in ornamenting his grounds, and kindly admitted strangers to come and enjoy the pleasure of lounging in the walks, or reposing in the arbours. A man in the costume of a military officer, accompanied by some women whose dress gave them the passport of gentlewomen, came one day to admire the lake, with its boat, its island, and its swans ; but instead of using the privilege as became persons of their appearance, how did this son of Mars and these daughters of Bellona amuse themselves ? They crowded into the little boat, as if embarking on some grand naval expedition, sailed to the island, and made an attack with clods and stones on the half-fledged cygnets that were disporting in the water, and left them wounded or dead. Whether they bore off any of the spoil *to be eaten,* or kept as a trophy, is not recorded ; neither has it been noted whether they took the thrush's nest with the young, which till then had been carefully guarded ; or whether the rare exotic, which by some sleight of hand was transported from the conservatory to the torrid clime of a lady's muff, was found in their possession.

Ἡμεις δε κλεος διον ἀκουομεν, οὐδε τι ἰδμεν'—HOM. B. 486.

" We only hear reports from flying *Fame.*"—OGILBY.

But this we know from better authority, that such acts as these generally cause the privilege of rambling in gentlemen's demesnes to be withdrawn, and hence so many of them are surrounded by high walls, as by a line of fortifications, obstructing the view and deforming the landscape.

The telescope may be sometimes as successfully employed to discover the forms, colours, motions of distant objects, as the microscope in the examination of the most minute. Children are delighted to behold objects that are altogether inaccessible to them—a ship, a fishing-boat, a beast, or a bird—apparently brought almost within their grasp, and a new world thus unfolded to their admiring and astonished gaze, by means of this instrument. To them, as to the naturalist, it furnishes a cheaper, a safer, a more innocent, and a far more instructive amusement, than a fowling-piece. Robert Ball, Esq. whose lecture on Ornithology has been already mentioned, (p. 178) has kindly furnished the author with the following appropriate and interesting extract from that lecture:—" I have often myself been a party in this inhuman, reckless sport, (shooting gulls in the breeding season,) but now find, when opportunity offers, immensely greater pleasure in levelling another, but an innocent tube, at the harmless tenants of the rocks, than I did before in pointing the destructive gun. I allude to the use of a telescope, or spy-glass, pompously called by Ornithologists an Ornithoscope. I cannot conceive any individual, who having once had a peep through such an instrument, would not wish for another, and find increased interest in each fresh view. The manners and personal deportment of birds can thus be ascertained when they are unconscious of the spectator. The view of a ledge of rocks, tenanted by some hundred individuals, occupied in incubation, and feeding their young, is as pleasing a spectacle as I have ever witnessed." Yes—such scenes are truly delightful, and in them may young people especially be best taught to become conversant with the God of nature and his works. The quiet contemplation of a spectacle like this must afford "immensely greater pleasure" to every true lover of nature, than it is possible to extract from the screams, the agony, and the slaughter of unoffending creatures; and in accordance with this sentiment, I may be permitted to repeat what I have elsewhere " sung or said :"

s

Ye feathered tribes,
Sing unmolested in your leafy bowers;
Ye finny nations, in your streams and lakes
And pearly grottos play; ye insect swarms,
Murmur melodious; turn your burnished wings
Bright-twinkling to the sun; at morn and eve,
With all your sportive myriads in the air,
Reel through the mazy dance—for in your mirth
My soul participates. Around your cliffs,
In many a playful curve, ye sea-birds, wheel;
Preen your gray wings;—along the level brine
Quick-diving plunge; or on the sunny swell
Float like smalll islets of embodied foam;
Stars of the sea, ye stud and beautify
Its azure waste, as th' empyrean fires
Gem and illume the ebon vault of night.
Who would not deem it an offence to heaven
To harm your joys, or from one little nook,
Their heritage from God, your wingless brood
Cruel dislodge? With man from God ye spring,
Are God's dependents—ratified as his
Your rights to share the bounty Nature gives,
Sport in the waves, or on your native rocks
To congregate and clamour as ye will.
Ye too perchance, as particles detached
From mind's pure essence, thro' full many a grade
Of still improving being, may advance
To life celestial. Shame pursue the wretch
That in your carnage finds a dire delight!
May heaven forfend he e'er should wield the sword,
Or turn his ire on man! Beneath my roof
O let him come not! Never may we ride
In skiff or car together! May he ne'er
See my lov'd rocks, nor with his hideous sight
Blast the pure air through which ye wing your way.
                    W. H. D.'s *Pleasures of Benevolence.*

The schoolmaster may ably second the benevolent designs of the parent: and he must have frequent opportunities of inculcating precepts of sympathy for the feathered creation, particularly in the season of nests. It may be profitable for his pupils to have their sensibility touched, and to contemplate, that they may avoid, the odious character of the truant and idler, that " would rob a poor bird of her young."

" The most ungentle of the tribe was he,
  No generous precept ever touched his heart;
With concord false, and hideous prosody,
  He scrawled his task and blundered o'er his part.

" On mischief bent, he marked with rav'nous eyes,
  Where wrapt in down the callous songsters lay,
Then rushing rudely seized the glittering prize,
  And bore it in his impious hands away."

The clergy, too, should act as auxiliaries in this good work. The influence derived from their office cannot be better employed, either in public or private, than in pre-

venting cruelty, and teaching their friends and auditors to
be humane. Divines often expatiate on the value of a
human soul, and declare that the whole solar system is of
less estimation. It is true indeed, inert matter is of value
only in its relation to animated beings; and this consideration should induce them to extend the idea to all living
creatures, even to the lowest species; as many parts of
the inanimate world have evidently been constructed with
a view to their peculiar habits and instincts.

Many years ago, a Presbyterian minister in the north
of Ireland, desirous of putting a stop to cock-fighting, a
barbarous custom to which the people of his parish were
addicted, particularly at the season of Easter, requested
their attendance to hear a discourse on a very interesting
subject. The congregation, of course, was crowded. He
chose for his text that passage of Matthew or Luke which
describes Peter as weeping bitterly when he heard the
cock crow; and discoursed upon it with such eloquence
and pathos, and made so judicious an application of the
subject, that his hearers from that day forth abandoned
the unchristian practice. Of how much good was this
single discourse productive? How much ribaldry, blas-
phemy, ebriety, gambling, and all such vices as are
commonly associated with cock-fighting, did it serve to
abolish? Will any one say that this minister went out
of his province in expatiating on such a theme? or that he
was not preaching Christ, when he was putting down a
vice so opposed to Christianity? He might have declaimed
for years on speculative points of faith, without any such
result. The best preacher of Christ is he who by his
discourses best promotes the practice of the Christian virtues. Would that such a laudable example were more
generally followed—that no minister of the gospel would
cease to denounce cruelty till it was banished—that no
priest would grant absolution to the cruel man, till he
had done due penance for his merciless deeds!

Humanity, mercy, compassion, are virtues especially
required and insisted on by Christianity, and their influence is not limited to the human race. It extends to the
whole worlds of reason, life, and sense; to the worm on the
ground and the shell-fish on the rock, as well as to the

wounded traveller, the widow, and the orphan. How much good might the clergy of all denominations effect, were they sometimes to insist on these truths? how much more than any legislature for the correction of inhumanity? Human laws may reach and punish a few of the most atrocious acts of cruelty which are exposed to observation; but there are thousands and ten thousands of such acts that escape their cognizance and defy their authority. To find a remedy for the evil, we must go to a higher source. We must appeal to the law of God. We must address the moral principles. We must bring the feelings of benevolence to operate on the conduct. We must instil the dews of compassion into the bosoms of our children. Humanity must elevate her voice and inculcate her precepts in the nursery—in the school—in the college—in the lecture-room—in the courts of justice—in the pulpit. She must speak aloud with a hundred tongues, by the mouths of orators and poets, philosophers and divines, by mothers to their daughters, and by fathers to their sons, and by masters and mistresses to their male and female servants. She must invoke THE PRESS to stamp her dictates in the indelible characters of ink and type, and give them a passport to the extremities of the world. She must implore it to brand, with a disreputable stigma, every cruel deed; that those who are not to be allured to mercy by high and generous motives, may be deterred from cruelty by the dread of shame.

CHAPTER XI.

SHALL ANIMALS EXIST HEREAFTER?

> ———— Passimque soluti
> Per campos pascuntur equi : quæ gratia currum
> Armorumque fuit vivis, quæ cura nitentes
> Pascere equos ; eadem sequitur tellure repostos.—VIRG.
>
> Their steeds around,
> Free from their harness, graze the flow'ry ground ;
> The love of horses which they had alive
> And care of chariots after death survive.—DRYDEN.
>
> And thinks, admitted to that equal sky,
> His faithful dog shall bear him company.—POPE.

Such are the ideas entertained "by savage and by sage" of the world to come. They who have no idea of happiness beyond the gratification of the senses, think that man's future bliss will consist in the enjoyment of such sensual pleasures as gratified him most upon earth. Hence Virgil's warriors delight in steeds and chariots; and Pope's Indian in a dog, a bottle, and a wife. These notions clearly imply a belief in the immortality of the souls of animals as well as of men. Christians generally entertain a more exalted notion of the joys of hereafter, and though one class would confine them to the contracted circle of their own denomination, another would extend them not only to all of their own species, but to the whole of animated being—a doctrine which is at least more accordant with the benevolent spirit of Christianity, than that which would sentence the majority of the human race to everlasting burnings.

Various and contradictory are the opinions which have been formed of the metaphysical nature of animals. By one they are sunk to the level of insensate matter; by another exalted to immortality.

Some who are proud of their reason and their dignity in the scale of creation, but who are assuredly neither philosophers nor Christians, look down on animals with infinite scorn, and treat them as if they were automata or

s 2

self-moving machines, and seem scarcely willing to admit
that they are composed of nerve and muscle like themselves. They endeavour, too, to justify their violation of
the dictates of humanity on much the same principles, and
with the same regard to good feeling, that a slave-dealer
endeavours to justify his brutality to negroes, by pleading
the inferiority of their intellect; as if that very inferiority,
admitting it to exist, did not establish a claim to protection, instead of affording a plea for injury and abuse.
They proceed on wrong ground in supposing that they
exalt their reason and dignity by degrading animals. Allowing their own superiority, the more highly animals
are exalted, the higher, too, must be that superiority; as
the ruler of a civilized people holds a more honourable
station than a ruler among savages. Elaborate treatises
have been written to prove man a machine; and, indeed,
if the term be applicable to brutes, we see not how it can
be denied to man. But what propriety is there in the
application of the term to the one or to the other? What
are the points of identity or similarity? Has a machine
affections, passions, feelings? Is it grateful for being
wound up, or grieved if suffered to run down? Has
it memory? And will it expire with joy, like the dog
of Ulysses, to see its master, after a lapse of twenty
years? If diseased, will it seek a cathartic, like the sparrow, in a dose of spiders; or an emetic, like the dog, in a
medicinal grass? Will it help its digestion by swallow-
ing gravel, as birds; or raise a shrill cry to warn its companions of an approaching enemy? Does it change its
climate with the season; or rear a young progeny, and
delight in the indulgence of parental affection?

Granting that they are machines, is that any reason for
treating them with barbarity? Should we not rather try
to keep the springs and wheels of the machine in proper
trim and motion; and not derange them by too rapid
friction, or by laying on them a heavier burden than they
can sustain? Has God formed them with such exquisite
skill, only to be torn in pieces by human folly and wickedness? If they are short-lived by nature, should we render their lives shorter by injurious treatment? An argument for showing them kindness has been founded on

their short and fleeting existence. This life is their all; they have no " bright reversion in the skies." Their condition, therefore, should be rendered as comfortable as possible, and no injury offered them by which it can be curtailed.

Others again, taking into consideration the evils that animals are made to undergo in their present state, suppose that a bright futurity may be reserved for them, as well as for the virtuous sufferers among mankind. The author of the thirty-seventh number of " *The Adventurer*" says, that when he " considered the inequality with which happiness appears to be distributed among the brute creation, as different animals are in a different degree exposed to the capricious cruelty of mankind, in the fervour of my imagination I began to think it possible that they might participate in a future retribution ; especially as mere matter and motion approach no nearer to sensibility than to thought, and he who will not venture to deny that brutes have sensibility, should not hastily pronounce that they have only a material existence."

Father Bougeant, in a work entitled " *Philosophical Amusement*," discusses the question whether brutes have spiritual souls; and having come to the conclusion that they have, and this conclusion involving consequences dangerous, as he fears it might be supposed, to the doctrines of religion, to free himself from the difficulty, and answer the objection, he invents a hypothesis of his own, which has the sinister merit, at least, of surpassing all others in folly and absurdity. " Religion," he says, " teaches us that the devils, from the very moment they had sinned, were reprobate, and that they were doomed to burn for ever in hell; but the church has not as yet determined whether they do actually endure the torments to which they are condemned." He supposes that the execution of the verdict brought against them is reserved for the day of final judgment, and that " God, in order not to suffer so many legions of reprobate spirits to be of no use, has distributed them through the several spaces of the world, to serve the designs of his providence, and make his omnipotence to appear. Some continuing in their present state, busy themselves in tempting and tormenting men. God with the others makes millions of beasts of all kinds, which serve for the several uses of man. Hence it is easy to conceive how beasts can think, know, have sentiments, and a spiritual soul, without any way striking at the doctrines of religion. * * * As they are altogether strangers to human society, they can have no other appointment, but that of being useful and amusing. And what care we whether it be a devil, or any other creature, that serves and amuses us ? The thought of it, far from shocking, pleases me mightily. I with gratitude admire the goodness of the Creator, who gave me so many little devils to serve and amuse me. If I am told that these poor devils are doomed to suffer eternal tortures, I admire God's decrees; but I have no manner of share in this dreadful sentence. I leave the execution of it to the Sovereign Judge; and notwithstanding this, I live with my little devils, as I do with a multitude of people, of whom religion informs me that a great number shall be damned."

What shall we say to imaginations so monstrous and revolting ? A writer of our own, Granville Sharp, so far from admitting that animals have the souls of evil spirits, maintains that they are not even susceptible of demoniacal possession. Nay, he contends that they are superior to men, inasmuch as " they never commit suicide;" and he might have added, nor like the satanic host in Milton, fabricate gunpowder, nor bore cannon, that devilish enginery by which so many thousands are massacred for human glory. " They are never known," he continues, " to violate that universal principle, self-love, except it be for a *reasonable cause*, that they risk their own lives in defence of their young, to preserve their species, or through gratitude, as dogs will defend their masters, which surely is no depravity ! To what extraordinary cause then shall we attribute this very singular superiority of brutes, in a circumstance so necessary to happiness ? The cause is obvious : brutes have never been subjected to *spiritual delusions*, or been actuated by *infernal spirits*, since the time that the serpent deceived our first parents !"* (Tract on *The Law of Nature*, p. 177.)

---

* He allows, however, of one exception, the possession of the swine.

Wesley, in his sermon on Rom. viii. 19, 22, after giving us a romantic description of the moral and intellectual perfections of the first man, proceeds to speak of the original state of the brute creatures, and affirms that they had all a principle of *self-motion,* a degree of *understanding, will,* and *liberty.* The barrier between man and brute, he affirms, was not *reason;* for if, instead of this ambiguous term, we substitute understanding, we can deny them this no more than we can deny that they have sight and hearing. But man is capable of God; the inferior creatures are not. This is the essential difference. Like man, they were originally happy. They had some shadowy resemblance of moral goodness; and how beautiful they were, may be conjectured from the remnant of beauty which they still possess. They were also *immortal.* All the blessings in paradise flowed to them through man: but their fate was involved in his. By his fall they were precipitated from their state of bliss, and *made subject to vanity.* Only a few, those commonly termed domestic, retain more or less of their original disposition. How little shadow of good is now to be found in any part of the brute creation! On the contrary, what fierceness and cruelty, as in the tiger, the eagle, and the shark! The original beauty, too, of most of them is impaired, and they have become not only terrible, but grisly and deformed. Man is the enemy of them all. Even the gentle creatures do not escape his fury. The ocean shark gives pain to the creatures he devours from sheer necessity; the human shark gives gratuitous torment till death signs their release. But the day is approaching when they shall be delivered from the bondage of corruption into glorious liberty; even in measure, according to their capacity, of the liberty of the children of God. All their horrid deformities will be exchanged for their primeval beauty, their happiness will return, and their corruptible bodies having put on incorruption, they shall enjoy a happiness suited to their state, without interruption and without end.

This is a benevolent conclusion, for which we might almost pardon the fiction of the premises.* Happily for

* On this point his bitterest opponents agreed with him. " I will honestly

Wesley he was not under the ecclesiastical jurisdiction of authors like Antonio Le Grand, who condemns such opinions as *heresies* and Platonic figments already laid prostrate by the Fathers. Under this impression he asks some questions, which the followers of Wesley may answer :—" *Si æternæ sunt bestiarum animæ, et immortalitate donantur, quæ erit inter homines et cætera animantia distinctio ? An illa, sicut et nos interminata felicitas manet ? Sed ne de belluarum beatitudine simus solliciti, ubi animæ illæ degunt, quæ ab orbe condito extitere, quibus in locis reconduntur ? An iis peculiares campi Elisei assignati sunt in quibus vagentur et excurrant ? Quid de pulicibus, muscis, variique generis insectis factum est quibus olim Ægyptii divexati sunt ? Quæ illis post interitum officia ? Quem in finem asservantur ? Aut quam universo orbi utilitatem adferunt ?*"—Diss. *de Carentia Sensus et Cognitionis in Brutis*, p. 8.

Wesley was by no means singular in his opinion. Many others have maintained, that "man forfeited both for us and them the blessed privileges of our primitive state and condition."* They have unwarrantably extended to the whole animal world the text, Rom. viii. 22, " We know that the whole creation groaneth and travaileth in pain together until now." But the learned reader will clearly see, that the Apostle's expression, πασα η κτισις, every creature, or the whole creation, must be limited to the rational creation. This will be evident from comparing it with Mark, xvi. 15; Col. i. 23; in which the phrase occurs, and signifies all mankind. The whole context exposes the absurdity of extending the phrase to brute animals.—*See* TAYLOR *on the Romans*, in loc. *Macknight, Whitby, Belsham, &c.*

As to the question in Ecclesiastes, iii. 21.—" Who knoweth the spirit (breath) of man that goeth upward, and the spirit (breath) of the beast that goeth downward to the earth ?" we can draw from it nothing decisive. We

---

confess," says Toplady, " that I never heard one single argument urged against the immortality of brutes, which, if admitted, would not, *mutatis mutandis*, be equally conclusive against the immortality of man."—See SOUTHEY's *Life of Wesley*, vol. ii. p. 191.

* HILDROP, p. 227.

are told in a preceding verse that beasts and men " have all one breath, (spirit) so that a man hath no pre-eminence above a beast." The curious reader may see a long and laboured explanation of the text in Brown's " *Procedure of the Understanding*," p. 357, which is referred to by Parkhurst; but it would be beside our present purpose here to enter into its examination. Bishop Patrick's paraphrase may also be consulted with advantage. The expression in the 12th verse of the 49th Psalm, " The beasts that perish," is equally indecisive as to the point in question; for in a verse almost immediately preceding, " the fool and the brutish man" are also said to " perish," *i. e.* to die and be as little regarded or deplored as beasts ; but would it not push the meaning to an unwarranted extremity, to affirm that it implies the total annihilation of either the one or the other ?

While some, with Des Cartes and Malebranche, pronounce animals to be mere automata, others, with the chevalier Ramsay, think they have souls that were placed in them for crimes committed in a pre-existent state. The Epicureans maintained that there are two species of souls, the sensitive and the rational, *anima* and *animus.* Hence the distinction noticed by Juvenal :—

Sensum a cœlesti demissum traximus arce,
Cujus egent prona et terram spectantia. Mundi
Principio indulsit communis conditor illis
Tantum animas, nobis animum quoque.—Juv. xv. 147.

We, from high heaven, deduce that better part,
That moral sense denied to creatures prone
And downward bent, and found with man alone :
For he who gave this vast machine to roll,
Breathed LIFE in them, in us a REASONING SOUL.—GIFFORD.

Similar is the distinction which we are in the habit of making between instinct and reason. As to the former, whether it be a blind influence impelling animals to act in a uniform, undeviating manner, or whether it be a species of reason, the same in kind though not in degree as in man, has long been a subject of enquiry. Some have endeavoured to prove that dogs can syllogize; and it is undeniable that animals can, to a certain extent, vary their modes of acting, and accommodate themselves to new circumstances, as birds are known not only to vary the materials of which they compose their nests, but some-times to choose places for nidification altogether foreign to their general habits.* Fothergill affirms that " they possess all the faculties of man, though in a limited degree, imagination alone perhaps excepted." " It seems to me as evident," says Locke, " that they do in some in-stances reason as that they have sense."† The late Dr. Brown of Edinburgh " believed that many of the lower animals have the sense of right and wrong; and that the metaphysical argument which proves the immortality of man, extends with equal force to the other orders of earthly creatures."‡ Many of them, it must be admitted, are endowed with properties so closely approximating to those of the creature which we call rational, that it is by no means easy to shew an essential difference. It cannot be denied that they possess moral affections, for they have gratitude; nor intellectual faculties, for they have memory; and that each of their powers conducts to the proper end with unerring certainty. Autobulus, one of the speakers in a dialogue of Plutarch, observes, that " reason is in the creature by nature, but right and perfect reason is attained by industry and education; so that, naturally, all creatures may be said to be rational. But if they look for per-fection of reason and true wisdom, they will hardly find these perfections in any man whatever."

Should we admit with Cicero, that whatever feels, wills, and acts with discernment and vigour, is celestial and divine, and therefore eternal, the question as to their im-

---

* Thus the herons in the island of Rathlin, where there are no trees, build their nests among the reeds of a lake.

† Hildrop affirms, that instances, if necessary, might be produced in which brutes " reason well, and discover more sense and better logic than many a stupid puppy with two legs, who lives at random, who pur-sues every appearance of pleasure, gratifies every appetite, submits to every demand of lust or fancy, without thought or reflection, and rushes with his eyes open into certain diseases, beggary, and damnation.''

‡ The biographer of this distinguished philosopher and poet says that " the tenderness and the quickness of his sympathy were such, that he could not bear to see any living thing in pain. The cold-hearted would have smiled, perhaps, had they seen the patient and anxious care with which he tried to relieve the sufferings of animals that to them would have appeared unworthy of a thought. He considered the duties which we owe to the brute creation a very important branch of ethics, and had he lived he would have published an essay upon the subject."—*Philosophy of the Human Mind.* Edin. 1828, p. 22.

mortality would be settled. "*Quicquid est illud quod sentit, quod sapit, quod viget, cœleste et divinum est, ideoque æternum.*"

Come to what conclusion we may on these subjects, if, as religion teaches, every man must hereafter give an account of the deeds done in the body, cruelty to animals is a crime that will not escape due chastisement; and whether reason be granted or refused to brutes, it will scarcely be denied that they can *feel :* for feeling does not depend on intellect, nor is the intensity of a man's sensations to be estimated by the strength of his reasoning powers. Shall we suppose that a philosopher feels more acutely than a clown? He may, indeed, from education be more sensible of indignity, but the sum of physical suffering, under similar circumstances, will in both be the the same. Stoicism taught Epictetus to express no sense of uneasiness, while his leg was undergoing the operation of a deliberate fracture. A similar operation could not be performed on any animal capable of sound or gesture, without shrieks and contortions ; whence the inference is obvious, that it is " mind which masters matter;" that reason alone, by a mighty effort, can subdue the sense of physical pain. When a patriot or a martyr is brought to the scaffold or the stake, he is enabled to endure the rack or the flame, by the high and holy thoughts which occupy his mind. The consciousness of his own rectitude, the *mens conscia recti,* arms him with invincible patience. He knows that he has the sympathy of the wise and good ; that he is contemplated by his friends with pity—by his enemies with admiration ; that his death may serve the cause for which he dies more effectually than his life ; and that even on earth he cannot *all die,* for his name will be embalmed in the poet's song or the historian's page. He looks up with confidence to the righteous Judge and merciful Parent of all, and cheered by the certain hope of passing into a state of felicity ineffable and immortal, he smiles in the midst of torture, and gives a joyous welcome to death. But what cheers a poor animal under the butcher's hatchet, or the epicure's crimping knife? What redress can it hope for its wrongs ? What resource does it enjoy in futurity ?

T

CHAPTER XII.

CRUELTY TO ANIMALS ADMITS OF NO DEFENCE.

"The merciful man doeth good to his own soul: but he that is cruel troubleth his own flesh."—*Prov.* xi. 17.

"Now they have no cloak for their sin."—*John* xv. 22. "They are without excuse."—*Rom.* i. 20.

PHOTIUS, the learned Patriarch of Constantinople, records an anecdote highly honourable to the humane character of the Athenians. "The senate of the Areopagites being assembled together on a mountain, without any roof but heaven, the senators perceived a bird of prey which pursued a little sparrow that came to save itself in the bosom of one of their company. This man, who naturally was harsh, threw it from him so roughly that he killed it; whereat the court was offended, and a decree was made, by which he was condemned, and banished from the senate: whereupon the Patriarch judiciously observes, that this company which was at that time one of the gravest in the world, did it not for the care they had to make a law concerning sparrows, but to show that clemency and merciful inclination were virtues so necessary in a state, that a man destitute of them was not worthy to hold any place in government, he having, as it were, renounced humanity." WANLEY'S *Wonders,* fol. 174.

There are so many acts of cruelty on record, that it is pleasing to meet with an anecdote like this, to prove that clemency is an instinctive sentiment of the heart; while its opposite vice, cruelty, is universally detested, especially when it affects the lives and liberties of men. The tyrant is an object of reprobation to the historian and the poet, to the old and the young. All who are in authority which they abuse—the master of a family, of a school, a city, a nation—all are censured and hated; they live unhonoured, and when they die, the people rejoice.

The same feelings of dislike extend to those who are

cruel to animals; and no one is known to treat them with inhumanity who does not suffer in the estimation of all the good and wise. We justly and naturally conclude, that he who maltreats his beasts or his birds, would also maltreat his fellow-creatures, if he dared. But happily, cruelty is a dastardly vice, and when confronted with courage, dreads to feel the pains it is so ready to inflict, and shrinks back into its own cowardice and deformity.

A tyrannical prince may often have some plausible pretext for his tyranny. He may plead the exigencies of his situation compelling him to lay heavy burdens on his people—to seize by violence what he cannot gain by entreaty, and the necessity of providing for his own safety by the exile, imprisonment, or death of those from whom he apprehends danger. He may plead not only his fears, but his wrongs. He has been provoked, insulted, threatened; his throne, his life, placed in jeopardy. He may argue for the good policy of striking terror into the bosoms of the disaffected, by examples of appalling severity. But what plausible pretext can the tyrant of animals offer, to palliate or justify his inhumanity? He cannot affirm that he is wronged by his sheep, his ox, or his ass; and still less, if possible, by other creatures with which he has no manner of connexion. He cannot plead that he dreads their conspiracy and rebellion; that they malign his character, and want only an opportunity to depose him and establish another in his place. He dares not make any such allegations as these. Wherefore, then, does he maltreat them, and play the tyrant? To make them more obedient, to stimulate them to greater exertion. But here he acts like a fool. Harshness never renders animals more obedient; on the contrary, it renders them more refractory and stubborn. Again; it is, for his own sake, unwise by cruel stimulants to compel an animal to a greater exertion of strength or fleetness than its nature can properly endure. It breaks down under labours disproportioned to its powers; or if wronged in its food, or otherwise ill treated in the pasture or the stall, it dies prematurely the victim of folly and cruelty; and he is justly punished by the loss of a servant, whom lenity and proper usage might have rendered valuable for years.

But this is an argument addressed only to the cold, selfish, calculating principle of profit and loss. There are higher considerations to lead men to the practice of humanity. Animals, it must be reiterated again and again, have their rights—rights chartered to them by their Creator, and not to be violated with impunity.

The very circumstance of animals being unable to appeal to any earthly tribunal to witness and avenge their wrongs, must influence every right-thinking mind in their behalf. The destitute, the friendless, the orphan are the most proper objects of compassion among our own species. The duty of yielding assistance increases with the urgency of the necessity. The more dependent an animal is on our care, the stronger is our obligation to yield it protection. But the very circumstance which elicits the generosity of noble minds, is that which induces the base and degenerate to be cruel. They are fond of shewing their superiority where there is no resistance; and are lavish of kicks and blows where they dread no retaliation. Wo to the animal that shews any inclination to reciprocate these rewards of its services! It is sure to receive tenfold chastisement from the rod or the lash of its exasperated dastardly owner. A man of generous mind, instead of resenting the use which an animal makes of the weapons which God has given it, in defending itself from aggression and injury, will hold it in respect; and appreciate even in a worm or a fly the virtues which he would honour in a man. Thus felt a gallant soldier, who having caught a mouse in his hand, was severely bitten by it. He could have crushed it instantly to death; but he acted more nobly in restoring it to freedom, as the reward of its courage.

Much more might be said on this topic, but time, the most constant and invincible of all antagonists, warns me to conclude.

In a word, then, Cruelty admits of no defence. It is opposed to the laws of God, and the interests of man; it is the worst passion of the breast; the perpetrator of the most detestable crimes; the darling attribute of the great adversary of Him whose name is Love. As benevolence delights in doing good, and participates in the enjoyment of all God's creatures; cruelty, on the other hand, rejoices in the infliction of pain and misery, and in the destruction of all that gratifies the gentle and amiable feelings of our nature. It is lamentable to reflect how extensive is the empire of this demon, and into what a number and variety of situations she intrudes. She dwelt with Cain, and with the giants of old, and polluted the earth with deeds of violence and blood. She had for her devoted worshippers the priests of pagan superstition; and prompted them to heap their altars with human victims. She rejoiced in the sports of the Roman amphitheatre, where not only beasts but men perished in thousands, as on a battle-field, by mutual wounds. Now you may behold her in the cock-pit, the bear garden, and the "Sparrow-Club;" or seated with bigotry in the halls and dungeons of the Inquisition, amidst racks, and wheels, and implements of torture; or in the vivi-dissector's class-room, witnessing the expiring agonies of dogs and cats. Sometimes you may see her with a stripling gunner shooting swallows on the wing, or with an angler impaling worms on a hook; now pursuing a poor wretch as he runs the gauntlet through a regiment of soldiers, or inflicting bloody stripes on a negro's back. There is no class of society, nor any situation, into which she does not occasionally force an entrance. You may find her in the court and in the camp; in the city and in the field; on the judge's bench, where justice should preside; and uttering her spells in the pulpit, where mercy alone should reign triumphant. The weapons she employs are as various as the situations in which she appears. Sometimes she wields a sceptre, and sometimes a sword; a carter's whip, or a pedagogue's rod; a rope or a scalpel. She is the companion, the instigator, and the slave of every bad passion; of gluttony and ebriety; of rape and murder. He who entertains her in any form must injure his happiness and reputation, and at last become a fit associate of the ruffian and assassin. As the senator was banished from the court of Areopagus for his harsh repulsion of the poor sparrow that sought his protection; so should cruelty, in every shape and disguise, be banished from all societies that pretend to the name of Christian, or have any claim to be considered as existing within the pale of civilization.

Cruelty holds the bad pre-eminence over all the vices which degrade our nature; it is deservedly the object of universal reprobation, and is utterly opposed to the spirit of Christianity. When directed against man, when it "grinds the faces of the poor," when it preys on the substance of the orphan and widow, or riots in a feast of blood, who is not ready to invoke earth and heaven to arrest it with their judgments? Shall we forbear, then, to deprecate it, when let loose on our more humble co-habitants of the earth? Does it lose its native hideous-ness by changing its object? Is the gloom in which it wraps itself less sullen, or the aspect it assumes less de-moniacal, when it stamps, and tears, and foams, and utters horrible blasphemies and imprecations? He who yields himself to its control loses all the nobler characteristics of man. He degrades himself beneath the creatures which he maims and wounds; and instances are not wanting to shew how his own passion becomes their avenger, by driv-ing him to acts of frantic desperation, or suddenly dis-severing the cord of life. How often does God punish men by their own scourge? And who that believes in the exercise of his righteous Providence, can doubt that he will, soon or late, render them responsible for every abuse of their power? HE, of whom mercy is the glori-ous attribute, will surely take cognizance of those inhuman deeds, which, as they disturb not the peace of society, are not subject to its laws; but which in the sight of HIM who judges not by the outward appearance but by the heart, may be not less deserving of punishment. For as there may be no less malice in the murder of a brute than in that of a man, though not cognizable at a human tribu-nal, how can it escape a just retribution from heaven?

As cruelty is, on the one hand, the most odious and detestable of vices, so is mercy, on the other, the most amiable and engaging of the virtues. The one has her abode in realms of woe, in scenes of discord and war, of pain and agony, amidst racks and tortures, and where there is "weeping, and wailing, and gnashing of teeth."

The other dwells by the throne of Eternal Love, whence she is deputed on messages of grace and pardon to the children of men. The one teaches us to thwart, as far as we can, the beneficent designs of Providence, to imprison what God made free, to deform what God made beautiful, to spread blood, and carnage, and sulphurous stench, and misery, and desolation, over scenes which God has enrished with verdure, and scented with flowers, and peopled with tribes of happy creatures. The other admonishes us to co-operate with divine benevolence; to use the powers entrusted to us, not in committing injury, but in diffusing benefits; to repair the ills which accident has caused, to rend the prisoner's chains asunder, to rescue innocence from destruction, to afford an asylum to the fugitive, bread to the hungry, clothing to the naked, medicine to the sick, instruction to the ignorant; to spread life and vegetation, and peace and plenty over a waste and depopulated land; to mitigate pain, to redress wrong, and console affliction wherever they are found. These are the acts of mercy. She comes to raise the fallen, to relieve the heavy-laden of their burdens, to bind up the wounds of the broken-hearted, to breathe hope into the bosom of despair, and to excite in the kindling imagination the glorious vision of beatified spirits, with their amaranth crowns and golden harps, standing before the throne, and chanting hallelujahs to HIM, the only wise, the only good, who liveth and reigneth for ever and ever. This is the delightful office of mercy. She comes to imbue us with her own hallowed spirit. She speaks as the herald of Jehovah. She desires us, if we would fulfil the design of our creation, and be happy in time and eternity, to " be merciful, even as our Heavenly Father is merciful," and never to contaminate our nature by a malevolent feeling, nor deform, by an act of cruelty, any part of that creation which is still redolent of airs from paradise, which God has mantled with beauty, and enriched with his blessing.

INDEX.

Webb and Chapman, Printers, Great Brunswick-street, Dublin.

Lightning Source UK Ltd.
Milton Keynes UK
UKHW020634060223
416537UK00012B/2666

9 780341 969815